Arthur Griffiths

Wellington & Waterloo

Arthur Griffiths

Wellington & Waterloo

ISBN/EAN: 9783337144357

Printed in Europe, USA, Canada, Australia, Japan

Cover: Foto ©ninafisch / pixelio.de

More available books at **www.hansebooks.com**

WELLINGTON & WATERLOO

— BY —

MAJOR ARTHUR GRIFFITHS.

WITH AN

INTRODUCTION BY

FIELD-MARSHAL VISCOUNT WOLSELEY, K.P., etc.

COMMANDER-IN-CHIEF OF THE ARMY.

THE "NAVY AND ARMY ILLUSTRATED" LIBRARY.

STORIES OF OUR NATIONAL HEROES.

ERRATA.

Portrait of Countess of Mornington (Frontispiece, facing p. 3)-

In first line of description, for "Garrett, second Earl of Mornington," read "Garrett, first Earl of Mornington."

Irish Rebellion, 1798 (Plate on p. 25)—

In Line 1, for "Dublin" read "Waterford."

Bridge at Constantino (Plate on p. 84)—

For "Noyales" read "Nogales."

Portrait of Colonel Thomas Graham (p. 127)—

For "Lawrence" read "Hoppner" as name of painter.

H.R.H. the Prince of Orange (Plate on p. 140)—

The last sentence is incorrect.

Portrait of Sir Stapleton Cotton (p. 143)—

For "Sir Stapleton Cotton" read "General Charles William Stewart, afterwards Marquis of Londonderry."

INTRODUCTION.

IN his selection of the "Fifteen Decisive Battles of the World," Sir Edward Creasy included two which saved Europe from the complete domination of France. Both were won by English Generals, helped by German Armies. Upon both occasions it was to the genius and striking individuality of those two Commanders that Europe owed her deliverance. In the first of these battles, that of Blenheim, Marlborough put an end to the impudent claim of Louis XIV. to universal dominion; in the second, Wellington finally destroyed Bonaparte, who had similarly tried to impose his despotic will upon all nations.

Marlborough won the earlier battle by a brilliant assault upon the French centre, and never did British soldiers prove more conclusively how irresistible they are in attack when directed by a master hand. The battle of a century later is a remarkable instance of that dogged and pertinacious pluck for which our soldiers have been distinguished in all ages. What English-speaking man or woman can read without pardonable pride of how our men that day stood unflinching whilst the enemy's round shot tore through their ranks, and of how they mocked as the most famous horsemen of France charged down upon them? To those who, after the manner of Plutarch, wish to compare Marlborough with Wellington, these two battles illustrate their respective modes of fighting. The former always took the offensive, the latter usually waited to be attacked. It should, however, be remembered that unavoidable circumstances, not preference, often influenced Wellington on this point. In the following pages it will be shown how brilliantly he could, upon suitable occasions, assume the offensive to pounce upon the adversary who had given him a good opportunity for attack. Nevertheless, whilst Marlborough will be remembered for his persistent and brilliant offensive, history will always couple Wellington's name with that of Fabius as a tactician.

Sir Edward Creasy tells us in graphic language of the great battles which, up to his time, had most influenced the course of history. Since he wrote, wars and revolutions have seriously altered the geographical distribution of European states, and have even called new kingdoms into existence. "The balance of power" no longer rests upon its old-established fulcrum. But Waterloo is still the great battle of this century, and perhaps of all ages. It is not to Englishmen only, but to all who are truly interested in human progress, that it appears in this light. A thousand circumstances combine to make it do so, for upon its result hung the interests of most European dynasties and the political independence of their subjects. It brought to a fatal end the brilliant but dishonest career of the world's greatest man. It practically killed the adventurer who had made France more powerful than all her legitimate Kings had ever done, and around whose memory the glamour of victory and the fascination which despotic power lends the great ruler still cling with an intensely romantic and increasing interest.

Eighty-three years have come and gone since Waterloo was fought, and yet we still hail with eagerness every newly-discovered incident that throws fresh light upon its events, or upon the lives of the two great battle-chiefs who met for the first time face to face upon that memorable day. So much hung upon its issue that it is only natural we should still seek for information about it, and try to measure and compare the talents and character of the two mighty opponents who there strove for victory. But this is not the place to draw any such comparison. Suffice it to say, that no two contemporary leaders of nations ever differed more in moral qualities nor in their respective aims.

If, therefore, Waterloo be still regarded as the most memorable of battles, it is not surprising that Wellington's name should still be revered wherever our tongue is spoken. The very fame of Napoleon but adds to the reputation of his conqueror; and when history extols the Corsican's great achievements, she thereby adds—it may be unconsciously—to the Englishman's renown.

As long as England values worth and honour, Wellington will be remembered for his unswerving love of truth and justice, unselfish loyalty and patriotism, and for his all-absorbing devotion to duty. Apart from his great achievements, we revere his memory because we find personified in him the high qualities and characteristics which constitute the English gentleman, and which we prize, perhaps all the more, because we believe them to be so peculiarly British. Indeed, his very faults are to us but national traits upon which we plume ourselves. When he died, all England mourned for him as her best friend, her most faithful servant, feeling she had lost a pillar of the Empire, the like of which she may never see again. Let us daily pray that when we have another Waterloo to fight we may have another Wellington to win it for us.

Admiral Calder's action with Villeneuve off Finisterre caused Napoleon to abandon for the time his rooted intention of invading England. But within a month, the army he had collected for that operation was on its march to great achievements on the Danube. Calder's action and Nelson's glorious victory at Trafalgar saved us then from invasion, but they did not save Austria or Russia from the destruction which so quickly overtook them. It may be truly averred that ten Nelsons and ten Trafalgars could not have done for

England or for Europe what Wellington effected at Waterloo I mean the final destruction of Bonaparte's power.

Waterloo not only dethroned the greatest King the world has ever known, but it restored peace and prosperity to Europe for a generation of men, and ensured to nations the privilege of working out their own destiny on lines of their own choosing. To Wellington, whose story is told in the following pages, Europe owes that victory. Had it not been for him, Bonaparte might have died in peace at the Tuileries, surrounded with all the pomp and etiquette he had invented for his brand-new Court, and sanctified by all the holy rites of the Roman church he had re-established.

What Wellington did for the Empire is not, I think, sufficiently well remembered in these days. But we hope that this earnest and painstaking record of his achievements will revive a fitting interest in the history of the greatest Englishman of our century.

In the following pages my friend Major Griffiths gives a lucid and interesting account of Wellington's great services. The story carries the reader along through his many campaigns from Assaye to Waterloo, making us realise the grave difficulties he encountered and admire the courage and ability with which he overcame them.

But it is not only as the leader of battles that Britain's tribute of praise and gratitude is here claimed for him. Our author describes to us the circumstances under which the great soldier-statesman threw himself patriotically into the troubled arena of political strife when he felt that his intervention was absolutely necessary in his country's interests.

Immense pains have been taken to illustrate the events described in these pages, and to give us good portraits of those who took part in them. Strong light is thrown upon the military and social life of the period by the contemporary prints and caricatures which are here reproduced. The original drawings of officers and artists, made on the spot whilst the operations described were in progress, together with engravings of scenes on the march, in bivouac and in battle, have been sought out and copied for this work.

In commending this volume to Wellington's fellow-countrymen, it is but right I should refer to the admirable manner in which that great man's history is here told. Major Griffiths is well known to the Army as a Staff College Officer of high professional attainments, and as a distinguished writer upon many subjects he has long been before the public. He has consequently been able to make this work not only instructive to the soldier, but intensely interesting to the general reader.

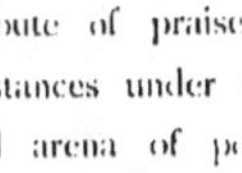

INDEX TO ILLUSTRATIONS.

Wellington and Waterloo.

Wellington and Waterloo.

"Navy and Army Illustrated" Library.
Edited by Commander CHARLES N. ROBINSON, R.N.,
Of the "Army and Navy Gazette."
OFFICES: 20, TAVISTOCK ST., COVENT GARDEN.

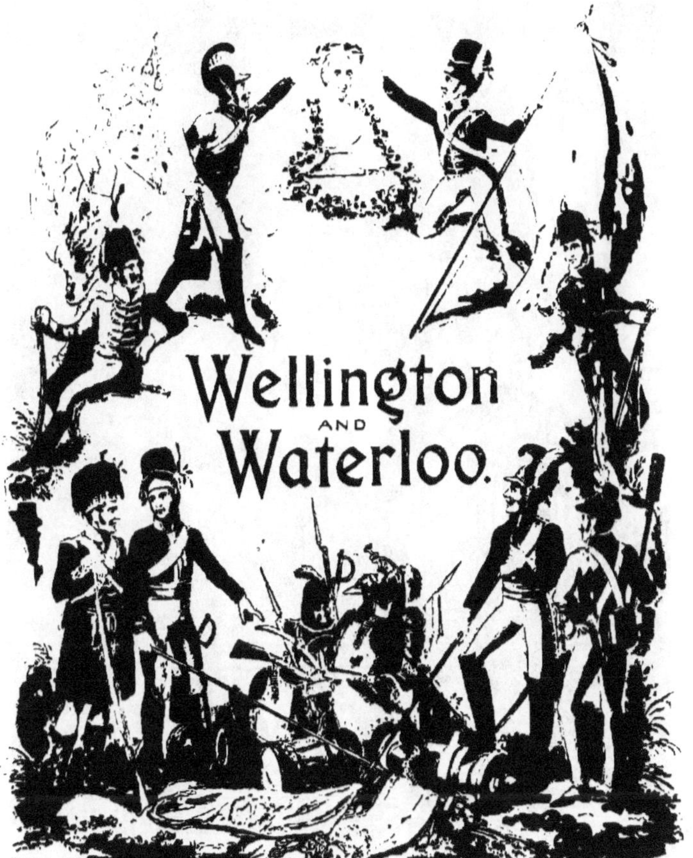

Printed by HUDSON & KEARNS, 83-87, Southwark Street, S.E.
Published by GEORGE NEWNES, Ltd., 8, 9, 10, and 11, Southampton Street, Strand, W.C.

THE COUNTESS OF MORNINGTON.

[illegible]

[illegible] Earl of Mornington [illegible] 175[illegible] and Arthur Wellesley was their fourth [illegible] family [illegible] discharged the trust faithfully. [illegible] to the highest distinction. [illegible]

Photo. [illegible] Copyright [illegible]

ROOM IN WHICH ARTHUR WELLESLEY IS SAID TO HAVE BEEN BORN

Now occupied by the Land Commission in Dublin.

WELLINGTON AND WATERLOO.

CHAPTER I.

Arthur Wellesley's birth and parentage. His early years. Educated at Eton and Angers. Joins Army in [illegible]. A.D.C. to Lord Westmoreland, Lord Lieutenant. Unpopular as a youth. Enters Irish Parliament as M.P. for Trim. [illegible] Commanding 33rd Regiment, after six years' service, aged 24. Proves an excellent Regimental officer. State of the Army at that time. [illegible] campaign under Duke of York in Flanders. [illegible] at Boxtel, where he shows great military skill, and in the general retreat. What he learnt in this campaign. His leaders and [illegible] Duke of York, Dundas and Abercromby.

MUCH obscurity hangs about the date and place of Arthur Wellesley's birth. One story [illegible] that he first saw the light at Dangan Castle, the seat of Lord Dungannon, in West Meath, while another gives Dublin the honour. The first is supported by the evidence of his mother's nurse, who [illegible] fixed the event on the 6th March, 1769. The last is generally believed to be the place; and the house is now occupied by the Irish Land Commission. A local chemist possesses a prescription written for Lady Mornington by her medical man about the time of her son Arthur's birth. The parish register of St. Peter's, Dublin, records his baptism on the 30th April; and, again, a letter from his mother gives the date as the 1st May. Wellington himself kept his birthday on the last-named date, and where the evidence is conflicting, that of mother and son may safely be preferred.

The great Duke seldom referred to his childhood. It had been unhappy, and the memory was displeasing. His mother lavished little affection on him. Gifted with an acute and powerful intellect, she could not tolerate what appeared to her the stupidity of her fourth son. For years Arthur was called the fool of the family; [illegible] beauty of feature that distinguished his brothers and sisters. The eldest, Richard, afterwards Marquis Wellesley, was one of the handsomest men of his time, and his sisters were beautiful women. Lady Mornington, as may seen in the fine portrait painted of her by Lady Burghersh as a venerable dame, shows the remains of great beauty, but she evidently had the strong features of the son whom she styled her ugly boy Arthur.

The real name of the Wellesleys, or Wesley, as they wrote it, until about 1798, was Colley or Cowley, an English family which passed over to Ireland in the reign of Henry VIII. A Colley, Richard, who took the name of Wesley, was ennobled as Baron Mornington, in 1747, in the peerage of Ireland; and his son Garrett became the father of the Duke of Wellington. He had married Anne Hill, daughter of Viscount Dungannon, in 1759, and became the year after Viscount Wellesley and Earl Mornington. He will be best remembered as a composer of sweet sounds, glees, songs, and more ambitious efforts in sacred music. He was also a fine performer on the organ and the violin.

Arthur Wellesley's Birthplace.
Now Office of the Land Commission, Dublin.

Arthur had the same taste; and the story goes that even when in the nurse's arms he delighted in his father's fiddling. One day when Dubourg, the eminent violinist, was about to play for Lord Mornington, the precocious infant protested against his father giving up the violin. But, so the story runs, when young Arthur had once heard Dubourg he would not suffer his father to play if Dubourg were present. This may sound apocryphal, but it is an undoubted fact that Arthur Wellesley loved the fiddle, and played it well himself until, with the increasing cares of duty and office, he felt that he must not waste time on such an engrossing amusement.

Lord Mornington has been taxed with a fondness for political intrigue. He may thus have gained higher rank in the peerage, but he made little else by it, and when he died in 1781, still young—no more than 46—he left his widow and children but poorly provided for. Lady Mornington lived in London, and, despite her straitened circumstances, sent her sons to Eton.

Arthur spent some little time at a preparatory school in Chelsea, and his career at Eton was brief and undistinguished. While Richard, the eldest, carried off school honours, and went on to take a high degree at Oxford, Arthur was credited with but ordinary abilities. He made no close friends at Eton; he played no games; he left no mark at Eton, except in his fight with "Bobus" Smith—his first battle and his first victory. Robert Smith, the famous Sydney Smith's brother, was bathing in the river, when Wellesley passed and proceeded to throw stones at him. Smith promised to thrash him if he did not stop, and was dared to do it. "Bobus" came out of the water, and, as he was, without clothes, struck in. He was beaten, as were most people who fought with Arthur Wellesley.

THE GREAT BRIDGE, ANGERS.
Ancient Bridge, with Cathedral of St. Maurice in the background.

We have no authentic knowledge of why he left Eton, but his stay there was short. It has been said that his mother declined to keep him at such an expensive school, where he was only wasting his opportunities. Another version is that influential friends had secured the promise of a subordinate office in the Customs for the youth who was destined for something better than a tide-waiter or a gauger. His bent and bias had always been towards the

Army, and now kinder friends intervened, offering to help him to a commission and to provide funds for his military education. This is the explanation of his stay at Angers, in France, where he studied for a time — no more than a year, according to his own account — and where he cannot have learnt much.

Pignerol, who kept the Academy, taught the military science, but it was not an exclusively military school, certainly not a Government school like that of Brienne, in which Napoleon was a cadet. Among Arthur Wellesley's schoolmates were Chateaubriand, as the Duke believed, but was never positively certain in after life, and one or two English boys.

QUAI DU ROI DE POLOGNE.

Riverside scene in Old Angers where Wellesley was at School.

Young Wellesley made many acquaintances in Angers, and was well received by the best people. He went into Society a great deal, and often dined with the Duc de Brissac, who kept open house at his fine chateau a little out of the town. The boys from Pignerol's school were welcome, and met many strange guests at table, priests and wandering monks among them. The fare was plentiful enough at the high table, but at the extremities meagre and inferior. In after years Wellington described an amusing scene at one dinner. The host called for the menu, and seeing there was a haunch of venison, asked for it.

There was none left. It had been placed before a certain Pere Basile — Father Basil — who had eaten the greater part of it. The Duc de Brissac shouted down the table asking what had become of the haunch. Had it come to life and run away? Pere Basile excused himself by saying he had helped many people to the dish, but it was believed that he had principally helped himself. This was not the end of the story. Some of the guests, the school-boys included, furious at losing their share of the venison, waited for the poor Father outside the chateau after dinner, and gave him a sound thrashing, to teach him to be less greedy in future.

WINDSOR BRIDGE.

The Thames at Windsor a year or two after Arthur Wellesley was at Eton.

Arthur Wellesley met many Frenchmen at Angers who were destined to fill a large place in history. One was the Abbé Sieyes, who became a prominent politician during the Republic, and materially helped to bring Napoleon Bonaparte into p[ower]. They met at the chateau of the Duc de Praslin, father of the Duke who forty years later murdered his [wife]. Other acquaintances of those days were D'Archambault, Talleyrand's brother, and Jaucourt, who became Secretary for Foreign Affairs under Louis XVIII. "Dix Huit," or "Des Huitres," as he was styled from his gourmandise tistes. Strange fate nearly brought the Duke of Wellington back to Angers at the head of his victorious army, when he invaded France in 1814. Had not peace been made, he must have advanced to the Loire, and Angers would probably have become his headquarters. Young Wellesley was gazetted as ensign in the 73rd Regiment on the 7th March, 1787, when barely eighteen years of age. The same year, when serving in Ireland, he was promoted lieutenant into the 76th, from which he exchanged into the 41st, then passed on to the cavalry. Four years later, on the 30th June, 1791, he was appointed captain in the 58th Foot, and presently exchanged to his old arm, to command a troop in the 18th Light Dragoons. These various changes are chronicled in the Army Lists, and were very common in those days, when young sprigs of nobility were pushed forward over the heads of older and often worthier men.

Arthur Wellesley was strongly backed. His brother Richard was in the English House of Commons and held office in Mr. Pitt's Government, and could do much for the aspiring young soldier. He had a staunch friend, too, in Lord Westmoreland, at that time Lord Lieutenant of Ireland, who presently made him one of his aides-de-camp. About the same time, too, when scarcely of age, he entered the Irish House of Commons as M.P. for Trim, a borough belonging to the Wellesleys, and for which the first Lord Mornington had sat.

The EARL OF MORNINGTON, K.P.

[illegible]

From a small [illegible] Apsley House. This [illegible]

[illegible] books.

His position was brilliant, and he rose to it. Till then he is spoken of as a shy, *gauche* lad, not very polished in manners or address, with teasing, ungracious ways that made him unpopular, especially with ladies. One positively declined to accept an invitation to a certain picnic until assured that "that mischievous boy Arthur Wellesley" was not to be of the party.

[illegible] the Hon. ARTHUR WELLESLEY.

[illegible]

[illegible] belonging to Apsley House [illegible]

Another, Lady Aldborough, who lived to see him a Duke and Field-Marshal, is said to have taken him with her to a ball, where he would neither dance or try to make himself agreeable, but hung about the band, revelling in the music. When it was time to go home, Lady Aldborough had already disappeared, and Arthur was glad to accept a lift in the car with the fiddlers. Her Ladyship is said to have reminded him of this incident long afterwards, willingly confessing that when she thus deserted him, she never thought he would come to play first fiddle himself.

To this period belongs another rather apocryphal story of his Mohock-like adventure with the Dublin "Charlies," or night watchmen, which ended, it is said, in his arrest and detention for the night in the Guard House. In any case a far from unusual termination to an evening's carouse at this time.

He came more prominently to the front, if he did not turn over a new leaf, when M.P. and A.D.C. on the Vice-regal Staff. He no doubt went with the times, which were loose, and the standard of morality in Dublin, following the example set by the Castle, was by no means high. The pace was [illegible] for Wellesley, who soon found himself threatened with money difficulties. It is told with much circumstantiality how a certain worthy woollen draper of Dublin came to his assistance and helped him to face his liabilities.

Another version gives it as his boot-maker, over whose shop he lodged in Great Ormond Street, who saw that he was hard pressed, and who offered him a loan, to be rewarded by the Duke's custom and he was very nice about the fit and number of his boots for the rest of their lives. Neither story can be quite implicitly believed.

Photo. [illegible] & [illegible] [illegible]

THE BATHING PLACE, ETON.

[illegible]

Probably Wellesley took a pull upon himself in good time. He always had a lively horror of debt, and said so repeatedly in later years. "Debt makes a slave of a man," he had been heard to say. "I have often known what it is to be in want of money, but I never got into debt." We shall see presently how he had resolved to give up the Army, the profession he so infinitely preferred, entirely because he feared it would be too expensive.

We have glimpses, distinct, but somewhat different in tone, of the young soldier in [illegible] Dublin, that "ancient and loyal Corporation," as it used to style itself, and where, by the way, he is still honoured by a statue commemorating his subsequent achievements. One is from a contemporary who knew and remembered him well, and who was in the gallery of the House at the opening of the session of 1793, with a friend at his elbow to point out each celebrity as he took his seat. "A young man dressed in a scarlet uniform with very large epaulets caught my eye, and I enquired who he was. 'That's Captain Wellesley, a brother of Lord Mornington's, and one of the A.D.C.'s of the Lord Lieutenant.' 'I suppose he never speaks?' I added. 'You are wrong. He does speak sometimes, and when he does, believe me, it is always to the purpose.' . . . Presently a debate was opened as to further concessions to the Roman Catholics, and grew very animated. . . . Captain Wellesley spoke on this occasion, and his remarks were [illegible] and pertinent, his [illegible] and his manner [illegible].

"On another occasion," goes on the same authority, "when a property qualification for members . . . was discussed. A certain Hon. John Monk Mason vehemently opposed it. He held a large [illegible] which he flourished vehemently, to the manifest alarm of the members immediately beside [illegible]. [illegible] speech, he emphatically concluded by saying, 'I give my [illegible] opposition to this, as [illegible] of all the young brothers in the House,' striking Captain Wellesley, who sat beside him, so soundly [illegible] between

Photo. C. Hawtrey [illegible]

THE PLAYING FIELDS, ETON.

Wellington and Waterloo.

the shoulders with his parchment baton as to be distinctly heard in the gallery. The occurrence produced an instant and uproarious burst of laughter throughout the House."

The other picture is not so flattering. It is drawn by the well-known Sir Jonah Barrington, whose personal sketches of his own times in Dublin form one of the most interesting books of memoirs extant. He was Judge of the Admiralty Court, but at this time, 1790, a leader at the Bar, and very prominent in Dublin Society. "I occasionally gave splendid dinners," he says, naively, but modesty was not in him, and on one occasion he had asked the Speaker of the Irish House of Commons, and many other M.P.'s; Sir John Parnell (the Speaker) came late, and brought with him two uninvited guests, Captain Wellesley and Mr. Stewart, whom he was certain Barrington would cordially welcome, as he did. The first was the future Duke of Wellington, the second became Lord Castlereagh.

A FOOT SOLDIER IN 1791.
After H. Bunbury

Barrington describes Arthur Wellesley as "ruddy-faced and juvenile in appearance, and popular enough among the young men of his age and station. His address was unpolished; he occasionally spoke in Parliament, but not successfully, and never on any important subjects; and evinced no promise of that unparalleled celebrity and splendour which he has since reached, and whereto intrepidity and decision, good luck and great military science, have justly combined to elevate him . . . ." "At the period to which I allude," says Barrington, "I feel confident nobody could have predicted that one of those young gentlemen would have become the most celebrated English general of his era, and the other one of the most mischievous statesmen and unfortunate Ministers that ever appeared in modern Europe." Sir Jonah goes on to observe that each owed much to the other. But for their personal intimacy and close friendship neither probably would have gone so far. "Sir Arthur Wellesley would never have had the chief command in Spain but for the Ministerial manœuvring and aid of Lord Castlereagh, and Lord Castlereagh could never have stood his ground as a Minister but for Lord Wellington's success."

Now further promotion came to the young soldier, and he reached in just six years the high and coveted position of regimental command. The campaign in Holland under the Duke of York, destined to end so ingloriously, was near at hand. Young Wellesley, eager to see service, had urgently petitioned his brother to get him appointed as major in a newly-formed battalion of Guards. This application was refused; but on the 30th April, 1793, he was gazetted as major into the 33rd, and six months later he purchased the lieutenant-colonelcy with funds provided by his brother, Mornington.

One of the Light Company of an Infantry Regiment.
After H. B[illegible]

It is pleasant to record the kindly act, still pleasanter to tell how the first use Wellesley made of the ample funds placed at his disposal by the rich booty found in Seringapatam was to repay his brother. Mornington, now Marquis Wellesley, protested that he would not take the money, that there could be no question of loans or indebtedness between brothers, and we do not know exactly how the matter was settled.

Wellington and Waterloo.

The boy colonel (he was barely twenty-four) was an ardent soldier, and threw himself heart and soul into [illegible] work. There was much to be done. His regiment was not in the highest order, and needed all his attention. He busied himself over its interior economy, improved the regimental system, gave it a code of "standing orders," still preserved in the [illegible] regiment, the "Duke of Wellington's Own," and drilled it incessantly.

It [illegible] distinguished as the best and smartest in any garrison, a model [illegible] up to others [illegible] imitation, and it maintained this proud pre-eminence wherever it went, to Holland and the Far East. When General (afterwards Lord) Harris [illegible] it in India, shortly before Seringapatam, he declared that [illegible] equipment, for courage, for discipline or good conduct, it was above all praise.

The British Army was rather strangely constituted in those days. The private men were mostly the scum and sweepings of Society, the vagrants and ne'er-do-wells, who sought enlistment as a last resource in life. They were held under an iron discipline, backed by ruthless punishment, were badly cared for, absurdly dressed, and always at the mercy of imperious and tyrannical superiors. The officers [illegible] canes, the sergeants rattans, and both were used [illegible] upon [illegible] men's shoulders on parade or anywhere [illegible] in any small infraction [illegible] rule.

THE EARL OF WESTMORELAND.

[illegible]

LORD WESTMORELAND AT BRIGHTON, 1837.

[illegible]

"When in the field," writes one who went through [illegible] [illegible] to the officer's instructions, [illegible] [illegible] with a volley of oaths, [illegible] [illegible] general consent [illegible] making [illegible] ation. If you resist you are liable to receive many hundred lashes." [illegible] extreme. Flogging was the principal penalty, inflicted with terrible [illegible] methods of punishment were [illegible], such as riding the wooden horse, the strappado, tying neck and heels, clubbing, cobbing, booting, bottling. But "running the gauntlet," [illegible] "gantlope," was still in force in 1787, when Arthur Wellesley joined, and the whole regiment acted as [illegible], each soldier giving the culprit a stroke with a switch, in turn, as he passed the halberds. By degrees the [illegible] and degrading duty fell exclusively upon the drummers, under the teaching and strict supervision of the drum major.

The dread cat-o'-nine-tails, with its nine lashes of knotted whipcord, replaced the switch about 1770. For generations the "cat" reigned supreme in the British Army. It was used for all offences, light and serious, the only distinction being in the number of lashes awarded. "A soldier has been flogged for being unsteady in the ranks to the extent of brushing away a troublesome fly from his face; another because through careless tying his pigtail fell off on parade." Soldiers who would not tell where they got liquor were

GREAT COURTYARD OF DUBLIN CASTLE.

The Lord Lieutenant's Residence and the [illegible] Dublin, 1791.

given twenty lashes a day till they confessed. Deserters were sentenced to a thousand lashes, and, to prolong the torture, five was counted between each stroke.

The "cats" were pickled in brine and washed in it during the infliction of punishment. To drown the cries of the victims the drummers not flogging kept up a roulade on their drums. Right and left handed drummers were employed. Men were brought back again to the halberds, with their flesh scarcely healed, to undergo a penalty [illegible] in instalments. It was [illegible] to see the drum-major keep the drummers up to their duty by thrashing them with his rattan; the adjutant, [illegible], stood behind the drum major and "[illegible]" the [illegible] with his [illegible]. "The practice of [illegible] did not fall into [illegible] disuse for several years after the commencement of the present century."

THE PARLIAMENT HOUSE, DUBLIN 1795.

[illegible]

In which Arthur Wellesley sat as M.P. [illegible] Grattan, Curran, [illegible], Castlereagh.

[illegible] was [illegible] pensated for [illegible] and [illegible] well-being of the soldier. His poor pittance of pay barely sufficed for the commonest necessaries. It was subject to continual deductions for articles that should have been found by the State. "The Army is become very [illegible]," writes a soldier in his journal a little antecedent to this time, "by the many articles [illegible] that we are obliged to purchase. Our miserable pay is reduced to about a third of what it usually was. you cannot appear without white stockings, leather breeches, short gaiters, hair powdered."

The soldier's subsistence was so very meagre and uncertain, that military surgeons complained of its evil effect on physique. Some regiments kept their own butcher, and the men, who were left to provide their own messing, were obliged to buy a certain amount of meat daily. Commanding officers occasionally laid in fruit and vegetables in large quantities, which the men could purchase by retail, much as in the modern canteens, and which added "greatly to their healthfulness by avoiding scurvy."

A Grenadier of an Infantry Regiment in 1791.
After H. Bunbury

But the soldier's fare was generally scanty. William Cobbett, who served in the ranks, writes in 1785 that he was constantly half starved. Being resolved to carry on his studies, he could only buy pen and paper by foregoing a portion of his food. "A farthing then was a great sum to me. I was tall, and had great health and exercise." He tells us, with great pathos, how he cried when he lost a halfpenny which he had treasured up for the purchase of a red herring. Now and again the men were allowed to add to their pay by working at any handicraft they knew, or seeking employment when quartered in any town.

It is to be feared that a very general complaint might be made against the British officers of those days. They took but little interest in their men; they were indifferent to their duties, as a rule badly instructed in them. "Officers do not trouble their heads about the Service," is the opinion of an eminent foreign critic, Colonel Mauvillion, "and, with a few exceptions, understand nothing whatever about it; and this goes from ensign to general. Their home customs incline them to the indulgences of life, and nearly without exception they expect to have comfortable means of sleep. This disposes them to acts of neglect of duty which would sound incredible if repeated. To this is added a quiet natural nonchalance, which tempts them to despise the enemy as well as his danger."

KILMAINHAM HOSPITAL.
[illegible]
Was established in the time of Charles II. as a retreat for retired veterans, and is still kept up. A portion of the building has always been appropriated as a residence for the Commander of the Forces in Ireland, and is now occupied by Field-Marshal Lord Roberts.

The carelessness and want of zeal of the average officer of those days may perhaps be excused by the fact that they were not greatly encouraged to improve themselves; there was no certainty of rising by their own exertions. Money to purchase promotion was a first necessity; without it good men lingered for years in the junior ranks. Then interest at headquarters, political and social influence, continually pushed on young men, often in advance of their deserts, and always over the heads of seniors. The dissatisfaction they caused is the theme of many military writers of the time.

In the campaign of Flanders which was now in progress, and in which Wellesley was soon to receive his "baptism of fire," the complaint was frequent that the senior officers had been promoted prematurely. "The field officers

From [illegible] After [illegible] R.A.

FIELD-MARSHAL CONWAY.

The Right Hon. Henry Seymour Conway, a distinguished Military Officer, who held the post of Commander-in-Chief of the Army about 1782. He sat for years in the House of Commons, and was an active, prominent politician.

were many of them boys," writes Calvert (afterwards Sir Harry, and Adjutant-General of the Army), "who have attained their rank by means suggested by Government at home," and for whose youth and inexperience the Duke of York, unfortunate commander that he was, became responsible. That Flanders army which swore so well that its strong language became a by-word, was sadly neglected, and very imperfectly found for active service in the field.

"We want artillerymen," writes Calvert on another occasion; "we want a general officer at the head of the artillery; we want drivers and smiths; we want three major-generals of infantry; we want a commanding engineer of rank and experience; we want a total reform in our hospital; we want at least two out of the four brigades of mounted artillery with which his Grace of Richmond is amusing himself in England; we want a total stop put to that most pernicious mode of bestowing rank on officers . . . for merely raising" (by means of ample funds) "a certain number of men," so as "to relieve deserving officers from the intolerable grievance of seeing men without merit, without family, or the smallest pretensions to any military ability, pass over their heads and arrive at a very high, and, till now, very respectable rank in the Army, solely through the medium of a rascally crimp.

"The want of general officers to command brigades has in this army been an evil of the most serious nature, and has been attended by the very worst consequences." The chief evil was that the commands "devolved upon young men newly come into the Service, whose years and inexperience totally disqualified them for the situation. I could mention lads of one and twenty who had never been on service before."

Yet there was one young officer who reached the Low Countries about this time, and who might be classed, in point of years, with those thus severely condemned, but who in military character was very different from the rest. When troubles and disasters overtook the Duke of York's army in the summer of 1794, Lieutenant-Colonel Wellesley's regiment formed part of the reinforcement sent out under Lord Moira. Wellesley had gleefully resigned his seat as M.P. to take his place at the head of the 33rd, and he landed with it at Antwerp in July.

SCENES FROM THE MILITARY LIFE OF WILLIAM COBBETT.

[illegible]

This is the well-known radical and vehement political writer, who served for some years as a private soldier, from 1785.

The Duke of York, having been beaten at Oudenarde (the scene of one of Marlborough's great victories), was retrograding on Antwerp, and was again attacked at Malines, but made good his ground, thanks to Lord Moira's timely support. He was, however, soon compelled to continue his retreat; and, evacuating Antwerp, fell back first on Breda, and

FOOD FOR POWDER.

[illegible]

[illegible] of raising recruits at the end of last century [illegible] bounties and taking a linen ent [illegible] 17[illegible]

then to Bois le Duc. The French now sought to cut him off from the line of the River Meuse, and, seizing Boxtel, his most advanced post, threatened his right flank, and made his position untenable. The recovery of Boxtel was a matter of great moment, and the Duke entrusted the operation to General Abercromby, the great Sir Ralph, who, six years later, fell, after winning the victory at Aboukir. The affair at Boxtel might have proved a serious disaster but for the sound military judgment of Lieutenant-Colonel Arthur Wellesley. Abercromby had reconnoitred the French position, and deemed it too strong to attack. But the Duke of York persisted, and he himself sent forward the cavalry, supported by two battalions of Guards, with the 33rd and 44th Regiments. The assailants, meeting no opposition, were drawn on into a fir wood, from which a strong battery, masked, soon opened a murderous fire. Our men were checked abruptly, and presently fell back, pursued closely by a body of French Hussars.

The retreat was orderly until, in a narrow way, cavalry and infantry got mobbed together, and [illegible] ensued. The French charged forward, thinking to carry all before them, when they came unexpectedly upon a solid wall of redcoats drawn across the road. It was the 33rd, so formed by Wellesley. He had deployed, then opened his files to let the shattered cavalry pass through, and, reclosing, showed a firm front to the enemy, in "a thin red line." The French still came on with undiminished gallantry; but Wellesley, who had reserved his fire till they were within short range, now delivered a close and searching volley, effectually stopping them.

This repulse [illegible] French [illegible] British force from destruction, and [illegible] credit is due to the action of the young [illegible] who thus early exhibited the [illegible] genius for war which made him later [illegible] the first commanders of his own [illegible].

It was not the only occasion in this campaign in which the young [illegible] his capacity. His conduct at Boxtel had been noticed by Sir David Dundas—Dundas of the "Thirteen Manœuvres," the only drill

THE RECRUITING SERGEANT TAKEN IN.

After Dighton.

The Sergeant in his eagerness overlooks the fact that his recruit has a wooden leg. 1780-90.

book known to, and used by, the British Army of those remote times), and his skilful handling of troops in the field commended Colonel Wellesley to this great authority. It was through Dundas that the young colonel of the 33rd was appointed brigadier, and given command of the rear guard in the final retreat of the British in this wretched and inglorious campaign.

The brigade, which was composed of the 33rd, and two Highland regiments, the 42nd and 78th, was continually engaged with the enemy. Dundas, who had succeeded the Duke of York in the command of the British troops, Count Walmoden being General-in-Chief of the allied forces, strove to maintain the line of the Waal by taking the offensive. The brunt of it fell upon Colonel Wellesley, who at first lost some of his guns, and retreated; but gathering up his whole strength, he faced round, and, recovering his guns, made a good show at the village of Geldermalsen, which he held stoutly.

LORD CASTLEREAGH.

Robert Stewart, afterwards Viscount Castlereagh, and eventually Marquis of Londonderry, began political life brilliantly in the Irish House of Commons, and took an active part in carrying out the Union. He was Secretary for War under Pitt, and afterwards Foreign Secretary. On one occasion he fought a duel with Canning. He was extraordinarily quick and ready in debate, especially when attacked. In later life he fell into melancholy, and died by his own hand.

But the pursuing French were in greatly superior numbers. Continually reinforced, they pressed on and on, the British always retreating. Dundas first abandoned the line of the Waal, surrendering in turn all the cities and strong places Deventer, Arnheim, Amsterdam, Caerboden, Sneppen, Emden, and reaching the Yssel first and then the Ems, passed at length out of Holland. The season was mid-winter, a winter of phenomenal, almost Arctic, severity. The sufferings and hardships endured by the troops were intense.

It was a barren, inhospitable country; the peasantry gave no help to the soldiers, and there were frequent collisions between them whenever the latter went plundering in their great distress. One side broke into houses and burnt down villages, the other retaliated by killing the wounded and sickly who fell out by the way. The casualties of each day's march were numerous; there was no hope for the stragglers who from weakness or for marauding left the ranks. The supply departments had collapsed; the commissariat, in inefficient, dishonest hands, scarcely attempted to issue food. Medical care was almost entirely wanting; the sick were huddled into carts without warm clothing, medicines, or medical comforts. The army which eventually reached Bremen, and there embarked for England, was wasted by disease, suffering, and neglect, to half its original numbers.

Arthur Wellesley learnt many forcible and enduring lessons in this his first experience of war. He often referred in after life to the campaign, severely criticising the haphazard, happy-go-lucky way in which things were done. It was pitiable, he used to say, to see the want of foresight, the neglect of essentials, the incompetence of the staff,

H.R.H. THE DUKE OF YORK

As a young man

He became Major-General in 1782 at 19, and this portrait must be about this date.

the formality and red tape that hedged in the superior officers. If the Duke of York was at dinner, His Royal Highness could not be disturbed, whatever happened. If an important despatch came in from the Austrian headquarters while the wine was going round the table, the letter was tossed on one side, unopened, with the remark, "That will keep till the morning."

It was the same in the field—no proper precautions, a faulty system of outposts, rare reconnaissances, actions fought by accident without deliberate intention or real meaning. "I was on the Waal, I think, from October to January," he told Lord Stanhope, "and during all that time I only once saw one general from headquarters—they were not twenty-five miles distant—and that was old Sir David Dundas. We had letters from England, and I declare that these letters told us more of what was passing at headquarters than we learnt from headquarters ourselves. It has always been a marvel to me how any of us escaped," said Wellington, summing up the situation. If he learnt nothing good in the positive sense, he was taught negatively and in the most convincing fashion what he must avoid. "I learnt what one ought not to do, and that is always something."

He afterwards said he must have also imbibed, in the Low Countries, ideas that bore abundant fruit in after life, especially as regards supply. He now realised that no army—certainly no British army—can fight if it is not properly fed. The shortcomings of the commissariat were very glaring, as has been said, and the privations in that winter of 1794-95

From an Engraving. After P. J. de Loutherbourg, R.A.

THE SURRENDER OF VALENCIENNES.

In the allied campaign in Flanders against the French, H.R.H. the Duke of York besieged Valenciennes, a fortress built by Vauban, the famous military engineer, from May 27th to July 28th, 1793, when the garrison capitulated.

were only to be equalled by those in the Crimea in later years. Wellington never forgot this first lesson—that of food; as he said, when talking of India, his chief business there was to procure rice and bullocks. "If I had them I had men, and if I had men I knew I could beat the enemy."

LIGHT HORSEMAN, 1790–95.
After H. Bunbury.

Strange to say, for all Wellesley's successful *début* as a soldier, he was nearly lost to the Army after this first campaign. He wrote from Trim, where he was on leave, for his regiment was quartered at Harwich, to Lord Camden, the Lord Lieutenant of Ireland, seeking a civil appointment. He was encouraged, he said, by his brother, Mornington, to look for something in "the Revenue or Treasury Boards."

"If your Excellency," he goes on very modestly, "is of opinion that the offices at these boards are too high for me, of course you will say so; and as I am convinced that no man is so bad a judge of a claim as he who makes it, I trust you will not believe that I shall feel otherwise towards you than as I have always felt, with sentiments of the greatest regard. . . . . You will probably be surprised at my desiring a civil instead of a military office. It is certainly a departure from the line which I prefer, but I see the manner in which the military offices are filled, and I don't want to ask you for that which I know you cannot give me." The last sentence probably refers to his experience in Holland, where so many staff appointments and commands were held by incompetent men.

There were, no doubt, private reasons for this application. Some think that he was still oppressed by debt. Certainly his means were narrow, so much so at this period that they prevented him from marrying as he wished. He had already fallen in love with Lady Catherine Pakenham, one of the chief beauties of the Vice-regal Court, and the attachment was mutual. But young Wellesley was but a poor match, and Lord Longford, Lady Catherine's father, would not give his consent. It is more than probable that this application for a civil billet was to obtain a settled position with a sufficient income. As he did not succeed, the lovers separated without any positive engagement, but with the tacit understanding to be true to each other and wait for better fortune. In 1806, when Major-General Sir Arthur Wellesley and Chief Secretary for Ireland, he renewed his proposal, which was no longer refused.

LIFEGUARDSMAN, 1790.
After H. Bunbury.

It is almost idle to conjecture what would have followed Wellesley's transfer to civil life. That he would have made his mark in any line he adopted goes without saying. The qualities that produce the great commander will always raise a man to eminence in any profession. He (Wellesley) had a special gift for figures, and must have done well as a banker or financier, or, where he had sought employment, in the offices of the Revenue or Treasury. He showed this in his early Indian service, and was commended for it by his brother, the Governor-General. It was his own opinion too. "I think Nature intended me for a Chanceller of the Exchequer rather than a War Minister or Commander-in-Chief," he was heard to say, in after years.

On the other hand, he had already devoted much time and pains to the study of the military profession. As he told General Shaw Kennedy, he had made it his constant practice from the moment he first joined the Army to read

Wellington and Waterloo.

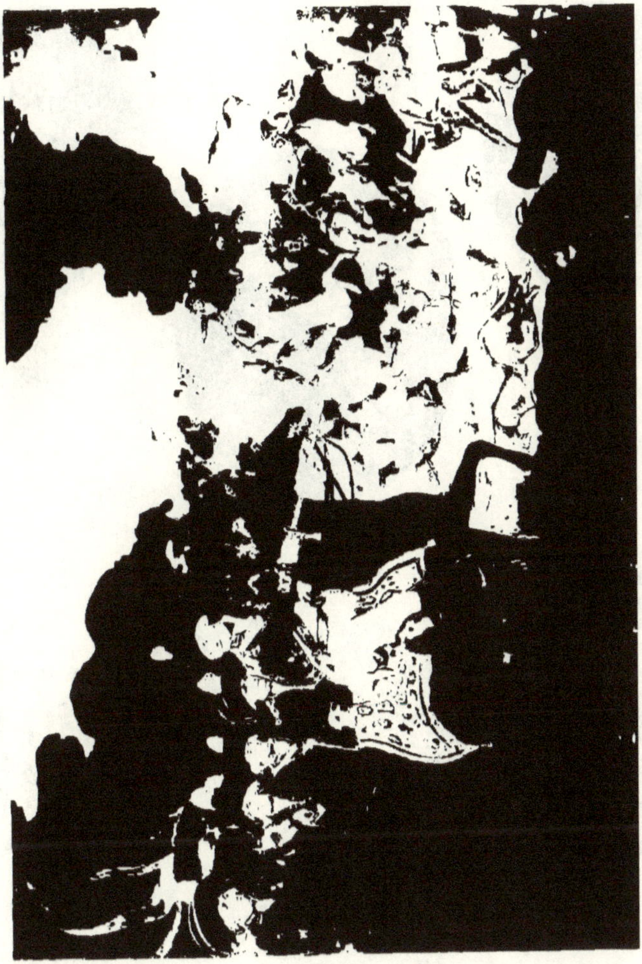

General Sir Ralph Abercromby.

[illegible]

Entered the Army in 1758, [illegible] the cavalry, and then the staff of Prince Ferdinand of Brunswick. Sat in House of Commons for some years. Served in Flanders as Lieutenant-General, captured many West India islands, went to Egypt in 1800 in command of expedition, and lost his life in the Battle of Alexandria, which he won.

H.R.H. THE DUKE OF YORK.

[illegible]

Was the second and favourite son of George III., and entered the Army as Colonel at a tender age, receiving promotion rapidly, but gaining his military education on the Continent, which at that time possessed the only military schools. He was appointed in due course Commander-in-Chief of the Army, and served with the army in Flanders, but showed no great skill as a General. He was, nevertheless, much disappointed that he did not receive the command in the Peninsula, and his relations with Wellington were in consequence never cordial. But the Duke of York did much for the well-being of the Army, and was generally known as the soldier's friend. His reputation suffered eclipse in later years from his supposed connection with the illicit sale of commissions by Mrs. Mary Anne Clarke, and he vacated the post of Commander-in-Chief for some years. A Parliamentary enquiry, however, exonerated him from any participation in the profits of this traffic, and he returned to the Horse Guards, retaining the command of the Army till some years after Waterloo.

General Sir DAVID DUNDAS.

[illegible]

Entered the Army as Lieutenant Fireworker in 1754, served afterwards with infantry, cavalry, and staff, and rose by his own exertions [illegible]. Wrote the first Drill Book for the British Army. Served at Toulon and in Flanders. Was Quartermaster-General of the British Army, and from 1809 to 1811 Commander-in-Chief.

Sir HARRY CALVERT.

[illegible]

General Sir HENRY CLINTON.

[illegible]

Entered the Army in 1787, was A.D.C. to the Duke of York in Flanders, served in Italy, India, Sicily, and the retreat from Corunna. Was always reckoned an excellent tactician and a safe divisional leader.

military literature for a certain number of hours every day, and he long kept up the practice. He was thus fortified by precedent and by the experience of the great masters in war when he was himself called upon to deal with important questions. In no other way, indeed, can we explain the breadth and correctness of his views, the conspicuous ability he showed in dealing with the most varied and intricate subjects, when still quite a young man. This is to be seen in every page of those Indian despatches which he was now to pen as he passed on into the wider and more exciting field of warfare and administration developing the Indian Empire.

DUKE OF YORK'S RETURN.
Caricature after Gillray

In spite of his early success, the Duke of York's campaign in Flanders was much derided at home. Yet its failures were not all traceable to him, and he showed great personal intrepidity in the field wherever and whenever he was engaged.

He was pardonably proud of these early Indian despatches. Long afterwards he spoke of them in terms which in a less eminent personage might have been called conceited. "I have been much amused in reading them over," he told Lord Stanhope; "the energy and activity are quite as great then as ever afterwards. I don't think I could write better now, with all my experience." And, again, to Lady Salisbury he said he was "surprised to find them so good they are as good as I could write now. They show the same attention to details, to the pursuit of all the means, however small, that could promote success."

It was indeed extraordinary how quickly he expanded into a shrewd, strong-minded counsellor and commentator on current events; how broad was his grasp, how close and almost intuitive his insight into great and momentous affairs with which, nevertheless, he had had but a short acquaintance. He wrote the most surprising minutes and memoranda, directly he arrived in India, on subjects of special local importance, quite outside his military business, and the intricate and quite novel details of which he had mastered, seemingly without effort.

A glance into these Indian despatches will show how masterfully and completely he dealt with such matters as the produce, commerce, taxation of the island of Pulo-Penang, the financial and industrial conditions of Bengal. He wrote at length on the best method of collecting an army in Madras, how grain and bullocks were to be obtained, how forts might be strengthened, how the native bazaars should be managed, with a mass of the most judicious orders and regulations for the government of the troops he commanded.

LORD SHEFFIELD'S DRAGOONS.

The 22nd Light Dragoons, or Sussex Regiment of Horse, were raised in 1779 entirely at the expense of Mr. J. North Holroyd, who had been a Captain in a cavalry regiment, and afterwards became first Earl of Sheffield.

No wonder that his brother, who soon followed him to India, trusted to him largely for advice, that General Harris, who commanded at Madras, wrote saying, "You will oblige me by your communications made in the fullest and freest manner. . . . . . In your opinion I am sure of honest zeal, not to flatter inability."

Yet at this time Arthur Wellesley had barely ten years' service, and was not twenty-eight years of age. But he had mastered already the whole business of soldiering, and in its highest and broadest lines. We may see this in these very despatches, still more in the orders he issued and the measures he adopted for maintaining the discipline and efficiency of the troops he commanded. No one could know more thoroughly the shortcomings of the Service, the weakness of the personnel.

All ranks had their grievances. The officer looked upon the private as an inferior being. His superiority was no more than that of caste—professionally he was no better, often worse, than the men he commanded.

The ignorance, idleness, and inefficiency of military officers is well hit off by Grose (who wrote

MANUAL EXERCISE WITH FIRELOCK (1780-1800.)

The handling of the musket was clumsy, and borrowed largely from the pike exercise. Many of the motions, however, survived for long, and one or two are still to be seen little modified in our present drill.

the "Military Antiquities") in his satirical advice to officers, published in 1782. He tells them to "be sure and grumble when ordered for guard and swear they have been taken out of their turn. Do not then appear on parade till the regiment has fallen in and been told off, and then come buttoning your gaiters or putting on some part of your dress. When on guard, invite your friends, get drunk, and make them drunk, then sing and make as much noise as possible. Never read the daily orders; it is beneath an officer of spirit to attend to any such nonsense. It will be sufficient to ask your sergeant if you are on duty. Think most of your dress; use your own ideas about the cut and fashion of your clothes. Never w[illegible] y[illegible] when you can avoid it; a green or a brown coat shows that you have others besides your regimentals [illegible] have the courage to disobey a standing order. If you have not an entire suit, at least [illegible] a round hat, or something unregimental or unmilitary."

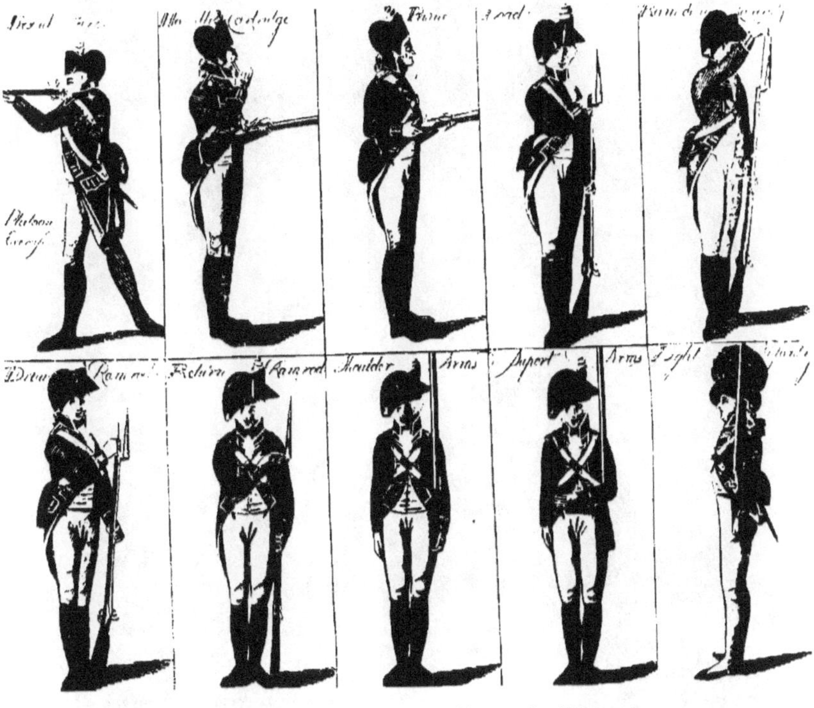

THE PLATOON OR FIRING EXERCISE (1780-1800).

The motions in this exercise were based upon the then conditions of loading and firing. The [illegible] ramrod, were altered first by the introduction of percussion caps and then by breech-loaders.

So we find General Wellesley, when he comes to command, enforcing regulations which, while they show an intimate knowledge of detail, prove also that he knows how to enforce discipline. His orders deal [illegible] with the most minute points; he can tell the picquets what to do; he will have no marauding [illegible] and good order by penalties, and always maintains a firm hand. He was, in fact, born to command, and [illegible] these early days fully proved it.

From an Engraving by C. Turner. *THE RECRUIT* (*CIRCA* 1798). After John Eckstein.

Eckstein, the artist, was a German by extraction, but a student of the Royal Academy, and known as a painter of military subjects. Copious drinking [illegible] the [illegible] to take the "Queen's Shilling," when the recruiting sergeant stood treat to all comers. The recruit himself was [illegible] over when he [illegible] to his friends.

IRISH REBELLION, 1798.

[illegible]

Strangely rapid movement of the Guards from London to Portsmouth [illegible] Dublin. [illegible]

CHAPTER II.

The 33rd embarks [illegible] Arthur Wellesley [illegible] the Cape of Good Hope [illegible] Lord Mornington becomes Governor-General. The new Viceroy's policy. Tippoo Sahib [illegible] Campaign of Seringapatam. [illegible] preparations. Siege begins. Wellesley's [illegible] Tippoo [illegible] Wellesley appointed Governor of Seringapatam and [illegible] East Mahratta War. [illegible] and Ahmednuggur. Victory of Assaye. Wellesley [illegible] Gawilghur. War ended. Bonaparte threatens invasion [illegible] England. Wellesley returns [illegible]

ARTHUR WELLESLEY, after the campaign in the Low Countries, served for a time [illegible] in Essex; and in the autumn of 1795 his regiment was among those selected to [illegible] intended for the West Indies. It embarked in October on board the fleet commanded by Admiral Christian, [illegible] never got out of the British Channel, meeting with the terrible gales still known as "Christian's Storm," which dispersed the ships to the four winds. Many were lost, and the rest returned to Spithead, after [illegible] battle with the elements, in a terribly dilapidated state. [illegible] expedition to the West Indies, a wasted [illegible] lost, was abandoned, and the 33rd [illegible] landed [illegible] Poole. It remained there till April, 1796, [illegible] for India. Wellesley thus happily [illegible] Ireland in the suppression of the [illegible] his native land, an[d] [illegible] strength of England. Reinforcements [illegible] the Channel in hot haste, and they were driven to Portsmouth in strangely-devised carriages, [illegible]

A MILITARY FLY.

[illegible]

Expeditious plan of moving troops [illegible] in the field, suggested in 1798 by [illegible]

Colonel Wellesley did not sail [illegible] East. He was kept back, so it is stated, [illegible] by severe indisposition. This [illegible] own account of himself, for he would have it, later in life, that he had never been ill, "I [illegible] for a day in my whole life since I had the measles as a child," he once said. "I [illegible] to do whatever duty there happened to be before me." He was reminded when he said this of the illness that prevented him from accompanying Baird's Expedition to the Red Sea, in 1800. But he persisted that it had not confined him to bed. "What I had then was the Malabar itch, a much worse kind of itch than ours—it would not yield to brimstone. I caught it on shipboard at Madras, in a man's bed that was given up to me."

"Through life I have avoided medicine as much as I could, but always eaten and drank very little." The Duke's abstemiousness was well known. He was a true Spartan in his way of life, taking much hard exercise till the last, and rising early. His famous apothegm will always survive:—"When one turns over in bed it is time to turn out." It was made in answer to a lady who asked him how he could sleep in a bed so small that there was hardly room in it to turn over. The fact remains that the 33rd sailed without him, and that, when well, he followed in a fast-sailing vessel, which picked up the regiment in September at the Cape of Good Hope. The passage onward was extraordinarily slow, for they did not reach Calcutta till February of the following year.

MARQUIS OF WELLESLEY, K.G., K.P.

Eldest brother of the Duke of Wellington. Entered House of Commons, advanced to the House of Lords as a British Peer in 1797. Went out to India as Governor-General in 1798, and was a chief agent in the rapid extension of our Indian Empire. Was created Marquis of Wellesley on leaving India.

An opportunity for active service seemed to open for Wellesley directly he arrived. Sir John Shore, the Governor-General, offered him the command of a brigade in the force about to be despatched for the capture of Manilla, but with his usual generosity Wellesley declined it until it had been ascertained that an officer senior to him and with greater claims, General Doyle, had made the refusal. Wellesley took it, as Doyle would not, and went with the expedition as far as Prince of Wales' Island, whence it was recalled.

THE DESERTER. By H. Bunbury

... professional artist, although his ... Rowlandson ... the latter ... lampoons. He was at ... an excellent amateur actor.

Great news soon reached Wellesley. He heard that his brother, Lord Mornington, had been appointed successor to Sir John Shore, having accepted the responsible post of Governor-General, very much at his brother Arthur's earnest solicitation. "I am convinced," the latter wrote when urging him to come to India, "that you will retain your health; nay, it is possible that its general state may be improved, and you will have the fairest opportunity of rendering material service to the public and of doing yourself credit." This keen-witted, capable young brother of his was to be of immense assistance to him in achieving his later distinction. There was a very close and affectionate bond of union between the two brothers. They thought all the world of

GENERAL LORD HARRIS.

Of Seringapatam and Mysore.

George Harris (born [illegible] died 1829) entered the Army [illegible] the war with the A[illegible] [illegible] and was [illegible] [illegible] [illegible] [illegible] of Madras [illegible] [illegible] [illegible] [illegible] [illegible] by sheer good fortune.

each other. The elder courted the opinion of the younger, listening with respect to his sound practical advice, and, using his high place, but not unduly, gave him opportunities for showing his worth. Arthur, in return, looked up to his brother and greatly admired his gifts, especially his scholarship.

GENERAL SIR DAVID BAIRD, BART.

[illegible] great distinction in India. [illegible] very cruelly treated. After [illegible] when it was [illegible] Egyptian desert [illegible] Cape of Good Hope in 1806, [illegible] South African Empire [illegible] the battle of Corunna, [illegible]

Even to the last the Duke showed him much deference. On one occasion Lord Wellesley was late in keeping an appointment at Apsley House (he was not a punctual man, to the despair of the renowned Carême, his cook), but the Duke tolerated it, saying, "We must wait for the Governor-General."

It was said by Lord Macaulay that no two men were more unlike: the one scorning all display, the other living for little else. Lord Wellesley, again, had none of the strong, calm self-reliance of Wellington. This was, perhaps, due to his health, which was always delicate, and which prevented him from speaking much in the House of Lords, although he could be very eloquent on great occasions. He was, however, very fastidious, took a great time to prepare a speech, and was never satisfied unless it was the best in the debate. His diffidence was shown in the most marked way when on the voyage out to assume the duties of Governor-General. He was so nervous about himself, that by the time he reached the Cape of Good Hope he had made up his mind to resign and return home. Only the most urgent entreaties and the strongest remonstrances from those around him, that his character must suffer much from such a step, prevailed upon him to proceed.

Arthur had preceded Lord Mornington to India by rather more than a year, and he had filled up the time by close and attentive study of the country and its political condition; he had correctly estimated the near perils that threatened British rule, and although by no means eager for war, he soon realised that it was nearly inevitable. Bold, vigorous measures must be taken with the most deadly dangerous enemy, the notorious Tippoo Sahib, Sultan of Mysore. This truculent despot was a strange mixture of courage and cowardice, of strength [illegible] of intrigue, and of unwearied patience in gaining his ends. He had some [illegible], and had endeavoured to adopt, through his European officers, modern methods of warfare.

[illegible] a ruling passion was a hatred of the English. "Caffres," "infidels," "hogs," were the

Wellington and Waterloo.

epithets he always applied to them; and in his desire to overthrow and expel them from the East he did not hesitate, although a fanatical Mussulman, to enter into relations with other Caffres. When Napoleon Bonaparte, who was just rising into prominence, offered him friendship and alliance against his hated foes, he gladly accepted the help of the French. Bonaparte's letter announcing the invasion of Egypt seemed to bring his new friends almost to his door. Terrible tales came over of the cruelties perpetrated by Tippoo; of the barbarous execution of his English prisoners, some of whom were murdered by having nails driven into their heads. One, General Matthews, was given poisoned food; many were torn limb from limb by tigers, for that fierce wild beast was Tippoo's favourite emblem, and the "tiger's stripes" were blazoned across his flag.

But now his cup was full; an avenging army was gradually collected to punish him for his shameful violation of treaties, and to prove that he could not affront the English with impunity. A portion of the force intended to invade Mysore came under the immediate control of Colonel Wellesley. His zeal and activity were remarkable, and produced great results. He soon revictualled the forts, gathered in transport animals, and arranged satisfactorily for ample supplies of grain. Above all, he drilled and practised his division so assiduously that when General Harris assumed supreme command he highly commended Colonel Wellesley.

BOMBAY GRENADIER.

From [illegible]

The early British settlement at Bombay had no territory on the mainland, but it kept up a military force for its protection, which was greatly developed at the time of the Mahratta wars.

It was a colossal undertaking to prepare an army for the field in those days. General Harris's whole force did not exceed 35,000 men; but there were 120,000 attendants and camp followers, and vast numbers of draught bullocks were needed: in Wellesley's division alone, some 40,000. The transport of the siege train was most cumbrous. Each iron 12-pounder was drawn by forty-four bullocks, nine sets of four abreast, and four pairs of leaders. To each gun there were a spare bullock and an elephant, the latter for use in bad places where the road was sandy, miry, or steep. These sagacious animals gave their aid of their own accord when needed, and even chastised the bullocks with their trunks if they flagged and did not pull heartily.

"When once set in motion," says a contemporary writer, "an Indian army presents the most varied and gorgeous spectacle: its nearly interminable array—men, horses, elephants, bullocks—is very imposing. The

MADRAS SEPOYS.

From [illegible]

The Madras Sepoys were the [illegible] East India Company. They were [illegible] 1748 [illegible]

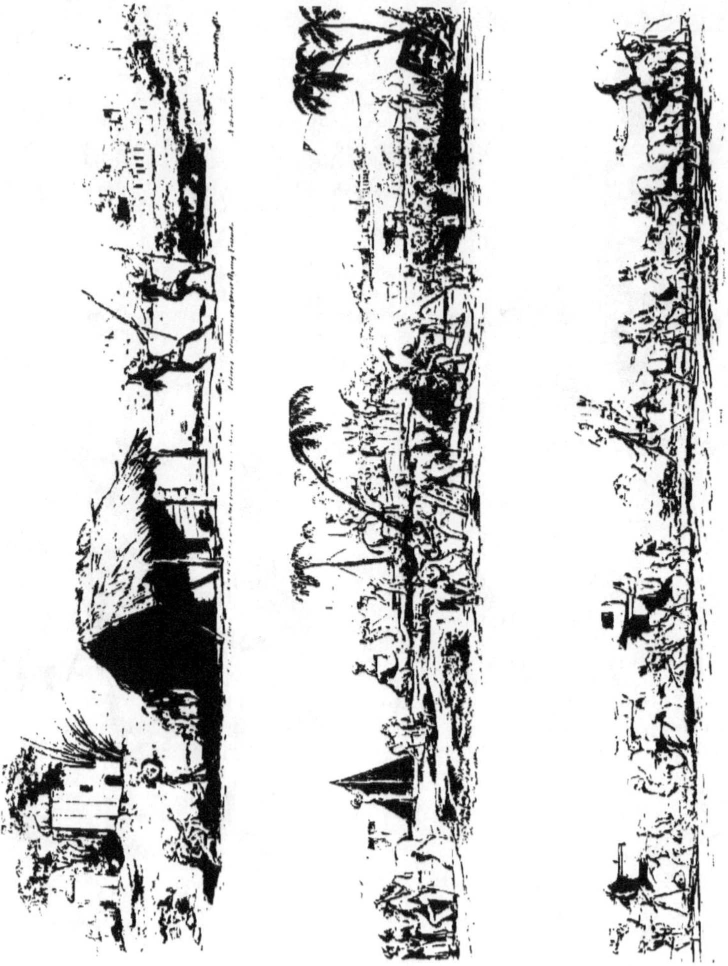

INDIAN MILITARY SCENES.

INDIAN MILITARY SCENES.

No. 4 represents a General in Command surrounded by his staff giving his orders from an elephant during an engagement. No. 5 shows the enemy matchlock men routed, artillery at the stretch galloping off. No. 6 shows the end of the engagement, the prisoners being brought in.

bright-coloured uniforms of the troops, the gay clothing of the native soldiery and attendants, the glitter of arms, the waving of pennons, all make up a mighty, motley pageant." "A body of Mysore horse, about 400, led in columns," adds this writer, who witnessed the march. "At some distance the advance guard was followed by the cavalry, with the new infantry picquets marching in their rear. The line of infantry followed, and after them the park, store, and provision carts. The guns of the allies closed the line of carriages. The ammunition and pack bullocks followed them with the rear guard, consisting of the old picquets. A squadron of cavalry moved on the reverse flank, and another body of 400 Mysoreans closed the line of march.

Lord Mornington (he did not get the title of Marquis of Wellesley for six years) went to Madras to be on the spot, but not to personally conduct the war against Tippoo. He had thought of joining the army in the field, but his brother strongly objected. "Your presence in camp, instead of giving confidence to the General, would, in fact, deprive him of the command. . . . If I were in General Harris's situation and you were to join the army I should quit it. . . . Your presence will diminish his power, at the same time that, as it is impossible that you can know anything of military matters, your powers will not answer the purpose."

This was not the only outspoken advice with which he favoured the Governor-General. Colonel Wellesley was always ready to give a plain piece of his mind to anyone, and he was equally strong in protesting against any encroachment on the Commander-in-Chief's patronage, or any failure to support him in what he did, whether he was right or wrong. "It is impossible to make him too respectable or to place him too high if he is to be the chief of an army in the field." Arthur Wellesley had, in truth, a very wise head on his still very young shoulders.

STORMING OF SERINGAPATAM, 1799.

After a Painting by Peter Kraft.

This represents the soldiers at the moment when the stormers, having crossed the wide and rocky channel of the Cauvery River, were scaling the ramparts, and met with fierce resistance.

Yet this siege of Seringapatam, which was now imminent, did not at first seem likely to add to his military reputation. It was the scene of his first and only failure in warfare. General Harris, after the first encounter with Tippoo in which Wellesley had been successfully engaged, desired to drive in the more advanced outposts at Saltaun-tope before investing Seringapatam. One attack was entrusted to Wellesley, with three white regiments and two of Sepoys. He came upon the enemy posted in an almost impenetrable jungle. The right attack, and the attacking column, becoming entangled amidst a network of irrigation canals, lost its way. Wellesley was unable to find the point of attack, and after some casualties withdrew his men.

In reporting this disaster, which has been much magnified to his discredit, he gave utterance to a fixed principle, which afterwards became an axiom in his life: "I have come to a determination [illegible] to suffer an attack to be made by night upon an enemy who is prepared and strongly posted, and whose [illegible] not been reconnoitred by daylight." He had weight enough, it seems, to impress this on his [illegible], at any rate, his influence served as a warning, for when the time was ripe to assault Seringapatam it was not made at night. If the Duke in later campaigns made night attacks upon Spanish fortresses, he had been very careful to observe the first preliminary — that of a daylight reconnaissance.

SURRENDER OF SONS OF TIPPOO SAHIB, 1789.

[illegible]

Tippoo Sahib having invaded the territory of [illegible] Lord Cornwallis and General [illegible] Seringapatam [illegible] Lord Cornwallis [illegible]

The story goes that he was utterly cast down by this petty disaster; that he went to Harris in despair, and then withdrew to his tent in great despondency. More, that when next morning arrangements were made up for a new assault by his brigade, he was absent from his post; and it is said that he owed the opportunity of retrieving his reputation to his [illegible], General Baird, who begged Harris to send for him and encourage him to go with the [illegible]. All these stories are surely apocryphal, the invention of a later date. What is at least certain is that Wellesley [illegible] command in the second attack on the Sultaun-tope, which was made early next morning and was [illegible].

The siege was actively prosecuted; batteries were armed, and soon opened a steady fire, by which [illegible] was effected in three days. Orders to storm the fort were now issued. The attack was to be made a little after midday, with troops furnished by contingents of the three armies engaged, [illegible] General Baird, who had volunteered to lead, was in chief command; Colonel Wellesley, with his [illegible] the trenches as a first reserve. The right column, under General Sherbrooke, had crossed the river and the ditch, had escaladed the parapet within seven minutes, and crossed the breach with the British flag. The left column was not so easily successful, and might have been in a critical condition but for the progress made by the right. Soon, however, the defenders began to break and fall back. Then, as an eye-witness describes, "I could not help exclaiming, 'Thank God! the business is done.'"

Tippoo Sahib was among the slain. When news came to him that the attack had [illegible] his dinner table, performed his ablutions, called for his horse, and rode to a point on the ramparts where, having dismounted, he could fire at his enemy with the carbines constantly loaded and handed [illegible]. At last, seeing that the day was going against him, he rode back into the city, and was [illegible] assailants crowding into a covered gateway. His horse was here killed, but his followers dragged him from under it, and placed him in his palanquin, where he was presently surrounded.

In a tussle with a redcoat whom he wounded he was shot through the head. His corpse, despoiled of everything valuable, fell among a heap of the slain, and was not found till pointed out by one of his servants. Both General Baird and Colonel Wellesley saw the body when it had been identified, and could not at first believe that the ill-fated Sultan was not still alive, so placid was the expression of his features, so life-like the appearance of the eyes.

The booty taken in Seringapatam was immense. Much never reached the prize agents, for many gold coins and valuable jewels were bartered by the soldiers, who were assiduous in looting the place. Still, the total amount divided was above a million sterling. Enormous quantities went for a song, even a bottle of spirits; thus, a couple of solid gold bangles, set with diamonds, bought from a soldier for a mere trifle, were found so valuable that a Hyderabad jeweller gave £32,000 for one, and was unable to name any price for the other, from the magnificence of the stones. The Sultan had secreted his treasure in the basement of the palace and other places. Besides the masses of jewels found, and valued at £100,000, there were upwards of five hundred camel loads of shawls, muslins, and rich stuffs, mirrors in great numbers, plate, and many finely-bound books.

A Soldier of Tippoo Sahib's Regular Infantry.

Seringapatam in the Distance.

The Sultan's throne was a splendid trophy, which had to be broken up and carried away piecemeal. It was a seat upon a tiger's back, under a canopy all of "sheet" gold. The fringe of the canopy was sewn with costly pearls, and it was surmounted by a gold bird whose beak was a large emerald, its eyes carbuncles, and its breast covered with diamonds; the tail was like a peacock's, the colours imitated in jewels. A more troublesome prize was Tippoo's zenana, in which were 650 wives, some of whom had been his father's, but they were eventually removed to the interior of the country and set at large. After the capture, Colonel Wellesley was appointed by General Harris Governor of Seringapatam; and, not strangely, the selection gave dire offence to General Baird. It is an unwritten, but accepted, rule that it is the leader of the assault, rather than the commander of the reserve, who should have the government of the stronghold which has been carried. Baird protested in bitter terms, implying that Harris had acted unfairly, in order to curry favour with the Governor-General. The Duke himself maintained that there were sound reasons why he should be preferred,

MYSOREAN CAVALRY ATTACKED BY BRITISH DRAGOONS.

After a Drawing [illegible]

the chief being that Baird was strongly prejudiced against the natives, and that the memory of his long imprisonment in Seringapatam still rankled in his mind.

There was more antagonism later between these two gallant soldiers, and now it was Wellesley's turn to repine. When the expedition for Egypt was planned in 1800, he was named to command, but [illegible] by Baird. It is pleasant to know that neither bore malice. Wellesley, writing to his brother, [illegible] in rather strong terms: "I have not been guilty of robbery or murder; and the Governor-G[illegible] changed his mind. I did not look for the appointment . . . . and I say that it would probably be more proper to give it to somebody else; but when it was given to me . . . . it would have been fair to allow me to hold it till I did something to deserve to lose it. . . . . However, I have lost neither my health, spirits, nor temper in consequence thereof. But it is useless to write any more upon a subject of which I wish to retain no remembrance whatever."

Gun Lascars, or Gunners of the Madras Artillery.

After [illegible]

As for Sir David Baird, his noble words deserve to be recorded. Long afterwards, in 1832, he said to Sir John Malcolm: "Times are changed. No one knows so well as you how severely I felt the preference given on several occasions to your friend Wellesley, but now I see all these things from a far different point of view. It is the highest pride of my life that anybody should ever have dreamed of my being put in the balance with him. His fame is now to me joy, and I may almost say glory." The Duke of Wellington heard this with undoubted satisfaction, and often said of Baird: "I don't believe there is a man who rejoiced more sincerely in my ultimate successes."

AN ELEPHANT ON DUTY.

After [illegible]

The intelligence of the artillery elephant was of great service in moving guns.

Wellington tackled the work of restoring confidence and order in Seringapatam with his usual promptitude and firmness. Here are some of his brief reports, sent hour by hour to the General-in Chief:—

"10 a.m., 5th May" (the day of his appointment, two days after the capture). "We are in such confusion still, that I recommend you not to come in till to-morrow, or at soonest late this evening." "Half-past twelve. I wish you could send the provost here and put him under my orders. Until some of the plunderers are hanged it is vain to expect to stop the plunder." "5th May" (no hour).—"Things are better than they were, but they are still very bad, and until the provost executes two or three people, it is impossible to expect order or, indeed, safety."

But the next day the calm, resolute master hand had prevailed, and he reports:—"May 6th.—Plunder is all stopped, the fires are all extinguished and the inhabitants are returning to their houses fast." Three days more, and the bazaars were open for all sorts of business; the streets were so crowded that the place had more the appearance of an Eastern fair than a city recently carried by force of arms. The last remaining trouble was with Tippoo's inconvenient pets. "There are some tigers here," writes Colonel Wellesley, "which I wish Meer Allim would send for, or else I must give orders to have them shot, as there is no food for them, nobody to attend to them, and they are getting violent."

Enlarged powers on a wider field soon fell to Colonel Wellesley. He was appointed Administrator of all the affairs in Mysore, with supreme civil and military control. He was so judicious, so fair and impartial, at the same time so firm and decided, that he quickly gained the goodwill of the people. But his work was also of the active kind he preferred; and he found himself called upon to take the field against a freebooter whose extensive depredations and increasing power were causing great alarm. This was a certain Doondiah Waugh, a "nameless

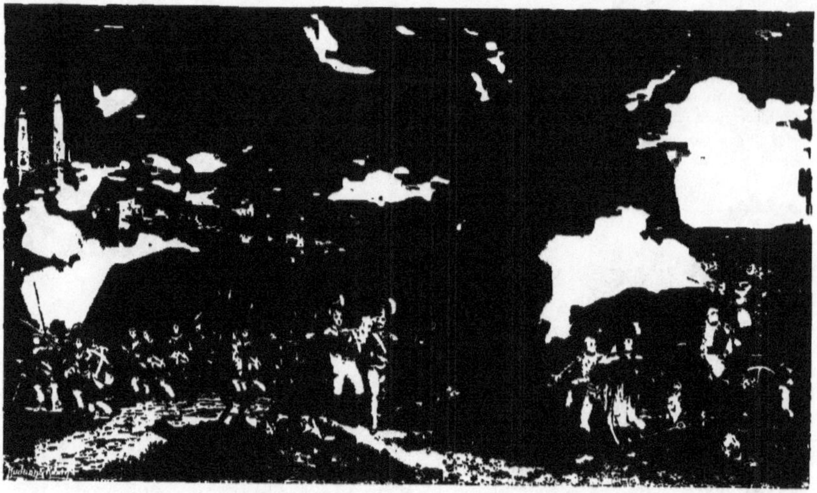

THE ATTACK ON SERINGAPATAM.

After the Painting by Robert Ker Porter.

This is one of three fine works by Sir Robert Porter, a famous painter of battle scenes. It is the right sheet, and shows the Highlanders fording the river. The assault was delivered in the afternoon, when the garrison were resting during the great heat of the day.

man," who had been a trooper in Hyder Ali's service, then deserted to rob and plunder on his own account. He had surrendered to Tippoo, who threw him into gaol, where he was found and released at the capture of Seringapatam. Directly he was free he gathered together many bold adventurers like himself—to the number of 40,000, indeed; and, being endowed with great personal courage, and some military skill, he soon grew into a dangerous scourge calling for suppression.

Colonel Wellesley was charged with his pursuit. Doondiah gave it out that he would carry off the English leader when in the hunting field, and Wellesley dared him to do it. At the same time, when a native offered to seek out Doondiah and stab him in his tent, Wellesley refused, declaring that "to offer a reward in a public proclamation for a man's head and to make a private bargain to kill him are two very different things." Doondiah, thus spared, daily grew more arrogant. He assumed the title of "King of the two Worlds," and claimed to be the coming

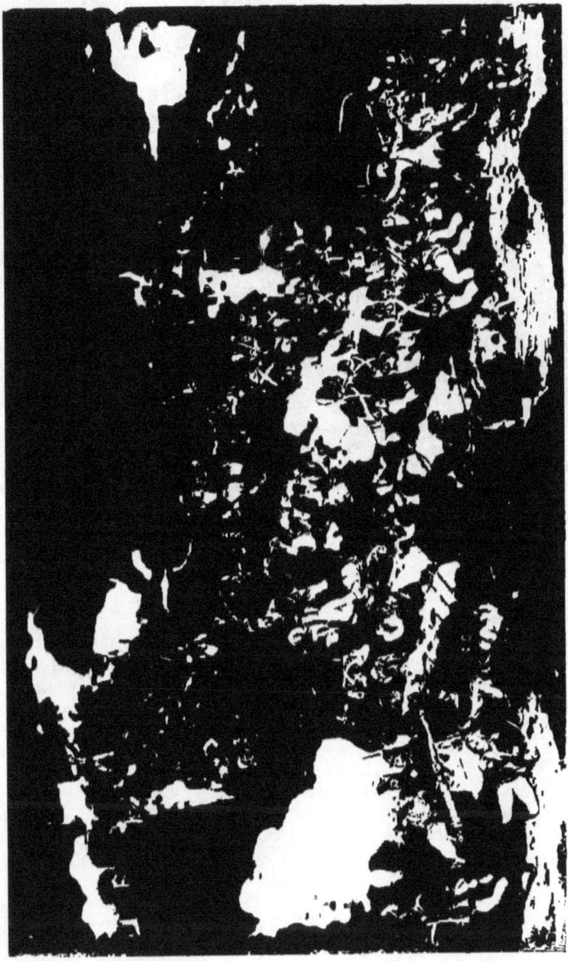

THE ATTACK ON SERINGAPATAM.

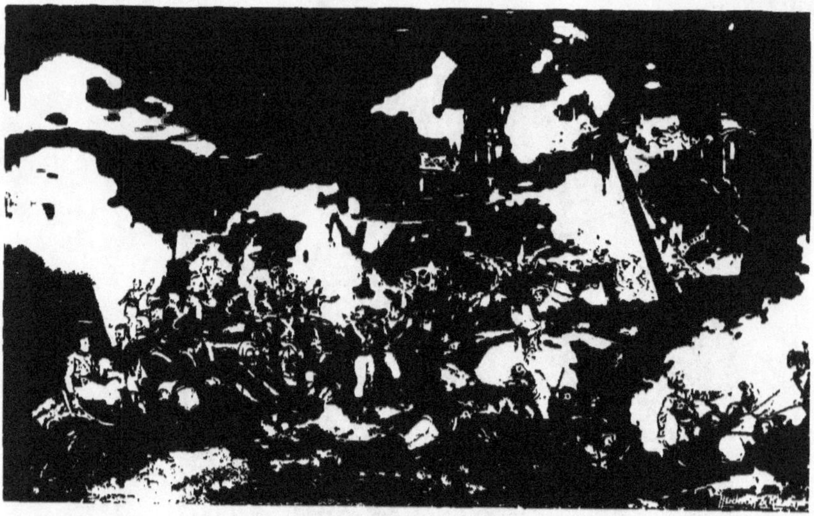

THE ATTACK ON SERINGAPATAM

After the Painting by Robert Ker Porter

The last effort made. The enemy are retreating, hard pressed, to the gate of the inner fort. Full credit must be given to the native troops, who are seen driving Tippoo's men across the bridge of the moat. It was within this inner gate that Tippoo Sahib, who fought valiantly to the end, was slain. This is the left sheet of the three which Sir R. Porter painted of the capture of Seringapatam.

liberator of India from the English. But the English under Wellesley were always at his heels, ever making extraordinarily rapid marches, and beating up his quarters continually.

The campaign became a race, and Wellesley with his troopers won it. He presently overtook Doondiah, who was some 5,000 strong, while the English were but 1,200. Attacked forthwith in a cavalry charge headed by Wellesley himself, which proved instantly and completely successful, Doondiah's followers broke and fled, the robber chieftain was slain, and his body brought into camp on a gun carriage. Another capture was that of Doondiah's son, and when the poor orphan was brought to Wellington he adopted him. Had Doondiah been taken alive, "his Majesty," as Wellesley styled him jestingly in his despatches, would undoubtedly have been hanged.

After this came the disappointment about Egypt, to which reference has already been made. As it proved, the luck was on Wellesley's side, for Baird saw no fighting, and in India the Mahratta War was close at hand. Space will not permit of any detailed account of the many intricate events that led to this campaign, the first in which Arthur Wellesley exercised a really independent command and won his first great victory. The Mahrattas were a warlike race who gained a decided preponderance among the native states, and as they increased in power the question soon arose whether they or the British should eventually be supreme in India.

The nominal head of the Mahratta confederacy was called the Peishwah, a feeble creature at this juncture, with no real authority over the most powerful chiefs he was supposed to control. The first of these was Scindiah, the next Holkar, the third the Rajah of Berar. Scindiah was the strongest. He had a large army disciplined upon a European model and under the command of Perron, a deserter from the French Marine. Holkar's force was principally cavalry, 80,000 strong. The Rajah of Berar had 20,000 cavalry and 10,000 infantry.

These turbulent leaders had fought among themselves who should make a puppet of the Peishwah, and Scindiah set up one of his own, while the real man sought refuge with the English at Be[illegible]. Th[illegible] about a reconciliation between Scindiah and Holkar, who joined forces and concentrated their armies [illegible] Hyderabad, ready to try conclusions with the British.

In the war which was now inevitable, Wellesley (but lately promoted to the rank of General) [illegible] the Southern operations. By his advice an army of observation was collected upon the [illegible] Madras Presidency, and when the command was given to him he began at once to show his [illegible] leader of men—he was ever great in organisation—and he displayed them now as fully as afterwards in Spain. He saw personally to every detail, arranged for the food and transport, the supplies of grain and bullocks, of [illegible] and forage, the carts, guns, and ammunition. He provided carefully for the comfort of his men, planned the hospital service most minutely, and, above all, cut down the baggage of the whole army. That allowed to officers was reduced to a bare minimum.

TIPPOO'S LAST EFFORT.

Tippoo Sahib fought to the last, disputing [illegible] wounded, and, taking from his horse, was placed [illegible] Tippoo struck [illegible] despoiled of every valuable, became [illegible]

Wellesley's great idea was to give his army the power of rapid movement. He did not wish to be hampered in his marches, nor at the mercy of the clouds of irregular horsemen, which were his enemy's principal strength. For the same reason he would encumber himself with no heavy guns; his largest in the siege train were 12-pounders. He caused pontoon trains to be prepared after a plan of his own, and was soon in a position to take the field with an active, mobile, and [illegible].

His first move was one of great daring, executed with surprising speed. [illegible] Poona, the Mahratta capital, which was occupied by one of Holkar's lieutenants, who threatened to burn it down, and after its seizure to reinstate the Peishwah. Wellesley, having advanced on the [illegible] March, 18[illegible]3, the Toombudra on the 12th, and then hearing, on the 19th, that Poona was in danger, he [illegible] cavalry and one battalion, with which he pressed to Poona in a forced march. [illegible] march, which he often spoke of as a great feat. "Seventy-two miles from five one [illegible] all fair marching," he said; "nor could there be any mistake as to distance, [illegible] with measuring wheels." He did not think highly of his men's powers as a rule, but [illegible] "they became good marchers from necessity." [illegible]

GENERAL SIR THOMAS MUNRO, K.C.B.

[illegible]

[illegible] in the Madras Army, and soon [illegible] held important posts, civil and military. He [illegible] Mysore after the fall of Tippoo Sahib, and his influence and authority were felt by Sir Arthur [illegible] Governor of the Presidency in 182[illegible] He greatly aided in the extension of the [illegible] He was a man of austere [illegible] won his high position by his own for troops to be in better order. . . . My marches are made at the rate of [illegible] and a few days ago I marched twenty-two and a-half miles in seven and a-half hours. [illegible] their legs from 6 a.m. till midnight, and on the very morning of [illegible] the burning sun.

He himself then and ever afterwards had extraordinary pow[illegible] day and ride seventeen miles to dinner, dance at a ball, ride [illegible] at his desk by noon next day. He thought nothing of galloping [illegible] sick in hospital. Once, returning from Lisbon to the front, he rode [illegible] in five days, and accomplished the last fifty miles, with relays of horses, [illegible]

Prompt measures were needed to cope with Scindiah and Holkar; to ensure despatch full powers, political and military, were given to General Wellesley. He was actually under the military orders of Lieutenant-General Stuart, the Commander-in-Chief in Madras, but that self-denying officer gave him *carte blanche* to act. Wellesley was very grateful for this permission to act quite independently, and at the end of the war publicly acknowledged the obligations he was under to General Stuart,

FINDING THE BODY.

[illegible] who never hampered him [illegible] gave him his confidence [illegible] Wellesley [illegible] of [illegible] Scindiah [illegible]

TIPPOO RECOGNISED BY HIS FAMILY.

made many shifts and excuses to gain time, but Wellesley was not [illegible] him to book. "I have offered you peace on terms of equality, honourable to all parties, [illegible] are responsible for all the consequences." Wellesley's first aim [illegible] the [illegible] Ahmednuggur, [illegible] desired to make safe his communications with Poona and Bombay. It [illegible] built of solid stone set in strong cement, and was armed with [illegible] His offer was refused, whereupon he at once [illegible] them Captain Duncan Grant, who had been driven in[illegible] officer in a duel. Grant was placed under arrest, and at the [illegible] the front, was the first to escalade the fort, and paid [illegible] with his life.

Wellington and Waterloo.

Meanwhile the main body of the enemy, evading Stevenson, who was co-operating with Wellesley from Arungabad, had crossed the Godavery and advanced, threatening Hyderabad. Wellesley moved up to join Stevenson, his object being to bring Scindiah as early as possible to a general action. The Mahratta Horse were most dangerous in desultory warfare, and so far their offensive operations were confined to hanging about the flanks of the opponents. But now, when Wellesley was at Arungabad and Stevenson at Jalna, the Mahrattas were joined by a large force of regular infantry with 100 guns, making up their total strength to some 50,000 men. They were posted in a strong position behind the Adjuntee Hills, and Wellesley promptly seized the opportunity to attack them in force.

TIPPOO'S TOMB.

After a Drawing by Captain Gold.

Hyder Ali, Tippoo's father, was a soldier of fortune, who rose from the meanest rank to be Sultan of Mysore. He beautified his capital with many fine buildings, and conspicuous among them was the Imperial Mausoleum.

The attack was to be made in two columns, Colonel Stevenson's taking the Western road, Wellesley's the Eastern, both of which pierce the mountain range. This division of forces has been condemned, but Wellesley defended it on the grounds that to use one defile only would have taken too much time; and that while his men were threading the one, the enemy might escape by the other. The result was that the whole brunt of the battle fell upon one column alone, Wellesley's, which, at noon upon the 23rd September, a day before that fixed for the reunion of the columns, came on the assembled Mahratta army in position by the River Kaitna.

Wellesley had to decide then and there between two hazardous courses — one was to advance boldly and fight, the other to withdraw and wait for Stevenson. The latter meant that he would be pursued and greatly harassed by the enemy's cavalry; he might possibly have lost his baggage; and in any case he would have missed the great battle, for the main body of the Mahrattas would have made off. He played the more desperate game, and resolved to attack an army three or four times stronger in infantry alone, with a vast quantity of cannon.

DEATH OF DOONDIAH.

After a Drawing in Maxwell's Wellington.

Doondiah was a noted robber, released from prison when Seringapatam fell, who set up the standard of revolt under the title of "King of two Worlds." Wellesley pursued him unceasingly, overtook him, charged the freebooters, dispersed them, and in the combat Doondiah was slain.

He quickly made his plan, and in this he was guided by his own ready wit. He saw that, to attack, he must cross the river, which had very steep banks and was called impassable by his guides. He could not well reconnoitre

THE LAST CHARGE AT ASSAYE.

After a Drawing by [illegible].

In the crisis of the action, Wellesley, who rode a handsome bay Arab, brought up his reserve of infantry and directed an advance with the bayonet, which broke the enemy utterly.

with less than his whole force, and, weak as it was, he took it boldly forward, relying from his own observation upon finding a ford. He had seen through his telescope that two villages stood opposite each other on either side of the river, and he at once concluded that there must be some regular means of communication between them. It was just as he thought. The ford was there; it was not occupied by the enemy, and he advanced boldly, covered on both flanks by cavalry, got his men and cavalry across, and was in a position to attack.

The Mahrattas had thrown back their left on the village of Assaye, and were posted in the angle between the Kaitna and another smaller river, the Juah. Wellesley now meant to fall upon the enemy's right, seeing that success on that flank would render Assaye untenable, but the officer commanding his picquets tried to rush that village, coming at once under a terrible fire of artillery. The 74th, sent to support them, also suffered great loss.

The moment was perilous. But now Wellesley brought up the cavalry, no doubt prematurely, but it was inevitable, and the splendid charge made by the 19th Dragoons, headed by the gallant Colonel Maxwell, restored the fight. The 74th rallied, and Assaye was taken at the point of the bayonet. Upon the right the struggle was still maintained; a large part of Scindiah's army had hardly been engaged, but our forces carried all

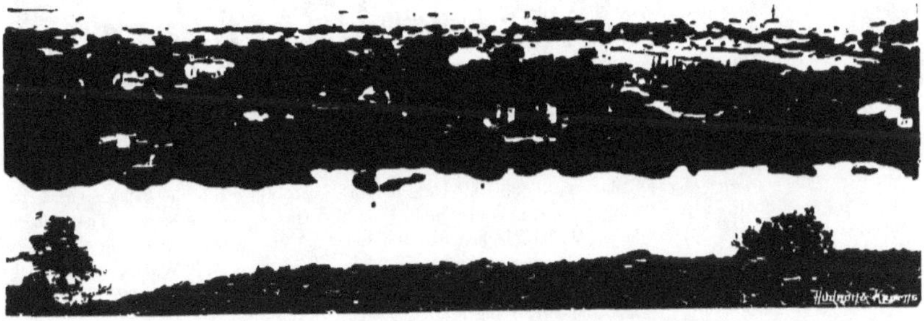

Photo. *POONA, FROM YEARODA HILL.* Copy.

before them. The only risk came from a trick of the Mahratta gunners, who lay down as if dead, and then, when passed in the charge, return to their guns. Again the cavalry decided the day, but Maxwell was killed, and the horsemen were too much broken to be of use in pursuit of the flying enemy.

Wellesley's opinion of Assaye was that it was "the bloodiest battle he ever saw." Yet the losses would have been only half as great but for the mistake in attacking the village too soon. History now admits that in this case "the most audacious course was the most prudent." No doubt Wellesley took the risks, as he often did afterwards, knowing exactly what they meant. He was in the thick of the fight himself, his orderly dragoon was killed at his side, and he lost two horses under him. In this his first battle he controlled every movement, and was always in the right place at the right time, a constant practice, and the secret of his general success in the field.

Of course he was well seconded by his troops at Assaye. They fought magnificently, although greatly worn by long marches and exposure to a tropical sun. The spirit of all ranks was superb. The General himself showed a fine example. His first remark on seeing the enemy drawn up in imposing array is said to have been, "They cannot escape us now." When in the advance he was told that the officer commanding the artillery could not get his guns forward, owing to the disablement of so many men and draught bullocks, he replied, "Then let us go on without them."

BATTLE OF ASSAYE.

After a Drawing by C[illegible]

The battle of Assaye was Wellesley's first victory as an independent commander. It was won by great daring, and after a bloodthirsty struggle.

ASSAULT OF FORT OF GAWILGHUR.

After a Drawing by Duncan Barr[illegible]

Wellesley, after a short siege, assaulted and captured this hill fort, hitherto deemed impregnable, thus ending the Mahratta War.

It is told of one officer, Captain Mackay, of the 19th Dragoons, who was attached to the Commissariat, and therefore in the rear with its people, that he asked permission to rejoin his regiment for the battle. The General positively refused it at first. Whereupon Mackay replied that "if he found his regiment going into action he would accompany it; even if he forfeited his commission, it would be with honour." "What can we do with such a fellow?" cried Wellesley. "I suppose he must have his own way." He had it, and it led him to a glorious death, charging with the leading squadron of the 19th Dragoons.

Overtures for peace were made after Assaye, and an armistice arranged, the conditions of which Scindiah

BONAPARTE'S THREATENED INVASION OF ENGLAND, 1804-5.

After a contemporary engraving, showing the details of boats assembled at [illegible]

broke by giving active help to the Rajah of Berar. This led to Wellesley's second great victory, that of Argaum. On the 30th November he found the confederate forces posted in front of a village, and, although the day was drawing on and his men had been marching since daylight, he decided to attack at once. He formed his men in two lines, infantry leading, cavalry in support. A delay occurred through the misconduct of some native troops, but the Highlanders of the 74th and 78th made short work of those opposed to them, and Scindiah's cavalry having charged, the left were repulsed. The enemy soon broke and fled, leaving all their guns behind them. They were promptly punished, even after the moon had risen, and were utterly confounded and cut up.

A gallant incident of this engagement has been preserved. Lieutenant Langlands, of the 74th, was wounded by an Arab, whose spear passed through the fleshy part of his leg. He quickly drew out the spear, and, using it against the Arab, pinned him to the ground. Whereupon a Grenadier Sepoy rushed out of the ranks, and, patting Langlands on the back, cried, "Well done, sir; very well done!" ("*Atcha Sahib; Bhot Atcha.*")

THE PREMATURE DISTRIBUTION OF THE SPOILS.

[illegible] the Napoleon [illegible] had landed in England and London was [illegible] soldiery.

After Argaum, Wellesley undertook the siege of Gawilghur, a hill fort, hitherto deemed impregnable, and which made a very sturdy defence. The brass guns alone could be employed in breaching, and they only slowly produced any effect upon the walls; but on the third day the breaches were reported practicable, and the assault was ordered. There was an outer and an inner fort. The first only was breached, and it was carried without much difficulty; but the [illegible] had [illegible] its walls intact, and was won by escalade. The forlorn-hope placed ladders against the place, and having got inside, opened the gates to the storming party. It was characteristic of this capture that the troops behaved with great moderation. There was no sack, no plundering: the men marched out of the fort as regularly as if they were only passing through it.

The Mahratta War was now ended, and with its close Wellesley's active service in India. He presently returned to Seringapatam, and was again engaged solely in civil administration. He was now the best-known, the most popular and respected officer in India. But he had had enough of India by this time. Six years' continuous service, much of it in the field, and all filled with arduous and anxious labours, began to tell upon his health. It is easy to believe that he was ambitious, eager to seek opportunity in a larger sphere than Indian warfare, to rise above the rank and status of "a General of Sepoys," as Napoleon contemptuously styled him after his first victories over the French. There was stirring work in progress upon the European continent, the near prospect of serious conflicts within the limits of these Isles.

[illegible] when Napoleon [illegible] his grand army and [illegible] flotilla of flat-bottomed boats at Boulogne and the neighbouring ports. All England had rushed to arms to meet the impending danger, every class was prepared to [illegible] their [illegible] Cabinet Ministers joined the volunteers; camps were formed round London; soldiering was the [illegible] All this may be seen in contemporary caricature.

ENROLLING THE SUPPLEMENTARY MILITIA.

After a G[illegible]

The general [illegible] [illegible]

HOW TO STOP AN INVADER.

"Boney" is seen advancing, and asking the way to London, when he meets the country people, who give him a characteristic reception.

Such BRITAIN was!
Such FLANDERS, SPAIN, HOLLAND, now is!
from such a sad reverse
O GRACIOUS GOD,
preserve Our
Country!!!
The Blessings of
PEACE,
DOMESTICK-HAPPINESS.)
The Curses of
WAR,
MASSACRE & DESOLATION

Wellington and Waterloo.

News of this national uprising, of the intense public excitement, reached India, and was not without its effect upon Wellesley. He saw with the prescient eye of true greatness that a dire and protracted struggle was inevitable; and not strangely he was anxious to get into the swim. It has been said that he already saw that the British plan of fighting in a two-deep line would be effective against the heavy columns used by the French; and this he predicted before leaving India. Undoubtedly he benefited greatly by this formation in the campaign he fought in Europe, but at the time he was credited with the remark he could hardly have known that he would be called to high command. It is certain, however, that he had closely studied and pondered on the theory and practice of war. We find constant evidence of this in his early despatches no less than in his conduct of operations in the field. He knew all the rules by heart, the axioms and broad principles which he applied with sound judgment to his own case. "A long defensive war will ruin us; we must avoid, if possible, entering upon a campaign at a distance of 700 miles from our own resources"; "if we begin by a long defensive war, and by looking after convoys which are scattered over the face of the earth, and do not attack briskly, we shall soon be in distress." As a commander he enforced the strictest discipline. He inculcated secrecy on all public matters, and, as to bribes, always took a very high line, insisting that every British officer should take even the bare offer as an insult. His thorough knowledge of detail, of all orders and regulations, enabled him to insist upon their close observance and keep his troops in the highest state of efficiency.

COLONEL OF CINQUE PORTS ARTILLERY DRILLING HIS REGIMENT.

After a Caricature Published by Fores.

The Right Hon. William Pitt, when Prime Minister, was colonel of a volunteer regiment. Two of his men are Charles James Fox, the stoutest, and Sheridan. The "fugleman" is a supporter of Mr. Pitt.

The Honest Private and the Great Colonel.

Fox and Pitt, with Sheridan as "fugleman."

After a Contemporary Caricature

He began to show in India that determination to look into everything for himself which was one of the secrets of his subsequent success. Indeed, we owe to Wellington the pregnant saying: "If you want a thing well done you must do it yourself." He never shirked the burden of this. "I am not afraid of responsibility, God knows, and I am ready to incur any personal risk for the public service." This was the keynote of his character, his duty to the public, to his sovereign and country, which he ever placed first in the objects of life. Thoroughness, promptitude, secrecy, a high sense of honour, were the governing principles that guided him in his great career.

ST. STEPHEN'S GREEN, DUBLIN.

[illegible]

The great park and public parade of the Irish capital; then, as now, a favourite resort.

CHAPTER III.

Sir Arthur Wellesley on return to England appointed to command brigade in Kent. Enters House of Commons, and becomes Chief Secretary for Ireland, under Duke of Richmond. Serves in Danish War, and present at bombardment of Copenhagen. Napoleon now seizes Spain and Portugal, but his hold is shaken by the widespread insurrection of the people, who ask for British help. The Government sends a force to Portugal, of which Wellesley has command at first, but is superseded by three other Generals. He lands, however, with the Expedition, and advancing without delay, fights and wins the battle of Roriça. This success might have been followed by the fall of Lisbon, but Burrard now interposes, forbidding pursuit [illegible]. The French, under Junot, however, take the offensive, and attack Wellesley at Vimiera, where he is in a naturally strong defensive position. He gains an easy victory, but is prevented from following up his victory by the veto of his superior, Dalrymple. Junot presently offers to capitulate, and enters into the Convention of Cintra, which brought such odium on all the Generals concerned—Dalrymple, Burrard, and Wellesley—that they were recalled and arraigned before a Court of Enquiry.

SIR ARTHUR WELLESLEY arrived in England on the 10th September, and at once renewed his acquaintance with his old friend Stuart, now Lord Castlereagh, President of the Indian Board of Control. His first business was to remove an unfavourable impression of his brother, Lord Wellesley, from Lord Castlereagh's mind. Then he saw the Duke of York, at that time Commander-in-Chief, who promised him early employment; and it came in the command of a brigade in Kent. The post was hardly worth the acceptance of a general who had led armies in the field; but Sir Arthur was ready to do his duty in whatever station he might find himself. As he put it, using an Indian phrase, he was a "nimmuck wallah"—one who had eaten the King's salt, and was always at the King's disposal.

While [illegible] in Kent, he was chosen to command a brigade, under Lord Cathcart, for service in Hanover—one of the [illegible] and generally fruitless military enterprises that were England's favourite device for carrying on [illegible] period. There had been forty-three such expeditions between 1793 and 1805, despatched [illegible]—East and West Indies, Holland, France, Naples, and the Mediterranean islands. [illegible] great expedition to Portugal, which gradually absorbed the chief military strength of [illegible], in 1809, came Walcheren, the greatest and most unfortunate that had ever [illegible]. It was [illegible] in mere fighting, but it was an utter failure through mismanagement.

Nothing came of the expedition to Hanover. It was effectually spoilt by the startling victories of Ulm and Austerlitz. But Wellesley on his return to England was again given a home brigade, now at Hastings. Now, too, he married the same Lady Catherine Pakenham whom he had courted before he went to India, and he had now no difficulty in gaining her parents' consent. There was no change in his sentiments, although the lady had, with much generosity, offered to release him altogether. In the years that had intervened she had been afflicted by that terrible scourge, small-pox, and had lost something of her early beauty. But Arthur Wellesley was too loyal a gentleman to be untrue to his word.

EARL CATHCART.

[illegible]

Served in the War of American Independence and with the Guards in Flanders. Commanded an abortive expedition into Hanover in 1805, and again in the attack on Copenhagen in 1807. Was British Military Commissioner with the Czar's armies in 1813-14.

About this time Sir Arthur Wellesley was returned for the borough of Rye, a town at no great distance from his brigade headquarters at Hastings. He entered the House of Commons in time to undertake the defence of his brother, whose administration as Governor-General was very virulently attacked. Lord Wellesley was charged with wasteful expenditure, misappropriation of funds, unjust wars and oppression. The debates extended over more than a year, and ended at last in a motion, carried by a large majority, entirely exonerating Lord Wellesley.

But Sir Arthur also took office, having been chosen by the new Viceroy, the Duke of Richmond, as Chief Secretary for Ireland—a post he continued to hold, but discharged by deputy, for some time after his departure for the Peninsula. He was cordially welcomed back to Dublin by many old friends, who saw in him the same Arthur Wellesley who had been only an aide-de-camp in the Vice-regal Court, but "Arthur Wellesley judiciously improved," says Sir Jonah Barrington. "He had not forgotten his friends and he had not forgotten himself. . . . During his residence in Ireland I did not have one complaint against any part of his conduct, either as a public or private man." Just before his departure for Spain in 1808 Barrington gave him a dinner party, and says that he never saw him more cheerful or more happy. But

GRAND TRIUMPHAL ENTRY OF THE FIRST CONSUL INTO LONDON.

After a Caricature [illegible]

When the invasion scare was at its height, Napoleon was [illegible] in British prints, and [illegible] by the London Press that he [illegible] against one [illegible].

NAPOLEON, EMPEROR OF THE FRENCH AND KING OF ITALY.

After an Italian Portrait, about [illegible].

Napoleon [illegible] the purple in May, 1804, with the title of Emperor of the French, the dignity being hereditary. He was [illegible] by the Pope in [illegible] December [illegible] King of Italy, in Milan, the following year. Then after having threatened England with invasion for [illegible] Boulogne, and transferred his vast army to Central Europe, where he took Ulm and then fought a series [illegible] the utter discomfiture of Austria, Prussia, and Russia [illegible] the first unquestionably his greatest [illegible] drawn battle fought in the depth of winter; but at [illegible] his star was again in the ascendant.

BOMBARDMENT OF COPENHAGEN, SEPTEMBER [illegible], 1807.

[illegible]

Fears that the Danish fleet might fall into the hands of the [illegible] Expedition under Admiral Gambier [illegible]. The Danes refused [illegible] fleet, and the capital was bombarded, with great loss of life and [illegible] capitulated, and the [illegible] given up [illegible] to England.

when, speaking of the bombardment of Copenhagen, of which more directly, Sir [illegible] bitterly against it, Sir Arthur Wellesley took him to task, asking what he meant, and speaking [illegible]

THE LION TURNED INTO A SNIPE.

[illegible]

The attack on the small State of Denmark was [illegible] cowardly and unworthy [illegible] the Government was [illegible]

was the action of Kioge, where he stormed the [illegible] recalled to Copenhagen in order to carry out the [illegible]

In accepting the appointment [illegible] Dublin he had stipulated that it should not interfere with "his military promotion and other pursuits," and now when another expedition was planned, that against Copenhagen, he claimed to take part in it, and was appointed to command a brigade, again under Lord Cathcart. The attack made by Great Britain on Denmark has been bitterly condemned as [illegible] of power. But at that time Denmark [illegible] coquetting with [illegible] fleet at [illegible] [illegible] [illegible] might have been [illegible] the [illegible] Copenhagen, besieged, made but a feeble resistance, would not capitulate [illegible] and partially burnt.

Sir Arthur Wellesley [illegible] and defeated the Danes [illegible] included [illegible] ships [illegible] in the port was one, an English-built frigate, which had been presented to the Crown Prince by King George III. This ship was not [illegible] with the rest, out of compliment to the donor. But the Crown Prince would not accept the concession. [illegible] to Caporit [illegible] ordered the ship to be manned by sixteen British sailors who had been taken prisoners, and sent over to England.

It is worth remembering that, of the two greatest soldiers who figured in the early part of this century, the one owed his chief fame, the other his first check and final downfall, to the

A STANDING TOAST IN THE ARMY.

[illegible]

Officers at a regimental mess table drinking confusion to General Whitelocke.

GENERAL WHITELOCKE.

[illegible]

war in the Peninsula. Wellington would never have risen in the first rank but for the chances it offered him of displaying his marvellous capacity. As for Napoleon, when, blind to truth and justice, he invaded Portugal and overran Spain, Talleyrand, a cynical but clear-sighted politician, prophesied that it was the beginning of the end. It was the opening of a malignant sore that was to eat into and consume the resources [illegible] of France. From first to last she sent some 350,000 men across the Pyrenees, and not a third of them returned home.

A CHARADE.

[illegible]

"My first the [illegible]
[illegible]
My whole [illegible]
[illegible]
A disgrace [illegible]"

Junot, who commanded the French advance, actually crossed the frontier, and, pausing only a moment at Salamanca, was again hurried forward to invade Portugal in November, 1807. The French settled down like locusts on Portugal. They had arrived almost in rags. The general [illegible] and laid their hands on anything they found [illegible] naked. Later on General Loison had shirts [illegible] taken from the beds in the royal palaces. [illegible] precious possessions were abandoned, [illegible] on the quay at Belem, and became [illegible] many other magnificent silver [illegible] and the pillage was wholesale and widespread. Meanwhile, farther back, Napoleon had made himself master of Spain. Two armies [illegible] followed Junot's march, 40,000 men in all, one of which had advanced to Vittoria, the other into Catalonia [illegible] the great high road from France to Madrid, the second took possession of Barcelona and its famous [illegible] Montjuich. It was Napoleon's first aim to occupy the fortresses; and by bribery and *finesse* he soon held San Sebastian, [illegible], Montjuich, and Pampeluna. The last was obtained by a contemptible trick. The Spanish garrison was playing at snowballs when the French arrived, and, being hospitably admitted, they joined in the sport, to [illegible] possession till 1813.

Soon Murat, having crossed the mountains with a fine force of cavalry a[illegible] Imperial Guard, [illegible] Madrid. The enslavement of Spain had been ca[illegible] without a blow being struck [illegible] warnings [illegible] But there was presently a rude awakening—sudden, startling, terrible. It was like an explosion, and set the whole country alight with devastating flames. Small riots and disturbances showed the direction of the current; but the great storm broke in Madrid upon the 2nd of May, 1808. The supposed abduction of the last of the Royal Family—[illegible]

CAPTURE OF THE CAPE OF GOOD HOPE BY SIR DAVID BAIRD. 1806.

[illegible]

The Cape Colony was first settled by the Dutch, [illegible] 1795 [illegible] from Holland [illegible] by British troops. British Government ruled it until 1802, when it was [illegible] Amiens [illegible] retaken by Sir David Baird in conjunction with Admiral Sir H[illegible]

FLIGHT OF THE COURT OF PORTUGAL BEFORE THE FRENCH INVASION.

When the French army under Junot invaded and occupied Portugal in 1808, the Court fled to Brazil. The Prince Regent was strongly urged to do this by Admiral Sir Sidney Smith, commanding the British fleet in the Tagus, who took him on board his ship and carried him away.

IV, and Ferdinand, the new King, were both in Napoleon's hands—kindled the insurrection. There was a fierce uprising. The Spaniard, when his passions are aroused, is savage and truculent. Numbers of unarmed French soldiers were slain, and there was much bloodshed in the streets. Murat suppressed this insurrection sternly—his lieutenants were more ruthless than he—and the result was an outburst of popular fury that went far beyond resistance to the intrusive French. The whole nation flew to arms. All Europe admired the courage and energy of a people hitherto deemed debased and unnerved, and in England especially deep sympathy was shown with

Soldiers of the 42nd Highlanders, the Black Watch.

From a series of drawings by William Walton, published in 1807.

Soldiers of the 95th, afterwards named the Rifle Brigade.

From a series of drawings by William Walton, published in 1807.

VALDES.

After a [illegible] Print.

A Spanish man who [illegible] guerilla warfare, was [illegible] shot, [illegible] for many dozens of Frenchmen, 1808[illegible]. He was one of the many instances of [illegible] patriotic Spaniards who devoted their lives [illegible] the service of their country.

Insurrection in Madrid on the 2nd May (Dia dos de Mayo), 1808.

After [illegible] Print of the period.

The national uprising began in Madrid on the 2nd May, 1808, when it was thought that the last of the Spanish Royal Family were [illegible] to France. [illegible] the train. Some French soldiers were killed, their comrades [illegible] into the city, and a terrible massacre ensued. Murat exacted still further penalties, [illegible] was the fate of hundreds of patriots. From this time [illegible] spread through Spain.

Spain. Napoleon had no thought of yielding before the hatred and hostility of Spain. Resistance gave him the right to conquer, to annex the Peninsula as another appanage of his upstart Empire. He resolved to put a member of his own family upon the throne of Spain, and having failed with his brother Lucien, passed on the crown to Joseph, a weaker vessel, who went to Bayonne vainly protesting, and was summarily sent across the Pyrenees into Spain, to hold his kingdom at the point of the sword.

The successful defence of Zaragossa about this date was another blow to the French invaders. Much credit in this noble and intrepid feat is due to a young woman, the famous "Maid of Zaragossa," Manuela Sanchez, whose splendid example restored courage to her fellow-citizens. It is recorded of this brave girl that, on visiting a battery lately abandoned by the Spaniards, she herself seized a lighted match from a dead gunner's hand and fired on the advancing army. Her courageous spirit roused the fugitives to return, and the battery was recovered. But the French persisted in their attacks, and presently one-half of the city was captured, while the other still held out. At this point the French

VIVA ESPANA
MUERA NAPOLEON.

"Viva España, muera Napoleon!"—*"Long live Spain, down with Napoleon!"*

[illegible] Spanish [illegible] French invaders is well shown in the [illegible]

THE MAID OF ZARAGOSSA.

[illegible]

general summoned the garrison to surrender, using the single word "Capitulate!" and received the well-known heroic refusal, "*Guerra al cuchillo*" ("War to the knife"). The murderous conflict was now renewed, and maintained to the bitter end; it was fought out street by street, inch by inch, and ended in victory to the defenders. The French were forced to give up the ground they had gained, and withdrew.

Staggered by these reverses, which culminated in the surrender at Baylen, the new King, Joseph Bonaparte, forthwith fled from his capital, and retired, with his Court, to Vittoria. He gave the scattered French columns orders to concentrate; and, under the shadowy pretence of seeking more healthy quarters, fell back towards Bayonne. Junot, five hundred miles away in distant Portugal, was left to hold his own as best he could, reaping the harvest he had sown. For his occupation of the country had been carried out with such oppressive, ill-judged harshness, that he had to deal now with an implacably hostile people. Junot

Lieutenant-General Sir Arthur Wellesley, K.B., 1808.
After [illegible]

H.R.H. THE DUKE OF YORK (17[illegible]).
After an Engraving by [illegible] Seeton.
For many years and until his death Commander-in-Chief of the Army. He succeeded Sir David Dundas in that post.

himself was detested. A man of good parts, but uneven in [illegible] of judgment, he had failed as a military [illegible]. The Spanish insurrection spread into Portugal, and the Spanish troops who had marched with Junot into that country mutinied. Those in Oporto joined the Galician patriots, but others under Junot's own eye in Lisbon were made prisoners bodily, and thrown for safe custody into hulks upon the Tagus. The Portuguese were [illegible] for revolt, but were in part [illegible] columns of French troops. Now [illegible] him. He was menaced from [illegible] England was about to enter [illegible] tentative fashion [illegible] military forces in puny [illegible] fighting returns, except in the capture of the Cape of Good Hope from the Dutch in 1806 [illegible] Baird, who [illegible] the foundations of our vast and valuable South African Empire. But against [illegible] ventures, and the quite recent disaster in Monte Video had left the whole

AT THE SIEGE OF ZARAGOSSA

[illegible] with [illegible]. Various events in South America—early disaster partly retrieved by small successes—led the British Government in 1807 to concentrate a large force at Monte Video for the reduction of Buenos Ayres. The supreme command was given to Lieutenant-General Whitelocke, an unfortunate man placed in a position altogether beyond his capacity, and who eventually forfeited his commission and the very name of soldier. The Government abandoned the hapless General to his fate, although some share of responsibility must attach to those who chose him for command. Yet even Buenos Ayres afforded no pregnant lesson, and it was almost by accident that the conduct of their newest enterprise fell into such able hands. It may be asserted confidently that, but for Wellesley, the expedition to Portugal would scarcely have succeeded. The force was sent out imperfectly equipped and badly organised. It was deficient in cavalry, and little fitted for the arduous campaign that was undoubtedly before it.

GENERAL JUNOT.

[illegible] time [illegible] Paris.

[illegible]

[illegible] first attracted [illegible] by his [illegible] his [illegible] with his [illegible] Paris [illegible] He was [illegible]

All the Ministry could do was to put forward crude, ill-digested plans, plans that erred against every principle of the military art, and bound, if followed, to end in fresh disaster. They did not know what to be at, or whom to entrust with the command. Should the expedition land at Corunna, at Oporto, or Lisbon? Should young Sir Arthur Wellesley—at that time the most promising, the most successful of our military leaders [illegible] Should [illegible], although not necessarily [illegible]?

MARSHAL MURAT.

For some time King of Naples.

[illegible]

He was the son of an innkeeper who had charge of the stables. He entered the Revolutionary Army, and soon attracted the attention of Napoleon by his fiery valour. Handsome, fond of gay uniforms, a fine swordsman, and a splendid rider, he was the [illegible] of a cavalry leader, and his services were conspicuous. His mental calibre was not high. At the downfall of Napoleon, he fled from his throne, was recaptured, and shot by order of a Neapolitan Court-Martial.

[illegible] was, no doubt, much competition for this command. It [illegible] that the Duke of York, at that time Commander-in-Chief of the Army, looked for it, although his campaign in Flanders was not quite forgotten; and there were other grounds for doubting his fitness. But if he could not have it for himself, he was resolved [illegible] young soldier, certainly not to Wellesley, [illegible] India, and was a politician and member [illegible] holding civil office. There were [illegible], who had more claims, who [illegible] service and their intimate [illegible] work, than this "young sprig of aristocracy," as Wellesley was often called. [illegible] arguments prevailed over the staunch friendship of Castlereagh, who, [illegible] obliged to supersede him completely before he got well to sea.

BEGINNING OF THE PENINSULAR WAR.

Th[illegible] British expedition to Portugal under W[illegible] beg[illegible] [illegible] M[illegible] River [illegible] 1st August, 1808 [illegible] [illegible]

What the authorities did, they did thoroughly, as they thought [illegible] the military [illegible] [illegible]ities, that [illegible] all this it was the Duke of York who decided the point with a most re[illegible]tatness that could have been only possible in the favourite son of [a] personal Sovereign. Not one, but three, generals were [placed over] Wellesley's head. From supreme chief he was to be no more than fourth in command. The first [news] that reached him on [illegible] [reaching] the Spanish coast was a letter informing him that Sir Hew Dalrymple, Sir Harry Burrard, and Sir John Moore were appointed to serve with the expedition.

The first, Dalrymple, was at this time approaching his 60th year, and esteemed in the Service as a veteran soldier, no worse yet no better than a dozen others who attended the levees of the Duke of York. He was at this time G[overnor] of Gibraltar, [illegible] had [illegible] [illegible] [illegible] stimulation and supp[ort] to the Spanish [illegible] [illegible] [illegible] was a [illegible] [illegible] [illegible] [illegible] [illegible] yet [illegible] [illegible] [conspicuous] as before. The second, Sir Harry Bu[rrard] was also an [illegible] [illegible] officer, a Guardsman not without ex[perience] in the field, [illegible] very marked [illegible]

As to Sir John Moore, [unquestionably] no better [illegible] [illegible] have been made [illegible] [illegible] the third place. So [illegible] [illegible] was [illegible] based on good and [illegible] [illegible] that W[ellesley] [illegible]

ROYAL ART[ILLERY]MEN.

would have gladly accepted him as chief. He had won his spurs in Corsica and the West Indies; had served with Abercromby in Egypt as a general officer, and again in independent command in Sicily and Sweden. The sweetness of his nature shines forth in his fine features in all the pictures preserved of him; his courage, his constancy, his unalterable firmness under the sharpest adversity, place him high in the esteem of his fellow-countrymen.

BRITISH SOLDIERS DRILLING

After a Contemporary Caricature

This drawing was made at the period of greatest military activity in England during the Napoleonic war, [illegible] as a model for the [illegible].

These supersessions, although most mortifying to Wellesley, he took in good part. "I shall be the junior of the lieutenant-generals," he wrote to Lord Castlereagh. "However, I am ready to serve the Government wherever and as they please." He knew that Sir Hew Dalrymple was to carry out the scheme he (Sir Arthur) had planned. Yet, still, he was loyal. "Whether I am to command the army or not, or am to quit it, I shall do my best to secure its success, and you may depend upon it that I shall not hurry the operations or commence them one moment sooner than they ought to be commenced, in order that I may reap the credit of success."

There was nothing to be gained by waiting; quite the reverse, for the troops cooped up on board ship would be better on shore, and the organisation of the army for the field could then be pushed forward. The place of disembarkation was much discussed. Wellesley first visited the British Admiral, Cotton, who was lying off the mouth of the Tagus, and conferred with him as to whether it would be safe to [illegible] Lisbon direct. [illegible] movement [illegible] Admiral [illegible] under [illegible] army, probably crippled, and "certainly in a not very effective state," would [illegible] effective force of the French. There could be no co-operation from the

Second Phase of the Battle of Roliça, on 17th August, 1808.

After a [illegible]

The French centre was strongly posted on steep ground covered by ravines full of rocks and brushwood, and the British attack was long and desperately resisted. The position had to be at last abandoned, owing to Wellesley's outflanking movement on the right.

Portuguese, for Wellesley did not yet realise what incapable and useless allies he had, and still looked for their help. So he resolved to concentrate at the Mondego River, the mouth of which was already [illegible] the disembarkation commenced on the 1st August, 1808, Admiral Cotton and his officers and men [illegible]

It was a tedious business, owing to the swell, in which the transports rolled as heavily as in a gale of wind, but it was completed in four days, using country boats and those of the fleet. Several craft were upset and men and horses nearly lost in landing on the steep shelving shore. The fifth day, General Spencer, who had landed in Southern Spain, arrived, having been recalled by Wellesley, because "the essential object was to drive the French from Portugal," and the British were not strong enough for the work unless combined and concentrated. Two other brigades, Acland's and Anstruther's, had left England and were

The Last Harvest or British Threshers Making French Crops.

[illegible]

now close at hand. A large contingent, 12,000 strong, which had been employed in a wild goose chase to Sweden, under Sir John Moore, had now returned to England, and was also on its way to Portugal. With the number in hand and these reinforcements approaching, Wellesley was in a position to take the offensive, and there were strong [illegible] why he should do so with all despatch. [illegible] with autumn would come tempestuous weather, when the fleet could not safely remain on this rockbound coast, [illegible] his true base, the sea and England [illegible]

It was very necessary to strike a blow soon. Although the French forces were still dispersed about the country, they would [illegible] soon concentrate to oppose him. Accordingly Wellesley prepared to [illegible] forward at once. He had 13,000 men all told, almost entirely infantry; but only a handful of cavalry—200 [illegible] —and he was greatly hampered by [illegible] impossible to reconnoitre or [illegible] count upon the Portuguese [illegible] people, whose [illegible] loyal to us. The fact was, [illegible] great stomach for [illegible] British support [illegible] tally expecting our defeat in the first battle, were [illegible] the other side. [illegible] Bernardim [illegible]

General Sir Hew Dalrymple, Bart.

[illegible]

This distinguished [illegible] born 175[illegible], died 18[illegible] served with the Duke of York in Flanders, and was afterwards Lieutenant-Governor [illegible] Governor of Gibraltar in 1808 [illegible] helped the Spanish insurrection, and was sent [illegible] the command of the army [illegible] in correspondence with Burrard and Wellesley [illegible] Convention of Cintra [illegible] He was arraigned with his colleagues [illegible] Chelsea and censured, although [illegible] He [illegible] no subsequent command.

Wellesley, but proposed to act [illegible] Only [illegible] was at last [illegible] column. This lukewarmness did much mischief, and especially in the matter of supp[illegible] obtained. Freire, who had seized and appropriated to his [illegible] large magazines, [illegible] W[illegible]y to feed his troops. The British commissariat was inexperienced, not to say inefficient, and it could hardly meet Wellesley's own necessities. Indeed, when his force advanced, they had no more than eighteen days' rations, and of these the troops carried three in their haversacks, thus adding to the weight carried by the men. Junot knew, on the 2nd August, of Wellesley's landing, and prepared to meet him; but through his chief lieutenant, not in person, for Lisbon was so hostile he did not like to leave the capital himself. One general, Loison, was sent by the south side of the Tagus to Abrantes; another, Laborde, advanced directly north, towards Leiria, where he was to watch the approaching British and cover Loison. The two French columns were to combine about Leiria, but Sir Arthur forestalled them there, having entered that place in strength on the 11th August. Laborde was then no nearer than Batalha, eight miles distant, and Loison was still some five-and-twenty miles away, with wearied men who had wasted their strength in forced marches, aiming at an impossible junction with Laborde.

Dragoons and Lancers of the French Imperial Guard.

From Horace Vernet's French Uniforms

Laborde now sought for a position in which to give battle, but could find nothing suitable here at Batalha, the site of one of the most splendid monasteries of ancient Portugal, a marvel, indeed, of church architecture. He fell back to Alcobaça, another famous monastery, then to Obidos, always closely followed by the British, who, on the 15th, attacked and drove in his picquets. This was the first blood drawn in the Peninsula, and an English officer, Lieutenant Bunbury, of the 95th (Rifles), was killed, together with a few of the men. On the 16th August, Laborde stood fast at Roleia, or Rorica, but he was in a position of much difficulty and danger. Loison was too far away to help him; and by falling back he increased that distance. If he drew towards Loison he uncovered the shortest road to Lisbon; and, lastly, by standing his ground he exposed himself to be attacked by three times his numbers. Undoubtedly Wellesley knew all this too, and pressed forward hotly, for the advantage lay with him. Early on the morning of the 17th he began the combat of Roleia, his first victory over the French.

PIONEER AND DRUMMER.

From Horace Vernet's French Uniforms.

The pioneer in the bearskin belonged to a French Light Infantry Regiment, the drummer to a regiment of the Line.

Wellesley's plan of battle was to turn the enemy's right flank, the side on which Loison might be expected to come up, then throw his chief weight upon Laborde's centre, while a smaller force of Portuguese menaced his left. Sir Arthur led the centre in person, having under him Hill's, Nightingale's, Craufurd's, and Fane's brigades; General Ferguson commanded the turning movement, on the left (French right); Colonel Trant was with the Portuguese on the other flank. These dispositions were completed with great precision, while the French looked on, according to an eye-witness, surprised and uneasy. General Foy, who afterwards wrote an account from the French point of view, says that his men, largely conscripts, who had as yet engaged only Portuguese irregulars, were much impressed by the stern soldierly bearing of these worthier foes. The firm, steady march of the British infantry, who never lost their formation even on rough ground, showed them to be troops of a fine quality.

Laborde did not wait for the attack; but, finding his position compromising, he drew off "with the dexterity of a practised warrior," and took a fresh, but far more formidable, position on the heights of Zambugeira, a mile to the rear. Wellesley followed, continuing the same plan, still outflanking the enemy's right, and pressing upon his

JOSEPH BONAPARTE, KING OF SPAIN.

[illegible]

[illegible]

centre. The ground was steep, the ascent by narrow paths winding through deep ravines, crossed with masses of rock, and entangled with a dense growth of evergreens. The French defended these ravines desperately; and Laborde, clinging always to the hope of reinforcements by Loison on his right, greatly strengthened this side. He fell thus with great impetus upon two British regiments—the 9th and 29th—whose eager ardour had carried them far forward, and whom Laborde attacked fiercely, driving them back down the cliffs. The 29th were taken in flank while making a front attack, and their right wing was nearly destroyed. But they were rallied on their left wing, the 9th made a new show, and, being reinforced by the 5th, they regained foothold above, at another part of the hill. Where the 95th were engaged, the French held two small houses, from which they kept up a galling fire. The rifle skirmishers suffered much; and at last one man rose, crying to his comrades "Over, over!" whereon the whole line cried "Over, over!" and carried the buildings at the bayonet's point. But now Ferguson's out-flanking movement on the right again told with great effect, and Laborde was everywhere forced to give way.

The French were beaten, but Laborde had handled them with such skill that he was able to draw off with no great loss. He was strong in cavalry, and he used it admirably to cover his retreat, being considerably helped by Wellesley's weakness in that arm. His retreat was towards Bombarral, a point five miles to the rear, where he found Loison waiting, and the French forces were once more united, but with the road to Lisbon, *viâ* Torres Vedras, uncovered.

Sir Arthur Wellesley would now have pushed on, and probably secured the capital; but, hearing that reinforcements and a strong fleet of store ships had reached the coast, he paused to cover their disembarkation. He again retreated, therefore, behind the Maceira River, meaning, when all were on shore, to renew his advance towards Torres Vedras and Lisbon. At the same time he wrote to Sir Harry Burrard, who was hourly expected, and begged that when Sir John Moore arrived with his division, they might be directed on Santarem and the Tagus. Wellesley's plan was to attack Junot in front, while Moore intercepted his best line of retreat and cut him off from the other French armies in the north of Spain. Burrard, unfortunately, turned up at this juncture, and forbade Wellesley's further advance. They must wait for Moore, he said; the cavalry was weak, the artillery badly horsed, it was dangerous to get too far from the coast and the ships—the only certain source of supply. It would be safer not to fight.

BATTLE OF VIMIERA.

From Westall's "Victories of Wellington."

This engagement was not so great a triumph as it should have been, for Wellesley was superseded on the field and the pursuit checked.

"Whether we advance or not," replied Wellesley, "we shall have to fight. For the French will certainly attack us if we do not attack them." The soundness of this forecast was soon proved. Junot was bound to assume the offensive; and he had already left Lisbon, on the 15th August, having taken what precautions he could to overawe the city, and leaving it with a garrison of 7,000 men. He reached Torres Vedras, where he met Loison on the evening of the 18th; and next day (the 19th) he was joined by Laborde, and the very day after by his reserves. Thus concentrated, he girt up his loins to fight, whilst his numerous cavalry formed such an impenetrable screen around him, that Wellesley had no news of his position or his movements. As has been said, Sir Harry Burrard would not suffer Wellesley to advance and fight the enemy wherever he found him. Fortunately, General Junot was obliging enough to save him the trouble by taking the initiative himself.

This brought on the Battle of Vimiera. The British position had been occupied the previous evening more for convenience as a bivouac than for defensive purposes. Yet it was naturally strong. One flank, the right and southern, was on hills that ended in the sea; the centre, at Vimiera, was posted on a high hill in front of that village; the left extended, rather weakly held, to the north and the road to Lourinham. Here the men slept fully accoutred, and under orders to stand to their arms at daybreak, 3 a.m. But they were spared the till now inevitable rule for every parade, of hair dressing and "hair tying"—an operation always grievous to be borne. The approach of the French was detected about midnight by a German dragoon officer, who heard the news from a servant of an innkeeper.

FRENCH CONSCRIPTS FLYING TO JOIN THE ARMY.

From the Literary Panorama.

The strong disinclination of the French nation to military service is well illustrated by this caricature.

It was reported at once to Sir Arthur Wellesley. The General, it is said, was sitting on a table, swinging his legs to and fro, alert enough; but he hardly believed the news. When day broke, and there were no signs of the French, he was still incredulous. But about 7 a.m. clouds of dust betrayed their march, and its direction was plainly apparent. Several columns, in order of battle, were crossing the whole British front, and aiming at the left. Whereupon Wellesley, seeing that his right was not yet threatened, withdrew four of his brigades from that flank, and sent them under cover of a convenient range of hills to strengthen the left. Fane and Anstruther still stood firm in the centre, and Hill with one brigade was on the right.

Junot's plan was to assail both the centre and left, the latter seeming an almost naked front, for he had no knowledge of Wellesley's masterly move towards it. Moreover, he did not realise, till he was committed to it, that on this side the ground was much cut up with ravines and nearly impervious to attack. Laborde attacked the centre, Brennier, supported by Loison, the left, Kellerman was in reserve behind Loison. Laborde came on with 5,000 men against Anstruther, and was soon sharply checked. Reinforced by Kellerman's grenadiers, they renewed the attack against the gallant 43rd, who fell back upon a churchyard on the hill, from which they could not be dislodged; and presently charged out in their turn so furiously that the French were driven back. In this hand to hand fight the struggle was so fierce that a sergeant of the 43rd and a French soldier were afterwards found dead "still grasping their muskets, with the bayonets driven through each body from breast to back."

French Dragoon.

From Horace Vernet's French Uniforms.

Conscript of the Imperial Guard.

Musketry and artillery fire had meanwhile so shattered the attacking columns that they could make no impression, and now the small handful of British dragoons, under their intrepid leader, Colonel Taylor, charged the broken enemy, but were met by a far superior force of French cavalry, and lost their chief and half their numbers. The French attack on this central part of the field had decidedly failed; but Wellesley, fearing the cavalry, which "rode stiffly between the two armies and were not to be lightly meddled with," and Kellerman, still intact in a pinewood, restrained his men from pursuit

The battle might be going well on this side, but it was by no means finally decided there. On the left, however, more marked success was already achieved. Selignac had attacked with great impetuosity, but had been met with unshaken confidence by greatly superior numbers, in fact, by the brigades astutely sent by Wellesley to reinforce this flank. Seligmac was soon driven back with many wounded, including himself, and the loss of his guns. Now Brennier with another French column, which had been entangled in the rough ground, got through and made a spirited attack still more to the left. He also was repulsed, and, in the counter-charge made by the 71st and 92nd, suffered severely, being himself taken prisoner.

It was in this charge that the intrepid piper of the 71st, who was wounded in the thigh, still blew his pibroch seated on the ground, stoutly declaring that "the lads should nae want music to their wark." It was a day in

BATTLE OF VIMIERA, 1808.

Another representation, after a Picture by L'Evêque

[illegible] Wellesley, hoping to drive the British into the sea. His main effort was against the left, which [illegible] that the French were defeated and General Brennier taken prisoner, [illegible] English had still [illegible] continued, Junot must have been destroyed.

which all ranks showed much courage and self-reliance. A message came to General Anstruther when seemingly hard pressed that Sir Arthur would send him supports. "I want no assistance," was his steady reply. "I am beating the French, and I am able to beat them wherever I find them." There [illegible] truer saying. The capture of General Brenier [illegible] told Wellesley that the French had [illegible] their strength. For when Brenier [illegible] "whether Kellerman had charged [illegible] Sir Arthur, knowing that he had done [illegible], guessed also that this was the last French reserve. It was victory all along the line, a victory completed early in the day with men in hand and to spare. Two British brigades had not fired a shot; one (Hill's) was two miles nearer Torres Vedras than the French. A prompt advance on one side must have destroyed the defeated and disorganised French, on the other Lisbon lay within reach of a vigorous blow. With the unerring eye of a great leader Wellesley saw his advantage, and yet was forbidden to seize it. Sir Harry Burrard, who had so far generously abstained from exercising command, now came upon the ground and interposed his authority, peremptorily ordering a halt.

Wellesley's Headquarters the Night before the Battle of Vimiera.
From a Contemporary Print.

In vain did Wellesley use every argument, the clearest and most forcible. His superior officer would not admit the advantage, and only saw the risks. It was the same story—they must wait till Moore arrived, the French were still strong, it would be rash to pursue them, unsafe to be drawn too far from the coast. Burrard was very much abused for his excessive caution; but it is only fair to say that he was borne out in his views by both the adjutant and the quartermaster-general, and that Wellesley, although furious at the time, admitted afterwards that Burrard "decided upon fair military grounds." What Wellesley's temper was may be judged from the language he used when the halt was made. One story is that he turned to his staff with the contemptuous remark, "There is nothing left for us, gentlemen, but to hunt red-legged partridges." The speech is differently reported, and another version is that he told his aide-de-camp to go and see about dinner, "for there is nothing more for soldiers to do to-day."

Further and deeper mortification was in store for Sir Arthur Wellesley. Not only was he denied the fruit of his victory, but he was involved in the odium that soon overtook those who superseded him, and for whose action he could not fairly be held responsible. There was to be no more fighting on this occasion. Junot was in such hard case that he offered to capitulate if given a safe conduct for himself and his troops to France. He sent Kellerman directly after Vimiera to ask for an armistice, and although Wellesley disapproved, it was granted by Sir H. Dalrymple, who had now arrived, and in turn superseded Sir Harry Burrard. Negotiations [illegible] which ended in the notorious Convention of Cintra, which pleased no one, and in England [illegible]

THE CONVENT OF BATALHA, PORTUGAL.
After a Picture [illegible]

This magnificent edifice was, with the Convent of Alcobaça, one of the [illegible] specimens of church architecture in Portugal. [illegible] not merely a church or a palace, but some fine city of Romance. [illegible] injured by the French in this war.

"THE CONVENTION OF CINTRA. A PORTUGUESE GAMBOL FOR THE AMUSEMENT OF JOHN BULL."

of indignation and disgust. Rejoicing at the recent success was now suddenly quenched, and public feeling ran riot in the opposite direction. The Government were loudly called upon to annul the treaty, which, it was declared, had ignored the interests of an ally, and given terms to an enemy who was on the eve of unconditional surrender. The Press was uproarious, journals of all shades of opinion denounced the Convention and all who had a hand in it. Some papers refused to disgrace their columns by printing the treaty; others published it within broad black mourning lines; one or two headed it with rough woodcuts, in which were three gibbets and a general pendant from each. The three victims to the popular clamour were Dalrymple, Burrard, and Wellesley. No distinction was made between them, and yet Sir Arthur clearly showed that he was not responsible in any degree for the terms in which it was framed or for any of its provisions. He had signed it, yes, but at the special desire of Sir Hew Dalrymple. Never had a successful General ever been treated in such monstrous fashion. After Vimiera, Wellesley was greatly dissatisfied, and had, no doubt, just ground for complaint. He was reduced to the fourth place in rank, and although the chief had been advised to rely upon him largely, Sir Hew does not seem to have liked his powerful lieutenant or to have consulted or confided in him. Wellesley was much hurt, and his letters of this date show it. He writes from Portugal to Castlereagh:—"I assure you, my dear Lord, matters are not prospering here, and I feel an earnest desire to quit the Army. I have been too successful with this Army ever to serve with it, in a subordinate situation, with satisfaction to the person who shall command it, and, of course, not to myself. However, I shall do whatever the Government may wish."

Again he writes:—"It is quite impossible for me to continue any longer with this Army, and I wish, therefore, you would allow me to return home and resume the duties of my office. . . . . If not that I should remain upon the staff in England, or, if that should not be practicable, that I should remain without employment. You will hear from others of the various causes which I must have for being dissatisfied, not only with the military and public measures of the Commander-in-Chief (Dalrymple), but with his treatment of myself. I am convinced it is better for him, for the Army, and for me, that I should go away, and the sooner I go the better."

He had strong sympathisers among his comrades in Portugal, and they showed it plainly. While a general feeling of disgust pervaded all ranks, based on their want of confidence in their new leaders, some of the senior officers combined to give Wellesley a public mark of their esteem. The generals who had served under him subscribed 1,000 guineas for the purchase of a piece of plate, which was presented him with a very flattering address, conveying the high respect they felt for him as a man, "and the unbounded confidence they placed in him as an officer." Wellesley's reply showed how deeply he was touched by this testimonial, and proves that he was not the cold, hard man he is so often represented.

CINTRA.

After a Drawing by the Rev. Mr. Bradford.

Steamers outward bound to Gibraltar obtain a fine view of this picturesque town.

Shortly after this, and when Junot's army had been embarked and sent to France, Sir Arthur asked and obtained leave of absence to return to England. As he wrote a friend, nothing would have induced him to go away if he had "thought there was the smallest prospect of early active employment for the army." His feeling against Sir Hew Dalrymple was one of deep disappointment. He was hurt that his chief would not accept his services more cordially. "I think I could have been of as much use to him as I believe I have been to other officers under whose orders I have served. He is the only one of whom I have not been the right hand for some years past." No doubt Sir Hew was either jealous of him or prejudiced against him. And yet his great subordinate stood by him in the trouble that was impending. For now the popular clamour at home culminated in a court of enquiry, and the three generals implicated, Dalrymple, Burrard, and Wellesley, were put on their trial before a board of officers at Chelsea Hospital. The absurdity of this was exposed by Napoleon, who, when he heard of the trial, said that "he had intended to send Junot before a court martial; but the English by arraigning their own generals had spared him the pain of punishing an old friend."

CINTRA, FROM THE LISBON ROAD.

After a Drawing by the Rev. Mr. Bradford.

Cintra, the scene of the Convention, although it was actually signed at some distance; it is now the favourite summer resort of the people of Lisbon.

It was the able and judicial statements made by Wellesley before the Chelsea Board that put the whole affair in a proper light and proved that the Convention of Cintra was no such grievous mistake.

Junot's position was by no means desperate; he could have fought his way out of Portugal northward, and the quiet repossession of the country was a very distinct gain.

There was nothing to justify the outcry raised at home against the Convention; and the Board practically came to that conclusion, although their report is a feeble, colourless document that neither praised nor blamed. The net result was that, while Dalrymple and Burrard were never again actively employed, Sir Arthur Wellesley, after resuming his seat in the House of Commons for a short time, returned to Portugal in April, 1809.

Wellington and Waterloo.

ROYAL ARTILLERY ON THE MARCH.

[illegible]

At [illegible] time the drivers were constituted as a distinct corps under their own officers, and known as the "Drivers and Waggon Corps."

CHAPTER IV.

After the recall of Wellesley to England to answer for the Convention of Cintra, the command of the Peninsular Army devolves upon Moore, who is ordered by the British Government to advance into Spain [illegible] and the Spanish armies. Moore is [illegible] misled as to their strength, and, being threatened by the French under Napoleon in overpowering numbers, he retreats hastily upon Corunna, where he fights and wins a victory at the cost of his own life. Wellesley is re-appointed, and reopens the war in Portugal with a new army; but the command is sought by H.R.H. the Duke of York, who [illegible] at the same time involved in some unpleasant scandal connected with the [illegible] of his patronage by Mrs. Mary Anne Clarke. Wellesley [illegible] [illegible] Aprl. 1809, and promptly proceeds to attack Soult. The [illegible] of Wellesley's [illegible] [illegible] followed by the [illegible] defeat of Soult, who narrowly escapes complete destruction.

AFTER the expulsion of the French from Portugal and the recall of the incriminated English Generals, the command of the army in that country was given to Sir John Moore, a first-class soldier, who might under happier auspices have achieved a brilliant reputation. It has often been said that there would have been no Duke of Wellington had Moore lived. No one, indeed, had a higher opinion of him than the General, who rose after he fell. There is a letter of Sir Arthur Wellesley's written to Moore, in which he assures him that he looks with confidence to his taking the command, and expresses the delight it would give him to serve with and under him. The same [illegible] prevailed throughout the Army; and even in the worst hours of that most disastrous retreat to Corunna, when suffering and grievous hardships tried [illegible] sorely, all ranks were still loyal to Moore. The blame of that failure does not rest with him, but with the Government that blindly committed the army to a really hopeless enterprise, relying on the vain promises of a foolish, faithless ally.

Had Spain been left to herself she must soon have succumbed to [illegible] The first grand outburst of patriotism proved to be little [illegible] Early successes inspired an arrogance that [illegible] the armies in the field, and encouraged [illegible] fanfaronade mixed with puerile imbecility. [illegible] campaign, no attempt to organise the Spanish [illegible] to arm, equip, officer, and drill the [illegible] efficiency to the regular troops. It [illegible] wretched people Moore was sacrificed.

Officer and Private, 52nd Light Infantry.
From [illegible] "Costumes."

Yet England had been most generous in her subsidies. Money and supplies in kind had been poured into the country lavishly, recklessly, mainly to be seized and misappropriated with shameless dishonesty. A few figures will best show this. Within twelve months of the beginning of the war, Spain received two millions of British money in hard cash; she got besides 150 pieces of field artillery, 200,000 muskets, 23,000,000 cartridges and 6,000,000 leaden bullets, 15,000 barrels of gunpowder, 92,000 suits of uniform, 356,000 sets of accoutrements, 310,000 pairs of shoes, 40,000 tents, with great quantities of cloth, linen, camp equipage, canteen, haversacks, and great coats. With all this the Spanish armies in the field did not deserve the name; half the men were unarmed, many nearly naked. Theft, embezzlement, fraud were rampant on every side.

BETWEEN ABRANTES AND VILLA DEL REY.

After a Drawing by Robert Ker Porter.

This well known painter of battle scenes accompanied Sir John Moore in his advance into Spain, and also in the retreat on Corunna. The sketches made at the time are still preserved in the British Museum, and are interesting as giving a vivid presentment of the disasters which befell the troops.

It was to co-operate with such worthless troops under such incompetent leaders that the British Government, ignorant or wilfully blind to the real facts, late that autumn ordered Sir John Moore to march into Spain. The season for active operations was really past, and no attempt had been made to prepare magazines and depôts ahead for the supply of troops on the march. The roads, too, were infamously bad, and transport animals were very scarce. To meet all these difficulties, he moved forward from Portugal by several lines, [illegible] Salamanca as the point of concentration. He had an admirable little army, small and compact, well disciplined and well equipped, in p[illegible] health and spirits, encouraged by the successes of a recent campaign. When Sir David Baird, coming direct from England, landed his division of [illegible] at Corunna, and marched through Northern Spain to join Moore, the whole

PLACENCIA.

After a Drawing by Robert Ker Porter.

A thriving town on the line of Moore's advance upon Salamanca, and an important point in later operations as commanding the pass of Banos. Many exciting episodes took place here.

Wellington and Waterloo.

MAMELOUCKS OF THE GUARD.

From Horace Vernet's French Uniforms.

These Oriental soldiers were originally raised in Egypt by Bonaparte, but during the Empire were recruited, anyhow, from the East.

FRENCH GRENADIERS.

From Horace Vernet's French Uniforms.

These were the veterans, the backbone of Napoleon's army. It was on these men that Napoleon depended during the crisis of a battle; their discipline has never been surpassed.

force made up a total of 32,000 effective men. Moore entered Salamanca on the 13th November. At this time the Spanish forces, under Blake, Palafox, and Castaños, occupied a crescent-shaped line from the sea to Zaragossa, a shadowy screen possibly 130,000 strong. They were acting without concert; the extremities of their line were too widely apart to be readily reinforced, and each flank was thus exposed singly to attack by the superior numbers of an enemy of extreme mobility and very strong in cavalry. For the French were only quiescent with the portentous calm that precedes a storm. Napoleon had long since resolved to wipe out the affronts of Baylen and Cintra, and had already marshalled the many legions that waited on his absolute will to swoop down with irresistible fury upon Spain. "I am determined," he told the French Senate, "to carry on the war with the utmost activity, and to destroy the armies that England has disembarked in that country." He had already 60,000 men in the northern province securely based upon Bayonne, San Sebastian, and Pampeluna. To these he added a corps of the Imperial Guard, the veterans of Jena, Austerlitz, Friedland the very flower of his army. He gathered up other fine troops, and a host of cavalry and artillery, so that he had presently 200,000 men at his call beyond the Pyrenees, for he meant to lead them in person, and that alone seemed to make triumph secure. Under him many of his most famous marshals commanded corps: Victor, Bessières, Soult, Ney, and Gouvion St. Cyr.

The French made short work of all the Spaniards they met in their victorious advance. First Blake was utterly routed on the 6th November; Burgos fell that day, and Napoleon made it his headquarters. When the North of Spain had been thus cleared, Palafox was next defeated, and Lefebvre disposed of Castaños. A Spanish force, holding the Samosiena and covering Madrid, was now attacked, and routed by Napoleon in person, who pressed on to the Capital. Some thought to emulate the prowess of Zaragossa, but it

NAPOLEON BONAPARTE.

[illegible] by Delaroche.

The Emperor N[illegible] w in Spain in person, intent on re[illegible] He [illegible] recovered Madrid, and hearing of Moore's advance, turned north with overwhelming numbers, meaning [illegible] the British from Spain. Napoleon, it will be seen, [illegible] although inured to long hours in the [illegible] that the horses for his [illegible] His favourite was the famous grey Arab so frequently [illegible] pictorially.

NAPOLEON BY THE BIVOUAC

was not a defensible city, and Napoleon was peremptory in his demands for its immediate surrender. When it fell, as it did on the 4th December, the heart and centre of the country had been secured, and the Spanish forces were everywhere in full flight. And what of Moore meanwhile? He had held his ground at Salamanca, but with deep misgivings, that grew as he realised more fully the falsehood and untrustworthiness of the Spanish authorities. He was led astray, too, by the weak credulity of Mr. Frere, the British Minister, who still swallowed all he was told. There was no assistance forthcoming from Spain. His own position was insecure—how much so he could not know, for the news that Napoleon was across the Pyrenees with all his host did not reach him for weeks. He heard nothing of his Spanish allies (Romana excepted, who would make no move) until he learnt their armies were no longer in existence. The bent of his mind was to despondency at this time. He foresaw that a retreat was more than probable. "If the bubble bursts and Madrid falls, we shall have to run for it," and he began to form magazines along the shortest road, by Benavente, Astorga, Lugo, to the sea. Now,

SALAMANCA.

From an Original Drawing by Robert Ker Porter.

A famous city, owning two cathedrals and many splendid edifices. This view is interesting, as antecedent to the ruin of the place by the French in 1812, when reoccupied after Wellington's great victory and subsequent retreat from Burgos.

however, an urgent appeal was made on him to save Madrid, which, as we know, was incapable of defending itself; and he believed that his best plan would be to strike at the French line of communications, and so draw Napoleon to attack him, the Emperor being more anxious, he believed, to drive back the English than to seize the Capital. But even before Moore advanced, Madrid had fallen. Moore's only chance seemed to be in beating Soult, who was on the line of the Carrion, and in no great strength, before he could be reinforced. Moore moved forward on the 11th December, and on the 19th he was at Mayorga with 23,000 men, including 2,300 cavalry and 60 guns. Soult, in front of him, was weaker for the moment by some 5,000 men; but strong reinforcements were within a few days' march, and Napoleon in person was coming up in hot haste from Madrid. No sooner had he heard of Moore's advance, than he gave up all other plans, and concentrated every effort to fall upon the English and destroy them utterly. The news reached him on the 21st December, and next night he was at the foot of the rugged Guadarama with 50,000 men. The crossing of the mountains was greatly impeded by storms of hail and drifting snow; but Napoleon, braving the elements, placed himself at the head of his columns, and forced a passage. He was well on his way, fifty miles from Madrid, by the 24th, at Tordesillas on the Douro on the 26th,

M[illegible]S RETREAT UPON CORUNNA, 1808.

[illegible]

Th[illegible] to the last by our [illegible] cavalry.

an[illegible] English picquets. But Moore had escaped him. Breaking up from the [illegible] the 24th De[illegible] behind the Esla by the 26th, leaving his cavalry only to watch Soult. The [illegible] soon came into collision with our horsemen. Lord Paget, afterwards Lord Anglesea, who lost his leg at Waterloo, commanded the cavalry, a gallant force of 2,400 sabres, the 7th, 10th, 15th, and 18th Hussars, with the 3rd German Hussars, which had already tried conclusions with the French in the recent advance, and won the combat of Sahagun. Now, too, they held their own in several skirmishes with Soult's Horse.

Again, a little later, when Moore had drawn off the main army, and Lord Paget was left at Benevente covering the retreat, he had a smart affair with the French Cavalry of the Guard, some of the famous Chasseurs, who, since Austerlitz, had borne the proud sobriquet of the "Invincibles." General Lefebre-Desnouettes had rashly hurried forward, thinking he had only to do with the last piquets, but was stoutly resisted, until the 10th Hussars came up under Lord Paget, and charged with so much spirit that the French line was broken, and their General made prisoner. This defeat, under the very eyes of the Emperor, caused Napoleon the deepest chagrin. It had the effect, too, of inspiring respect for our cavalry, who now, with the whole rearguard, retired across the Esla, the river being so swollen that the water was nearly breast high at the fords.

Moore retreated first on Astorga, thence towards Lugo by the wretched roads of a most difficult mountainous country, making for Corunna, the intended port of embarkation. A part, the Light Brigade, under the intrepid General Robert Craufurd, moved separately on Orense, so as to embark at Vigo. This rapid and incessant retreat had the worst effect upon the temper and discipline of the British troops. Sulky and grievously discontented, suffering many hardships from the persistent inclemency of the weather, half-starved, shoeless, in rags, and soaked through to the skin, they broke out into terrible excesses, and everywhere disgraced their name in pillage, followed by brutal besotted drunkenness. The destruction of the great palace of the Duke d'Ossuna at Benevente by the troops was one of the most shameless acts ever perpetrated. All along the route it was necessary to abandon stores, roll ammunition carts down ravines, slaughter horses and baggage animals. The cavalry was rapidly becoming non-effective from the want of horseshoes; there were shoes enough, but no nails had been sent out with them from England.

BRITISH REARGUARD FORDING THE ESLA, December, 1808.

After a Drawing [illegible]

After a sharp skirmish between the English and French cavalry, and in which Napoleon's hitherto "invincible" Chasseurs of the Guard had been worsted, Lord Paget (afterwards Lord Anglesey) drew off the rearguard by fording the Esla, which was breast high.

Meanwhile the pursuit never slackened. Napoleon had entered Astorga on the 1st January, where he had collected, within ten days, some 70,000 infantry, 10,000 cavalry, and 200 guns. He was in a position, as it seemed, to utterly crush Moore's army, now no more than 10,000 strong, unless the British, having the start, could escape to the sea. But at Astorga he suddenly left his army to Soult, and returned in all haste to France, drawn thither, it is said, by startling news that Austria was on the point of declaring war. Of late years it has been thought that Napoleon was perhaps loth to risk his reputation on the chance of being defeated by an English General with an inferior force. This suggestion might be rejected were it not certain that, in after years, he never returned to

MOORE'S RETREAT UPON CORUNNA, 1808.
The British column on the line of retreat amid snow and ice.

Spain, although the war there was a constant nightmare to him, and he would have been glad to end it at almost any cost. Could he have been deterred by the possible risk of defeat in a conflict with Wellington? Yet he attacked him eagerly and confidently enough at Waterloo.

In any case Soult was left to pursue with 60,000 men and 91 guns; and he followed up the retreating English with great vigour. Moore has been blamed for not sooner facing round to fight: he passed many strong positions, and once he might have attacked Soult with a decided advantage. Even a victory, which was not assured, could not have done more than make embarkation easier, for it cannot be pretended that Moore's 20,000 men were able to make headway permanently against the 300,000 French that now filled Spain. But, having at length met a convoy with shoes and clothing for his suffering troops, he resolved to fight at Lugo.

Till now the British army had been in sore straits: the line of march might be traced by scenes of suffering; the white surface of the snowy ground was flecked with red spots; soldiers fallen by the way, dying from fatigue, privations, and cold; baggage waggons broken down, their contents destroyed; the soldiers' wives, who in those days accompanied the regiments into the field, poor women and children were left behind to be frozen to death. All this time the pursuit was unrelenting, and could not be stayed. Bridges were in part broken down, but could not be completely destroyed. This was the case at Constantino, near Noyales, at a naturally strong pass, where Moore in person took the command of the rearguard, and made so imposing a show, that the French believed a battle was imminent, and halted to bring up all their supports.

Under cover of this bold stand, Moore collected all his force at Lugo, and, strange to say, the army responded nobly to the call. Till now discipline had almost ceased; insubordination had been general and wild disorder. But the moment it became known that a battle was imminent the men, [illegible], returned quietly and cheerfully to their ranks, saw to their firelocks, fixed their flints, [illegible] their bayonets, and prepared to stand with great [illegible] and courage.

MOORE'S RETREAT UPON CORUNNA, 1808.
[illegible] country over which the retreat was made is graphically illustrated in this and the above sketch, done at the time by Sir Robert Ker Porter.

But Soult was too wary to fall in with his adversary's wishes. He [illegible] Moore [illegible] to attack [illegible] was in a strong position; and he had no thought of attacking except with [illegible] Moore [illegible] force on a battle except at terrible risk; he had no choice but to continue the retreat, and the [illegible] into a rabble. Once Moore halted a day, for he had outstripped the French, and once more [illegible] together; so that they entered Corunna on the 11th in tolerable order.

Moore looked in vain for his troopships. They were still wind-bound [illegible] hand at leisure was lost. They appeared on the 14th, the French also next day, and it was clear now that a battle must be fought to cover embarkation. Some of the English Generals were for negotiating, but Moore stood firm; and, having sent off all his sick and wounded with other encumbrances, he destroyed his reserves of powder in one tremendous explosion, and awaited the enemy's onslaught. In the afternoon of the 16th January the battle of Corunna was fought and won at the price of his life.

GENERAL THE HONOURABLE JOHN HOPE

[illegible]

Soult had 20,000 men, the English only 16,000; but the latter had been armed with new muskets that day, and had abundant supplies of ammunition, in which the French were deficient. The advantage of ground lay with Soult, who tried to turn the English right flank, when Moore's reserve came up, drove back all they met, and, getting on Soult's left, swept his line in reverse. A sharp contest occurred in the centre and on the left of the English line, in which the French were eventually repulsed, and their defeat must have ended in a serious disaster had the still untouched division of General Frazer been brought into action.

But Moore had been struck down by a mortal wound just as the fight in the centre had been won. He remained on the field with splendid courage until he knew the happy issue, and then was carried off in a blanket. It was now seen that his sword-hilt had entered his wound, and Captain Hardinge (afterwards Lord Hardinge and Commander-in-Chief of the Army) tried to remove the weapon. "No, no," said the intrepid soldier, "it is as well as it is. I had rather [illegible]" he said to his sorrowing staff, "You know I always wished to die [illegible]."

His last words were, "It is a great satisfaction to me to know we have [illegible] again, "I hope the people of England will be satisfied! I hope my country will [illegible] that he breathed his last.

Vile calumny and low political passions [illegible]

at his true worth: as a guileless, chivalrous, fearless soldier, who fought from first to last with noble zeal, and who had but one thought, one aim—to serve his country to the best of his great ability. He is a model to his countrymen for all time. The troops went straight home from Corunna, but their troubles were not yet over. The transports were scattered by a tremendous gale, many ships were wrecked, the rest ran for any port, and Moore's soldiers were landed at many points between Dover and Land's End. "Their haggard appearance, ragged clothing, and dirty accoutrements, things common enough in war, struck a people only used to the daintiness of parade with surprise." The miserable state of this remnant of an army caused universal indignation, and its dead leader was bitterly assailed for what was by no means his fault.

BRIDGE AT CONSTANTINO (NOYALES).

After a Painting by Adam Neale.

Moore continued to retreat, much harassed by the pursuit, until he reached Noyales, where he turned, holding the bridge of Constantino with such an imposing show that Soult halted to bring up his supports. The time thus gained served Moore to gather together all his strength at Lugo, further to the rear, and here he offered battle, which Soult declined.

MARSHAL BERESFORD.

[illegible]

Commanded a [illegible] under Sir John Moore in the [illegible] Corunna.

The country had but little confidence in its military leaders just then, for a great scandal had come to light in the supreme command of the Army, and the character of the Duke of York was very seriously impugned. The story of Mrs. Mary Anne Clarke, and the clandestine sale of Army Commissions, is written deep in the chronicles of the time. It was first brought before the public by a member of the House of Commons, Colonel Wardle, an officer of the Militia, who moved for an enquiry, which was presently held by a committee of the House.

This Mrs. Clarke was a woman of great personal attractions, who had for some years lived under the protection of the Duke of York. Her early life was not very reputable. She had been on the stage, and had played Portia at the Haymarket, in 1803. All at once she came out as the mistress of a fine house in Gloucester Place, living in great style, with a dozen horses in her stables, twenty servants and three male cooks, and she dined off plate that had belonged to a brother of the King of France. Her allowance from the Royal Duke was said to have been £1,000 per month; but it was not very punctually paid, and, in order to satisfy her creditors, she devised a system of traffic in patronage, which she carried to great lengths.

PASS OF MANZANAL, 36 LEAGUES FROM CORUNNA.

[illegible]

[illegible] ... witness, and the [illegible] ... amusement by the [illegible] and [illegible] with which [illegible]. The Duke was, [illegible] the end, exonerated from any charge of [illegible] [illegible] of Mrs. Clarke's; but it was proved that he knew of what she was doing, and permitted her to meet the expenses of her household by trading with his patronage. He was, therefore, acquitted of personal corruption, but the public feeling was so strong that he was obliged to resign his appointment as Commander-in-Chief. This withdrawal was never meant to be permanent, and the vacancy was accordingly [illegible] Sir David Dundas, who was expected to retire when the scandal had blown over, as he did two years after, in 1811.

This is the same Sir David Dundas who had commanded in Wellington's first campaign, that in Flanders. He was a gallant old soldier, who had made his own way in the world, and was not ashamed to admit that he had walked from Edinburgh to Woolwich in order to enter the Artillery. His first commission was as a "lieutenant fireworker," in 1754, for which he joined the staff of Prince Frederick of Brunswick, and under whom he served constantly abroad. Dundas devoted himself largely to the improvement of drill, and having studied the methods of Frederick the Great, and attended many manœuvres of the French armies, he drew up the first drill-book known in the British Army.

This was the famous "Eighteen Manœuvres" [illegible] which the soldiers of the Peninsular War were trained. It had the merit of introducing uniformity, and his system

THE BAY OF CORUNNA.

[illegible]

was approved of by Abercromby, Moore, and Wellington. Dundas is described [illegible] tall spare man, of an austere temper, [illegible] When a youngster his strange style [illegible] and peculiar ways exposed him [illegible] straightforward gentleman, and did his duty to the Army. The retreat on Corunna and the re-embarkation of the British troops did not end our interference with Peninsular affairs. Napoleon took it for granted that we were driven from the field and would never re-appear, but he was singularly ignorant of the extent of our resources, which were, indeed, lying latent. Still less did he appreciate the obstinacy [illegible] the British character.

SIR JOHN MOORE.

From [illegible]

LORD PAGET, 1808.

Lord Paget [illegible] the retreat on Corunna, and [illegible]

Despite Moore's failure, the British Government still believed that the contest might be renewed with advantage, and this mainly upon the advice of Sir Arthur Wellesley. When asked, he told Lord Castlereagh that he was satisfied Portugal at least could be defended against the French, and that to hold that country would be the best method of encouraging Spain to resist. With his profound military insight he had been quick to realise the natural strength of the Portuguese frontier. Portugal was guarded by its mountains as a citadel is by its works. He had recognised, too, the military aptitudes of the Portuguese, and thought that the native levies properly

EXPLOSION OF [illegible] MAGAZINES AT CORUNNA.

[illegible] power before he fought the last fight

SIR JOHN MOORE.

[illegible]

organised and led by English officers would soon constitute a fine body of troops. How right were his conclusions the event finally proved, but few at the time had any confidence in his views or reposed the smallest faith in his prophecies. Only Lord Castlereagh agreed with him so far as to put him in charge of the new enterprise. It was resolved to send Sir Arthur Wellesley back to Portugal and entrust him with the supreme command. He was to have an army made up of 26,000 men, of whom 6,000 were already in the country. The formation of a Portuguese contingent was also approved. General Beresford, a resolute, practical soldier, a firm disciplinarian and of great experience, was put at its head, and began work at once. Wellesley himself bent all his energies to preparing for the field. Foreseeing a long campaign, he resigned both his office as Chief Secretary for Ireland and his seat in the House of Commons. Nothing should distract his attention from the higher duty that lay before him. His correspondence, as shown in those marvellous despatches of his, bears witness to the activity of his mind, his mastery over detail, his power of dealing with the innumerable needs of an army in the field. He saw to everything—the provision of all stores, arms and ammunition; he studied the military situation, closely weighing all the chances for and against success. Sir Arthur sailed in April for Portugal, and at the very outset narrowly escaped shipwreck. The ship, H.M.S. "Surveillant," met with terrible weather, and was in imminent peril off the Isle of Wight. Yet the Admiral, though he thought the frigate would certainly go ashore, strongly advised Wellesley to stick to her, as there was no hope of getting ashore through the breakers. The ship missed stays, and was then providentially saved by a sudden shift of wind. This was one of many such chances that proved Wellington's good luck. He was ever fortunate throughout his career. Constantly exposed, he was yet never seriously wounded, although he had horses killed under him and received slight hurts himself. Fortune often played into his hand, too, in the conduct of his

DUKE OF YORK.

MRS. MARY ANNE CLARKE.

FREDERICA, DUCHESS OF YORK.

Daughter of Frederick William II. of Prussia, married Duke of York September 29th, 1791; died without issue, August 6th, 1820.

MRS. MARY ANNE CLARKE.

[illegible]

Mrs. Clarke was a woman of great personal attractions, who passed through many phases of life, but [illegible] fine house in Gloucester Place, with carriages and a large retinue of servants. She owed her affluence to the [illegible] allowance of £12,000 a year, not very regularly, by the [illegible]. She acted as [illegible] in the [illegible] service for all sorts and conditions of men; in fact, so [illegible] did she carry on the [illegible] became necessary.

campaigns, offered him great opportunities, showed him a safe way out of danger, emphasised success. To admit this is in nowise to detract from his genius. Luck may be better than good management, but Wellington commanded both.

THE NEW MILITARY ... Y ... BY WAY OF ... ME

Sir Arthur Wellesley landed at Lisbon on the 22nd April, amid unbounded enthusiasm. This handsome city was at that time the dirtiest, the most foul and villainous capital in Europe; it was unlighted save by an occasional candle at a shrine; it was most unsafe—assassination for robbery was a nightly occurrence. Those who escaped the knife might be torn to pieces by the hordes of wild dogs that infested the streets, or had drowned in the mud if not first run over. But the bells rang out on Wellesley's arrival, the town was illuminated, and he was appointed Marshal-General in the Portuguese Army.

MILITARY LEAP FROG, OR HINTS TO YOUNG GENTLEMEN.

He took on the supreme command at once from Sir John Cradock, and lost no time in preparing his plan of campaign. He had two courses open to him. Two French armies beset Portugal. Soult with one was on the Douro in occupation of Oporto; Victor with the other, based on Madrid, threatened Lisbon along the valley of the Tagus. It was impossible to make head against both, but he was in a central position at Lisbon, and by swift strategy he might strike a blow at each in turn, take each singly before they could combine. Should Soult or Victor be the first attacked? Victor was nearest, and perhaps most dangerous, but for this Wellesley must cooperate with the Spanish army under Cuesta, who was little to be relied upon. Soult, on the other hand, held the rich city of Oporto, the second in Portugal, the chief source of future supply, and it was only four days' march distant. Victor, to reinforce Soult, must take eighteen days. Wellesley, leaving a certain, if insufficient, force to face Victor, resolved to operate against Soult; and the short campaign of the Douro which now ensued is more like a military romance, a series of swift, stirring, startling adventures, than a sober prosaic episode of war.

... with what was known ... Army commissions by a ... H.R.H. the Duke ... as well as first ... the whole matter

A week after his arrival, he started northward with 25,000 men of all arms, but only 13,000 British troops, for 3,000 were German, 9,000 Portuguese.

On the 2nd May he was in Coimbra on the Mondego, and no rumour of his approach had as yet reached his enemy. Soult's army was undermined by disaffection; a body of conspirators had approached Wellesley, and offered to make Soult prisoner. But Wellesley would not traffic with these traitors, and pressed on. He marched by two lines; one of his columns, on the right, under Beresford, mostly of Portuguese, arrived at Lamego, high up the Douro, where he would cut off Soult's retreat; Wellesley led the other in person, by the left direct upon Oporto.

VIEW OF LISBON.

From a Co[illegible] Print [illegible]

The City of Lisbon was of imposing appearance, but had the character at that date of being the [illegible] and most [illegible] capital in Europe. The streets, knee deep in filth, were infested by [illegible] wild dogs. Something had been done to [illegible]

This rapid advance all but caught a large portion of Soult's force on the far or southern side [illegible] the operation was a failure, and the French withdrew after a sharp combat at Grijo. Soult still lay at O[illegible] [illegible] by a wide, deep [illegible] which there was now no [illegible] bridge, [illegible] as he hoped, by [illegible] all boats had been secured, and were safely guarded on the French side of the river. He had no notion that the whole British strength was close in front; but he had commenced his retreat, sending on his heavy artillery and baggage by the road to Amarante [illegible] to follow [illegible]

[illegible] But [illegible] had already been driven back by Beresford on the [illegible] and [illegible] he had given up Amarante, thus jeopardising Soult's line [illegible] the very day that Op[illegible] The British [illegible] behind [illegible]

VIEW OF CASTLE OF BELEM, LISBON.

From a C[illegible] Print [illegible]

Belem is a suburb of Lisbon, and its ancient castle [illegible] to defend the entrance to the Tagus. During the Peninsular War, B[illegible] the army, and the skulkers who filled its hospitals were called [illegible]

FRENCH AIDES-DE-CAMP.

From Horace Vernet's French Uniforms

Douro, in the early morning of the 12th. Soult was still quite unconscious of the nearness of the enemy. The conspirators helped to deceive him with false reports; his orders were disobeyed. He had, moreover, a fixed belief that the attack would be delivered on the lower river near its mouth, and that a part, at least, of the British were coming from the sea. No watch was kept at the point which Wellesley was reconnoitring, and where, with sudden daring, he meant to throw his men across.

From the rocky eminence already mentioned, crowned by a Franciscan convent, Sir Arthur made out clearly a large building on the far side, which was isolated, surrounded with high walls, yet having access from the river. An admirable stronghold, if only it could be seized and garrisoned. But how pass this river, which was deep and swift, and three hundred feet wide? At this momentous juncture a small skiff was found, in which the famous Colonel Waters, who became a most invaluable scouting officer, crossed to the far side, assisted by a priest and the barber who owned the skiff. Unperceived, they detached three great barges, and, still unperceived, brought them over. Now Wellesley began to act. He first sent General Murray with the Germans, and some cavalry and guns, higher up the stream to Avintas, where he was, at all hazards, to cross, while fourteen guns were massed in a battery upon the convent heights, so as to command the Seminary. Full of anxiety, he waited till the news came that Murray had found boats above; and at once he issued his orders to the force under his hand. "Let the men cross," he said, briefly, and one officer of the Buffs, with a party of twenty-five, silently and securely occupied the Seminary. A second and a third boatload crossed before the French took alarm; but now they swarmed out from all parts of the town, and furiously endeavoured to drive our men out of their stronghold. Wellesley's guns on the convent hill opened fire; General Hill, who was now in command within the Seminary, made a stout defence, and reinforcements constantly reached him. At the same time, the Portuguese brought over more boats, in which another British division, Sherbrook's, crossed lower down, and joined in the fight. Murray's men, too, now appeared from above, and the French began to give up hope. The attack on the Seminary slackened; a battery of French guns, coming up in support, was decimated by Hill's volleys, and a retreat, hasty and disordered, followed. Had Murray charged the enemy now, he must

MARSHAL OF FRANCE (Full Dress).

From Horace Vernet's French Uniforms

Napoleon created, or rather revived, this highest military grade in France when he became Emperor. His marshals, mostly excellent soldiers, were at once his strength and his weakness; under his own orders they helped him valiantly, but when alone or in combination with each other they often failed or ruined operations by their jealousies and quarrels.

VIEW OF OPORTO.

[illegible]

Oporto is a [illegible] spe[illegible] in [illegible] [illegible] during [illegible] 1832, and having a [illegible] [illegible] It is now [illegible] [illegible] and the second city in Portugal.

[illegible] inflict [illegible] terrible loss, but [illegible] [illegible] [illegible] [illegible] Campaign [illegible] [illegible] and loss [illegible] [illegible] [illegible] Only [illegible] [illegible] [illegible] of cavalry, [illegible] [illegible] be found.

Oporto was thus [illegible] a surprisingly fine [illegible] [illegible] a fitting completion [illegible] [illegible] days' splendid work. Between the [illegible] and the [illegible] May, the British troops had marched eighty miles, and had been in the presence of the enemy nearly all the time. Sir Arthur Wellesley had outdone all in the rapidity of his movements; for it was not more than twenty-six days since he had left Portsmouth, and now one of Napoleon's most [illegible] Marshals had been surprised in his quarters, and beaten out of them with serious loss. There was still worse in store for Soult, and

CAMPAIGN ON THE DOURO.

Soult, flying headlong after Oporto had been [illegible] [illegible] [illegible] [illegible] danger [illegible] being [illegible] [illegible] his line of retreat. The only bridge [illegible] of Misarella [illegible] [illegible] was [illegible] and repaired [illegible] Dalting, and in the night Soult [illegible] [illegible] [illegible]

ATTACK ON THE FRENCH REAR-GUARD, SALAMONDE.

[illegible]

Soult's rear-guard in the retreat from Oporto was caught up at [illegible] but not [illegible], and [illegible].

he only saved his army from surrender or complete destruction by his own indomitable spirit. Although in full retreat after a sharp disaster, his veteran troops had speedily recovered themselves, and the same evening were marching in regular order upon Amarante. Had that vital point been still held, all would have gone well; but Loison, as we know, had not stood firm, and Soult was called upon to change the direction of his retreat. The Marshal was in terrible pain, caused by a fall from his horse, which had reopened an old wound in his hip; but nothing could daunt his soul, not even accumulated misfortune, the murmurs of his army, nor his own physical suffering. He had heard of a steep goat path across the mountains, to his left, which would give him [illegible] other valleys, and lead him to another point on the frontier. [illegible] at [illegible] he destroyed his guns, abandoned his military chest, loaded his sick on mules, and took to the hills. The weather was most inclement, rain fell in torrents, and his troops were worn out with fatigue. But his firm will carried all through, and, on crossing the mountainous range, he found Loison, also Lorge's cavalry, and the army was again concentrated 20,000 strong. But he was not yet safe. He was at Convalino de Este on the evening of the 14 [illegible] May. But now Wellesley, who had halted to bring his guns and [illegible] fell [illegible] close, while Beresford still headed him, [illegible] his [illegible]. But he was a day to the good [illegible] reached Salamonde, where there [illegible] escape. [illegible] on Chaves, was said to be [illegible] shorter and more direct on M[illegible] could secure the bridge at Ponte

MARSHAL SOULT.

[illegible]

Marshal Soult, Duc de Dalmatie, entered the Revolutionary Army, and [illegible] General in 1794, when 25 years of age. He was with Napoleon at Marengo and Austerlitz, and throughout the Peninsular War was one of Wellington's doughtiest antagonists, but was never successful against him.

Wellington and Waterloo.

Nova, by this time in the hands of Portuguese irregulars, who had half destroyed it. A daring French officer, Major Dulong, was sent forward with a chosen band to recover the bridge and repair it. This perilous feat was successfully accomplished, and Soult's army filed across the narrow bridgeway in the night of the 15th, continuing their march on Montalegre. Another passage, that of the Salteador or Leapes, a single arch across a rushing torrent, had to be secured, and it was done by the brave Dulong. Soult was at Montalegre on the 17th, and two days later across the frontier; having only escaped by the skin of his teeth. He had lost every gun, all his baggage, and 6,000 men; but he had maintained his reputation as a stout soldier, whose firmness had spared his army a still more terrible disaster. Sir Arthur Wellesley has been blamed for rashness in forcing the passage of the Douro; blamed also for not organising a more active pursuit. The first was rather bold than rash, the prompt seizure of the chances given by the negligence of the French. He appears to have been ill-served by Beresford, who was at Chaves on the 17th, when Soult's rear-guard was still at Salamonde, and who should have stuck at that important point holding the bridges. As it is but one march from Chaves to Montalegre, he might have been there ahead of the enemy. Nevertheless, Wellesley's gain was great; in less than a month he had restored confidence in Portugal, held one French army (Victor's) at bay, defeated the other after an adventurous march, and sent it in headlong flight across the frontier. Wellesley had now to deal with Victor. Having made Portugal safe, he was free to enter Spain. There were two Spanish armies in the field, ready, as he believed, to coöperate against Madrid; that of Venegas to the south-east in La Mancha, that of Cuesta near at hand in the valley of the Tagus. The English General had not as yet been fully undeceived as to the worthlessness of his allies; even Sir John Moore's experiences had not taught him that the Spanish troops were not to be trusted. Moreover, he had not yet made acquaintance with Cuesta, who was incompetent as a General. "He had no military genius," Wellington said of him; a traitor withal, who presumed to dictate a military policy, and went to bed when asked to concert the details for an attack.

BRIDGE OF ALCANTARA, ON THE TAGUS.

After a Drawing by Robert Ker Porter.

ARCH OF BRIDGE OF ALCANTARA.

After a Drawing made on the spot by Robert Ker Porter.

The bridges over the Lower Tagus are mostly in a ruinous condition. The river proved of great importance during these operations, and both sides lamented the destruction of this the great Roman bridge of Alcantara, a stupendous work of the Emperor Trajan, built 105 A.D.

RECRUITING AND BILLETING IN ENGLAND.

[illegible]

[illegible] war with Napoleon was at its height England was one vast camp. Recruiting parties were [illegible] The troops were billeted mostly at the inns and ale houses, and the above painting depicts [illegible] cavalry regiments waiting for beer, the soldiers flirting with the pretty maid, while at [illegible]

A MILITARY BAGGAGE WAGGON.

(From Atkinson's "British Costumes.")

Troops on the line of march carried all their baggage with them, and the women of the regiment [illegible].

CHAPTER V.

While Wellesley fights in Spain with meagre numbers, the British Government still wastes its means on foolish and aimless expeditions; that to Walcheren in 1809 was a ghastly failure. Meanwhile Wellesley, having beaten Soult, turns on the French in the valley of the Tagus, relying too hopefully upon his Spanish allies. Cuesta is useless and incompetent, and in the great battle of Talavera the victory was entirely gained by the starving British troops. But its advantages were lost by the converging advances of several French armies, and Wellesley is forced to retreat with all speed into Portugal. His success is belittled at home, but he is created Lord Wellington, and is meanly supported by the Government. While holding the frontier of Portugal, a fresh French attack is organised under Massena, who, in June, 1810, invades Portugal with a large army. Wellington retires before him, a brilliant example of defensive warfare. He faces round once, and fights the successful battle of Busaco, then resumes his retreat into the impregnable lines of Torres Vedras.

THE utter defeat of Soult, in the campaign of the Douro, was the first of an unbroken series of successes, but the interval between this success and the full triumph was to be long and disappointing. For years to come Wellesley's victories in Spain were discounted by the apathy of his allies, the lukewarm support of the British Government, and its persistent resolve to break up the forces in many futile efforts instead of concentrating them in one capable man's hands. Wellesley was left weak to prosecute a war which promised well, while huge means were wickedly wasted in other directions.

At this moment, Napoleon's check at Essling inspired the idea that his power was tottering, and that it might be further shaken by blows struck at the extremities of his empire. One expedition was planned against Walcheren from England, the other against Italy from Sicily. The effect of this ignorant policy was to misdirect and lose the services of some 50,000 men, and to bring disgrace and discredit on the British arms. The failure of the Walcheren Expedition was, no doubt, largely due to the incompetence of one man, Lord Chatham, the General-in-Chief, but the Government, which planned it, was still more to blame. So vast an expedition had never before left our shores, yet never had enterprise been so meanly conceived, so improvidently arranged, so calamitously conducted. A whole army perished in the pestilential marshes of Walcheren.

The object of this expedition was to seize Flushing, on the island of Walcheren, with all the French warships, afloat or building, destroy the arsenal at Antwerp, and close the river Scheldt. The first part of the programme was, no doubt, accomplished. After much loss of time, Flushing was bombarded and captured; but, in the interval, the French and Dutch had made Antwerp safe, and withdrawn their fleet up the river. Lord Chatham moved forward so slowly that he did not touch the mainland till ten days after Flushing fell. This delay was lampooned by the contemporary satirists in the well-known doggerel:

> "The Earl of Chatham, with his sword drawn,
> Was waiting for Sir Richard Strahan;
> Sir Richard, longing to be at them,
> Was waiting for the Earl of Chatham."

Strahan, the Admiral, may however be exonerated from blame, for the British fleet did its work well and completely. It was Lord Chatham's childish incompetence and want of decision that caused the whole failure. By the time he had made up his mind to fight for what would have fallen into his mouth a month or two earlier, his force was laid low by fever and ague, and he was compelled to retire.

It was impossible to hold Flushing. The malaria of Walcheren was fatal to the troops. Half the garrison was in hospital, and the death-rate increased to 200 a week. Altogether 7,000 lives were sacrificed, but thousands more returned home with shattered constitutions, and long afterwards men sent on to serve in Spain still suffered from the Walcheren fever.

GENERAL SIR HUSSEY VIVIAN.

After a Contemporary Painting.

A distinguished cavalry officer, who served through a great part of the Peninsular War and at Waterloo. Was afterwards Lord Vivian.

Wellesley was now about to embark upon a second campaign, that in which he gained the great victory of Talavera. He now advanced, as had Moore, on the faith of Spanish promises, with but scanty means of transport and no magazines. But he had been assured that the country could well supply his troops, and he had been promised abundant provisions. Yet, when he fought the battle, his men were famished with hunger, and had had no food but a few grains of wheat for the previous twenty-four hours. The starving troops, on the very night before the battle, begged to be let loose against the enemy, because "when engaged they forgot their hunger."

CHARGE RETRAITE.

After a French Contemporary Caricature.

The expedition to Walcheren, in the Low Countries, was the largest that has ever left our shores. It was intended to destroy the arsenal of Antwerp and the French fleet in the Scheldt, but through the incompetence of the General in Command, the Earl of Chatham, it accomplished nothing. Presently the army was devastated by disease, and with wasted numbers had to make an inglorious retreat. This failure is lampooned in the French drawing.

His aim was to fall first upon Victor, and drive him back on Madrid. The Spanish armies of Cuesta and Venegas were to co-operate; the former was said to have 40,000 men, the latter 25,000. Wellesley, at Abrantes, had under his own orders 22,000, but he expected 3,000 more from Lisbon, and a portion reached him after the battle. He meant to co-operate along the valley of the Tagus, a wide, swift river, flowing in a rocky bed, impassable except where bridges stood. A rugged mountain chain guarded his left from Soult and the armies of the North, and this barrier was only pierced by two passes, which Cuesta had agreed to hold, but, of course, neglected. Wellesley was at Placencia early in July, and, still advancing, he united with Cuesta at Oropesa on the 20th of that month. It had been settled between them to make a joint attack upon Victor, who, for the moment,

LOVE AND HONOUR: THE SOLDIER'S DEPARTURE.

From an Engraving by Bartolozzi ... [illegible]

During the Nap[illegible] wars, when a martial spirit pervaded all ranks [illegible] the [illegible] [illegible] engraving must have been familiar and constant occurren[illegible] [illegible] [illegible] with his [illegible] [illegible] visit, accompanied by a comrade, to his native village, [illegible] [illegible] farewell to his sweetheart. [illegible] demands that he shall give himself to the service of his country.

was in greatly inferior strength, and must have endured a serious defeat. "Had we fought then," the Great Duke said, five-and-twenty years later, "it would have been as great a battle as Waterloo, and would have cleared Spain of the French for that time."

But that changeable, capricious old man, Cuesta, would not consent to attack when the moment was most opportune. Then, when Victor retired upon Toledo, he pursued with rash precipitation, and nearly fell into a trap. For now Joseph, coming up from Madrid, reinforced Victor, and on the 26th July there were 50,000 French, with ninety guns, concentrated within a few miles of Cuesta's outposts. Joseph was also in communication with Soult, who was on the move towards the passes before mentioned, and it looked as though, by a combined attack, the French might envelop and destroy the allies.

LORD WELLINGTON.

After a Painting by [illegible] Rato, Lisbon, 1809.

[illegible] appears to have been a Portuguese portrait painter established in Lisbon at this period.

This, indeed, Napoleon had anticipated, with the unerring instinct of a great soldier. Writing from Ratisbon in June, to confer upon Soult the supreme command of three army corps (despite the recent defeat on the Douro), he told him: "Wellesley will probably advance by the Tagus against Madrid; in that case, pass the mountains, fall on his flank and rear, and crush him." Wellesley himself was hardly alive to the nearness of the danger. He had not heard of Soult's new army, and he relied still upon the blocked passes, which were really no better than open doors.

Cuesta, although roughly handled, had escaped from the advancing French. But Wellesley felt he could count upon no help from the Spaniards, except in a good defensive position, and begged Cuesta to fall back upon Talavera. The obstinate old man would take no advice; he long refused to retire another yard; and when at last he yielded, it was only, as he insolently told his staff, because "the Englishman had gone down on his knees to him." It is asserted that this really happened, that Cuesta made it a condition, and that Wellesley did not hesitate, nobly believing that there was no humiliation in an act which provided for the safety of the army. The battle-ground of Talavera lies between the Tagus on the right, and the spurs of a mountain chain upon the left. The town, which is on the river, had been defended by a redoubt and some earthworks, their front covered by broken country and thick cork woods. The position extended along a low slope, which rose gradually into a high hill on the extreme left, the key of the position. Beyond this, an open valley intervened, at the foot of the farther mountains. Wellesley placed the Spaniards behind the fortifications, where they were almost unassailable. On their left came the English divisions—Campbell, Mackenzie, Sherbroke, and lastly, Hill—

BATTLE OF TALAVERA.

on the highest ground. The British cavalry was in the valley, closing the left, and behind them, a little more to the centre, was Albuquerque and the Spanish horse.

The French came on rapidly. By 1 p.m. on the 27th July their advance had crossed the Alberche, and, driving in the picquets, nearly captured Sir Arthur Wellesley. He had dismounted, and was reconnoitring the approaching enemy from the roof of a tumble-down house, when the French actually arrived; and, but for the steady demeanour of the English troops, the General would hardly have got away. As it was, he had to gallop for it, and all went in hot haste to the rear.

The next event was a complete stampede among the Spaniards, some 10,000 of whom, abashed by the French artillery fire, abandoned their work and fled. Cuesta went with them in his coach and six. Men threw away their guns, gunners carried off their horses, the paymasters their money chests, the baggage was scattered far and wide. But for the promptitude with which Wellesley sent up some British squadrons, and the fire opened by the few Spaniards who stood firm, there might have been a serious disaster. During the night, the fugitives were in part rallied, and resumed their position; but the Spanish army was 6,000 short in the battle next day.

FRENCH HORSE ARTILLERY.
(Artillerie-à-Cheval.)
From ... French Uniforms.

There was a preliminary fight that evening. The sun was setting, but Marshal Victor, encouraged by the panic among the Spaniards, seeing that the high hill on our extreme left was weakly held, tried to seize it by a *coup de main*. Two French divisions attacked, and a third made a diversion, but Hill came up with supports; the enemy became entangled in a ravine, and were repulsed as darkness fell.

TALAVERA.
From Historical Prints, 1829.
The town of Talavera rests on the one side on the river Tagus, on the other it is flanked by high hills. The valley between is much broken and covered with thick cork woods.

About daylight on the morning of the 28th, another combat preluded the great engagement. Victor again attacked the hill on the left. It was an obstinate hand-to-hand fight, greatly prolonged, which ended in a new defeat for the French. Wellesley now saw that he must strengthen this flank, and, borrowing one Spanish division from Cuesta, placed it on the spur of the opposite mountains, while the British cavalry circled round to look farther into the valley, and was supported by Albuquerque's squadrons.

There were divided counsels now among the French generals. Marshal Jourdan, the King's chief adviser, was for withdrawing behind the Alberche, and waiting Soult's pressure on the allied rear. Victor scouted the idea of retreat, and insisted on an immediate general attack. It was the worst policy, but the King (Joseph), still wavering and undecided, resolved to try the chances of a battle.

WILLIAM HANNUM.

Provost Marshal of H.M. Guards.

[illegible]

The Provost Marshal was [illegible] with great powers, [illegible] and in some cases [illegible]

FOOT GUARDS.

[illegible]

A brigade of Guards, [illegible] Guards, were [illegible] battle of Talavera.

Meanwhile, the English rested in their lines, tightening their belts to silence the pangs of hunger. The Spaniards were disheartened, dreading the fight. Cuesta, it was said, but not truly, had opened a traitorous commerce with the enemy, and Albuquerque, who hated him, sent Wellesley word that he was being betrayed. The story goes that this disquieting news reached the English General as he stood with his telescope examining the enemy once more on the move. He listened quietly, and, without turning his head, merely replied to Colonel Donkin, the bearer of the message, "Very well, you may return to your brigade."

THE ENGLISH HOSPITAL AND THE CONVENT OF ALMAIDA.

[illegible]

View of [illegible] the English [illegible] hospital [illegible] the [illegible]

The attack on the high hill on the [illegible], the [illegible] key of the position, although made by a whole corps (the 4th), was [illegible] [illegible] intrepid dragoons were broken and nearly massacred, but their heroic self-sacrifice had checked the turning movement, and by its extraordinary daring had carried dismay into the French ranks. Meanwhile the fight had been steadily maintained in the centre, but at last the Guards triumphed, and drove back the French in great disorder. Elated by their success, they were drawn on too far in rash pursuit, and fell in with the French reserves, which came up with so much purpose that they restored the balance. The British centre was pierced and in confusion. It was the critical moment, and had not Wellesley, who watched every phase of the battle intently, now interposed with a masterly hand, the issue might have been very different.

He had seen the mistaken ardour of the Guards, and, foreseeing trouble, had sent across a fresh regiment, the 48th, one of the finest in the Service, which arrived at the threatened point just in the nick of time. They advanced like a solid wall, and, at the word of command, opened files to let the disorganised crowds pass through, then resumed their unbroken line and swept gallantly forward. Once more the French were checked, and made no further progress in the centre.

On the left the great hill was still intact; Cotton's cavalry came up with an imposing show backed by strong reserves. The French had lost ten guns; they had lost heart, too, and Joseph was not the man to restore confidence by organising a fresh battle. There was nothing left but to retreat; 44,000 men, of whom only 19,000 deserved to be called soldiers, had withstood nearly 50,000 French veterans, 7,000 of them excellent cavalry, the artillery being about equal on both sides.

But Wellesley's army had suffered severely; barely 14,000 sabres and bayonets remained. The losses included two generals killed and three wounded, and the total number disabled in all ranks was 6,000. That of the French was computed at 7,000. The gain to the English was in prestige, for this was the first great European victory our troops had gained since Marlborough's time, and it was won against the first military nation in the world. It was won, moreover, by starving soldiers; men who, for a whole week past, had not received one-third of their full rations; men, too, who were largely recruited from the militia, and who still carried the number and devices of their old regiments. As if to emphasise the prowess of British infantry, Crauford's Light Brigade, the nucleus of the soon-to-be-renowned Light Division, appeared on the field on the day after the battle, having accomplished an astonishing march from the coast. His three regiments, the 43rd, 52nd, and 95th (afterwards the Rifle Brigade), had been halted near Placencia, when the Spaniards, flying from

1. Starting to Join.

2. Taking his Breakfast.

3. Introduced to his Colonel.

MILITARY ADVENTURES OF JOHNNY NEWCOME.

Verse by an "Officer." Caricatures by Rowlandson.

The episodes in the career of this imaginary young gentleman show admirably the lights and shades of military life at this period.

MARSHAL BERESFORD.

Commander-in-Chief of the Portuguese Army, which he [illegible]

Talavera, brought the false report of a rout. Craufurd rose to the occasion, and, fearing the worst, hurried forward to reinforce Wellesley. Some fifty of his weakest men were withdrawn from the ranks, and then he started on a march, which lasted for six-and-twenty hours, with no more than short intervals of rest. In that short space of time he covered sixty-two English miles in the hottest season of the year, his men carrying knapsacks and ammunition, a total weight of fifty or sixty pounds. Only seventeen stragglers had been left behind, and the brigade crossed the field in a close and compact body, in the full view and to the admiration of the whole army.

Immediately after Talavera, Wellesley was forced to retreat. Soult had come through the Pass of Baños on the 31st July, and was approaching Placencia with at least 30,000 fresh troops. At 5 p.m. on the 3rd August, Wellesley

PENAMACOR, PORTUGAL.

From an Original Drawing by Major St. C[illegible] Officer on the Staff of the Peninsular Army.

A mountain town [illegible] within the [illegible] of Portugal, and an important point on the [illegible] from North to South, from the Douro to the Tagus.

heard he was at Naval Moral, having cut him from the bridge at Almaraz; an hour later Cuesta reported that King [illegible] advancing. He promptly decided, and it was his only chance of safety, to cross the Tagus at [illegible] towards Badajos and the south.

Cuesta [illegible], and would have stayed to fight. Wellesley persisted, and on the morning of the 4th, the English [illegible] across the river. Craufurd was sent by forced marches along the left (southern) bank to hold that side of the bridge of Almaraz, and prevent Soult from interfering with the retreat. Cuesta stood fast for a time to cover the English hospitals in Talavera, then abandoned to the enemy, and narrowly escaped being [illegible] Soult.

It had been a narrow shave for Wellesley. The imminence of the danger was felt not by him alone, but was

SIR BANASTRE TARLETON.

[illegible]

General Banastre Tarleton served during the American War. [illegible] House of Common[illegible] led him to find fault with his generalship. He condemned [illegible] and Vimeiro, and [illegible] Talavera. [illegible] apparent "to every soldier in the British ranks, and produced a general disquietude." The General himself confessed, "We were in a bad scrape, and I really believe, if I had not determined to retire at the moment I did, all retreat would have been cut off from us both" (Cuesta and himself). After this he would have no more dealings with the Spanish authorities. They had shamelessly thrown him over in the matter of supplies, had promised him provisions and full magazines, and gave him none. "They allowed a brave army," as he wrote, upbraiding them bitterly, "that was rendering gratuitous service to Spain, that was able and willing to pay for everything it received, to starve in the centre of their country, and to be reduced by want almost to a state of inefficiency."

SIR BANASTRE TARLETON.

[illegible]

It troubled their chief terribly. "A starving army is worse than none," he cried; "the soldiers lose their discipline and their spirit. . . . . . a fortnight ago they beat double their numbers. I should hesitate now to meet a French corps of half their strength." No wonder that these poor fellows were tempted to rob and plunder on every side. In this last retreat, when the army was threading a wood, they came upon large herds of swine, and the soldiers broke their ranks to kill all they could reach, "shooting, stabbing like men possessed, cutting off the flesh while the beasts were still alive." For this and other deplorable excesses condign punishment was ever at hand. Wellesley ruled firmly, and his provost-marshals spared no marauders. The "cat" was constantly heard, and the gallows often bore its ghastly burden. It was necessary that order should be maintained, lest the army should degenerate into a mere rabble; yet no one can withhold pity from the victims, for their crimes were instigated by the imperious needs of nature.

GENERAL SIR DAVID DUNDAS.

Commander-in-Chief, 1809-11.

[illegible]

General Sir David Dundas was a tall, spare man, crabbed and austere, dry in his books and demeanour, and there were peculiarities in his habits and style which excited some ridicule among young officers. He was born in 1735 and died in 1820.

Wellesley's experience was akin to Moore's, but happily he survived to adopt another line with his faithless allies. In a letter to his brother, Lord Wellesley, now the British Minister to the Cortes at Cadiz, he plainly declares that until "the evils of which I have reason to complain are remedied, till I shall see magazines established, and a regular system adopted for keeping them filled . . . . . I cannot enter upon any [illegible] of cooperation with the Spanish armies." Again: "The [illegible] neither numbers, efficiency, discipline, bravery, nor [illegible] contest." He adopts the same tone to the Government at home, [illegible] claims to be "justified from all blame" (with regard to his retreat), "excepting that of having trusted the Spanish General in anything." From henceforth he had done with the Spaniards, and would [illegible] every [illegible] the defence of Portugal alone. He was prepared to carry the whole burden [illegible] what it meant, and yet did not shrink from it. "I believe there never was any officer, certainly never a British officer, placed in so difficult a position as I am." He had to meet it all, and "if I fail, God will, I hope, have mercy on me, for no one else will."

He had still many enemies and detractors at home. His true character was by no means appreciated; many denied him military capacity, and the proposal to confer a peerage and pension on him was strongly opposed in both Houses of Parliament. The Corporation of the City of London actually presented a petition against the grant, and begged the King to prevent his Ministers from "rewarding one who, in the campaign of Talavera, had exhibited with equal rashness and ostentation nothing but a useless valour." This bitter language is in amusing contrast with the City's offering, six years

PASSAGE OF THE TAGUS AT VILLA VELHA.

After an Original [illegible]

This boat-bridge, established by Wellington, [illegible] him [illegible] to either side of the Tagus. [illegible] Villa Velha was very [illegible]

MARCH OF BAGGAGE FOLLOWING THE ARMY.

After [illegible]

From first to last Wellington's chief difficulty in the Peninsula was [illegible]. He [illegible] employed pack-mules, [illegible] their own

THE FORTRESS OF ELVAS AND SURROUNDING COUNTRY.

[illegible]

later, of a great gold shield emblazoned with his victories. The strictures passed upon his generalship were absurd. Some speakers condemned his operations as rash and silly; Lord Grey presumed to find fault with his dispositions at Talavera, just as at the time of the Cintra Convention General Banastre Tarleton found fault with both Roleia and Vimiera. This famous personage, who had served with some distinction in the war with the American Colonies, where he had commanded a British legion, but who was now a bitter political partisan, declared that there was "something rash" in the first battle and "something wrong" in the second. Yet Roleia was fought with the odds altogether in Wellesley's favour, and Vimiera was a great victory, nevertheless, which would have been greater but for his untimely supersession.

VIEW OF ELVAS.

[illegible]

[illegible] l, within view of Badajoz on the Spanish [illegible] during the Peninsular War, although

Tarleton's bitterness has been traced to the same cause as that which made the Duke of York so hostile to Wellington. Both sought the command in Spain, and both, as we know, were disappointed. Tarleton had, no doubt, done good work, but chiefly as a leader of irregular cavalry. He showed great activity at Charlestown, when, having lost all his horses on the voyage, he mounted his men on ponies or anything that would carry a saddle; and he was strongly against that cooping up of the army on the York River that led to its ignominious surrender. He was a Liverpool man, and represented that borough, always strongly supporting the slave trade.

BATTLE OF BUSACO, SEPTEMBER 27, 1810.

Despite this rancorous opposition, Sir Arthur Wellesley became Lord Wellington in August, 1809. Within five years he had reached the topmost grade in the peerage, and when he entered the House of Lords for the first time in June, 1814, he was hailed successively as "Baron," "Viscount," "Earl," "Marquis," and finally as "Duke." He had alike conquered the highest rank and the highest place in the public esteem.

But now, in 1810, he was only beginning the great task that was to bring him such substantial and well-merited rewards. In this year he was faced with difficulties and dangers that might have appalled anyone less capable and self-reliant. It was his firm resolve to defend Portugal at all costs, and he had formed his great scheme, of which more directly, and trusted to it implicitly. Yet the odds against him seemed nearly overwhelming. Peace in Central Europe had released Napoleon's legions, and he forthwith filled Spain with reinforcements, more than ever determined to drive the English into the sea.

By June in this year, the total of the French forces in Spain had reached the enormous figure of 366,000.

BATTLE OF BUSACO.

After a Painting by ...

An episode in ... engagement: Crauford's Division charging Ney's corps.

Wellington, on the other hand, had but 25,000 British and Germans in Portugal, north of the Tagus. But Hill had 5,000 more on the south side, with as many more Portuguese, and Beresford's Portuguese army, nearly 30,000 men, now fast becoming an efficient force under the command of English officers, garrisoned the [illegible] fortresses, and was held as a reserve. For the invasion of Portugal, Napoleon selected Massena, Prince [illegible] Essling, whose [illegible] success had gained him the proud title of the "spoilt child of victory." He was to have three Corps d'Armée under his orders, with a total of 80,000 men. Two of these, Ney's and Junot's, were in and about Salamanca and Valladolid; the third, under Reynier, was in the valley of the Tagus, facing General Hill. Wellington always said that Massena, after Napoleon, was the ablest French general he had encountered. They met, these two doughty antagonists, years afterwards, in Paris, and Wellington's own words shall be used to describe this interesting event.

"Massena was much excited at first seeing me," the Duke told Lord Stanhope; "made a great noise, and greeted me very cordially. 'Ah! M. le Maréchal, what a bad time you gave me.' And he declared to me that I had not left him one black hair on his body; he had turned gray, he said, all over. I answered that I thought we had been pretty even, things nearly balanced between us. 'No,' he said, 'how near you were taking me two or three times'—which I was," added the Duke.

MARSHAL MASSENA.

[illegible]

Marshal Massena, Prince [illegible] Napoleon's most intimate and [illegible] most trusted lieutenants. [illegible] Army to the rank of general, and [illegible] he rendered loyal allegiance. He [illegible] [illegible] victory [illegible] in his [illegible] in the field. [illegible] Wagram and Essling [illegible] was deposed, and [illegible] [illegible] to Napoleon.

Massena was one of the most remarkable products of the French Revolution. The son of an innkeeper, who kept the little tavern at La Turbie, on the hill above Monte Carlo, a place familiar to all modern visitors to the Riviera, he rose rapidly in the Revolutionary Army, and was at one time a rival of Napoleon. But he soon yielded to the superior genius of his great master, whom he served well on many hard fought fields. Lodi, Rivoli, the conquest of Switzerland, were among his early claims to distinction, and later, Wagram and Essling, the latter of which gave him the title of Prince. Wellington's great system against the coming invasion was vast in conception, terrible in execution. Anticipating the similar practised by the Russians in 1812, he insisted that the Portuguese should lay their country waste, destroy roads, remove boats, break down bridges, abandon their dwellings, and carry off with them everything that could minister to the needs of the advancing army—crops, cattle, food, fodder, all kinds of supplies. The Fr[illegible]

MAJOR-GENERAL SIR DENIS PACK.

[illegible]

Sir Denis Pack was present at the capture of the Cape of Good Hope, at Buenos Ayres, Vimiera, Corunna, and Walcheren. He served in the Portuguese Army, and at Waterloo he commanded a brigade.

drawn on through a howling inhospitable wilderness, while he, slowly retiring, took refuge at last in the impregnable citadel of Torres Vedras.

He had early realised the defensive value of the mountains covering Lisbon. The famous "lines," which the English engineers built under his initiative and control, had been suggested by plans made by others, but Wellington alone gave them effect. It was he who carried out this gigantic undertaking, who built the entrenchments, inundations, and redoubts that made one fortress of 500 square miles of mountainous country lying between the Tagus and the ocean. These colossal lines were threefold, and consisted of 114 forts strongly built and enclosed, so that each must be attacked by regular siege operations. Every advantage was taken of the ground, all passages were closed by trenches, abattis, and chevaux de frise.

Nothing redounds more to Wellington's credit than the construction of these lines of Torres Vedras. From first to last he kept his own counsel; no one but his engineers knew what he was doing, and they hardly fathomed his object. That works were being built could not be concealed when thousands of labourers were employed, but no one fathomed their great importance. No whispers reached the enemy, even although the French had friends still in Portugal; no one reported that Wellington was at work on this marvellous and impassable barrier.

It is said that Massena sharply rebuked the Portuguese who were in his suite for having failed to tell him of this. They retorted that it was his business, not theirs, to find out what Wellington was doing. "But Wellington did not make the mountains," cried Massena, meaning that he should have been informed of the natural strength of the country. Massena moved forward very leisurely [illegible] in [illegible] Then he attacked! [illegible] on

SKIRMISH ON THE RETREAT FROM BUSACO.

After a drawing in Maxwell's "Life of Wellington."

GENERAL REYNIER, DUKE DE MASSAS.

After a Drawing by Guerin.

General Reynier commanded the 2nd French Corps in the valley of the Tagus, and joined Massena just before the battle of Busaco, in which he attacked the British right, but failed. His troops fought with extraordinary vigour and resolution, overthrowing all before them; they established themselves on the top of the crest, but Wellington caused two guns to open upon them, and then the 45th and 88th Regiments [illegible] the [illegible] so furiously that they were driven down the hill in confusion.

the Coa, and nearly compromised it. But the intrepid general, backed by the gallantry of his troops, drew them off by one narrow bridge, after sacrificing many lives. At this time Wellington's main force was behind the Mondego. When, however, Massena, still slow in his movements, yet having taken Almeida, drew Reynier towards him, and at last showed a clear intention of advancing on Coimbra, Wellington resolved to bar his

1. Smells powder for the first time.

2. Writes an account of the battle home.

passage. Hill was ordered up in all haste, but that judicious leader had anticipated his orders when relieved of Reynier's presence, and was already on the march. He joined Wellington on the 26th September, as did Leith from Thomar. The English army was now concentrated at Basaco, a strong position on the mountain side, which Wellington had chosen as admirably adapted for a defensive fight. This brought on the battle of Busaco, an engagement for fighting which Wellington has been blamed. It has been called a "useless battle." But Wellington defended it on the grounds that it was indispensable to give confidence to his troops, especially the Portuguese. A general impression prevailed that the English meant to fight no more, but would soon embark and sail away, and the event justified Wellington's decision, for Basaco, as he put it, "gave the Portuguese a taste for an amusement (fighting) to which they were not before accustomed."

It was necessary to fight, although he could not bring 50,000 men into line, many of whom were untried soldiers, while Massena had 70,000 veterans under his command. But Wellington's position was a high ridge with a steep slope towards the enemy, the front being covered by deep gorges, and intersected by craggy defiles only practicable for mountain goats; his right rested on the Mondego, the left extended as far as the Sierra de Caramula. A road along the crest gave easy communication between the divisions, which yet stood far apart, for the position was some sixteen miles wide. There were commanding points on which to plant artillery, while the assailants must move in a cramped

3. Hallucinations. Short commons.

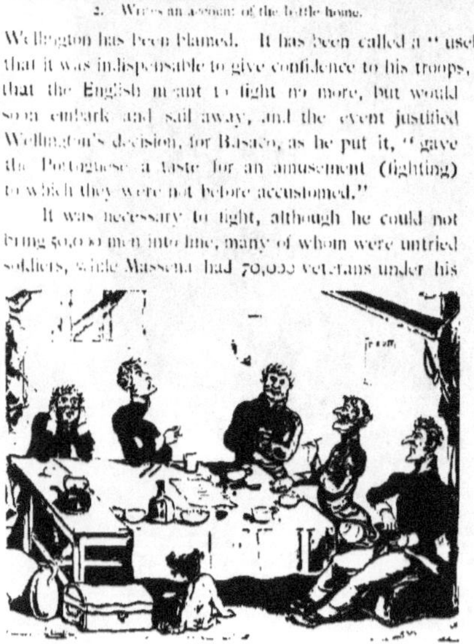

4. Learns to smoke.

FURTHER MILITARY ADVENTURES OF JOHNNY NEWCOME.
After Caricatures by Rowlandson.

COLONEL MELLISH.

After a Painting by Marshy

A well-known friend and ally of the Prince Regent (George IV.) and a dashing officer in his time.

space so that their columns could have full play. The position was so formidable that it was thought Massena would not dare to attack. "But if he does I shall beat him," said Wellington, with his customary imperturbable self-possession.

Ney came upon the 26th, early, and was for immediate onslaught. He saw that the allies were only moving into their places, and not without disorder; the natural confusion attending the occupation of new ground. Reynier coincided with Ney, and a despatch was sent to Massena urging prompt action. Massena kept the aide-de-camp waiting two hours for an audience, then said nothing should be done till he arrived, which did not happen till noon.

By this time the situation had changed. Wellington's whole force had come into line. The great ridge was held by six British divisions, and a number of Portuguese. Ney was not for giving battle now, but Massena, encouraged by Reynier, who thought he had only to do with a rearguard, resolved to attack at daybreak on the 27th. Ney and Reynier, with the 2nd and 6th Corps, were to assault whatever lay in front of them, while the 8th Corps, the cavalry and artillery, remained in reserve. The brunt of the battle thus fell upon Picton opposite Reynier, and Craufurd opposed to Ney.

Reynier began the action from San Antonio de Cantara with two columns, and, having the easiest ground to cover, he got in among Picton's people before he was seen. He quickly scaled the mountain, and pierced the right centre of the 3rd Division. Some of the French got to the higher cliff and stuck there; others, wheeling to the right, would have swept along the crest, but now Wellington brought two guns to bear upon them with grape, and Picton's "Fighting 3rd," having rallied, "charged so furiously that even fresh men could not have resisted the shock." The French gave way, and "both parties went mingled together down the mountain-side with a mighty clamour and confusion."

Meanwhile, the enemy above on the crest still stood firm, and had reserves been near, they would have gained the position. But Leith, who with the 5th Division stood next to Picton, had come with a brigade to his assistance, and skilfully using the 9th and 38th Regiments, he drove the French out of the rocks, and cleared the crest. Victory was now assured on this side, for Leith's 2nd Brigade was close at hand and Hill's division approaching, so that the English strength was too much for Reynier, and he retired discomfited.

On the other flank Ney had thrown his skirmishers forward

COLONEL TORRENS.

Military Secretary to the Commander-in Chief.

After a Painting by Thomson.

Sir Henry Torrens was for many years Military Secretary at the Horse Guards, and practically controlled the patronage during the Peninsular War, under the Duke of York and Sir David Dundas.

before it was light, and then came on in three heavy columns. One tried to turn Craufurd's right, a second smote him in front, the third remained in reserve. The 2nd Column came on with dauntless courage till they were close to the summit of the ridge, when Craufurd, "standing alone on one of the rocks," gauged the right moment, and sent forward two fresh regiments at the charge. "Next moment a horrid shout startled the French column, and 1,800 British bayonets went sparkling over the hill."

This ended, practically, Ney's attack. There was more fighting, fierce but desultory, and about 2 p.m. the battle was ended.

It was costly to the French, who had been repulsed with great loss, having in all some 4,500 killed and wounded. The English and Portuguese came off more cheaply; they had the advantage of position, and lost no more than 1,300 men.

LORD WELLINGTON'S LINES COVERING LISBON.

After a Drawing by G. Cumberland.

Next morning (the 28th) skirmishing was renewed, but only to cover a flanking movement made by Massena. He had learnt of a rugged mountain path across the Caramula Range, by which he could turn Wellington's left, and before evening he had moved his whole army round. Wellington is described by an eye-witness as being much put out when he saw what had happened. He had stationed some Portuguese troops on the far side of the Caramula to close the road, and they had failed to stop the French.

TORRES VEDRAS FROM THE NORTHWEST.

After a Drawing by the Rev. Mr. Bradford.

This picture and the one above show the famous lines of Torres Vedras, which were Wellington's last and [illegible] He had quite realised the natural strength of the position, and had, on his [illegible] that kept the French army at bay. The lines were threefold [illegible] attacked by regular operations. Here he lay sheltered and snug, while [illegible]

When they were first descried winding over the distant mountains towards his left, Wellington watched them with great earnestness. "He seemed uneasy; his countenance bore a fierce, angry expression, and, suddenly mounting his horse, he rode away without speaking. One hour afterwards the whole army was in movement." It was a race now for the Mondego, for Coimbra, Leria, and Lisbon. Massena followed fast, never doubting but that the English were making for their ships. He pressed on, although his heart must have failed him as he saw the desolation around, and [illegible] unless he was soon successful in the preoccupation of Lisbon, his men must starve. "The enemy [illegible] and disease [illegible] positions. [illegible] is subsisted on [illegible] and cattle; [illegible] women [illegible] the army [illegible] [illegible] only [illegible] only hope for the future, was to pass through the "lines," and gain Lisbon or the far side of the Tagus. A last and in

HUSSAR TRUMPETERS SOUNDING THE CHARGE

From [illegible] Contemporary British Uniforms [illegible]

After Busaco the cavalry were constantly employed in covering the rear.

startling shock was reserved for Massena. It fell upon him when, with increasing confidence that his English enemies could not escape him, he was brought to a full stop by the unexpected barrier of Torres Vedras. It was one of the most dramatic surprises in war. At the moment when he thought to reap a full harvest of success his prey slipped through his fingers, and, safely ensconced behind these stupendous works, was in every way unapproachable.

"FUNICULUS TRIPLEX DIFFICILE RUMPITUR"

After a Contemporary Print, 1810

George III. entrusting sword to Lord Wellington to defend [illegible]

THE SOLDIER'S RETURN.

From an Engraving by Ward. After Wheatley.

The war is at an end, and the soldier returns to claim the reward of valour at the hands of beauty. His sweetheart, who has waited patiently for her lover through long years of anxious suspense, coyly it may appear, but at heart cheerfully, listens to his pleadings. The old father, himself a veteran, adds his appeals to those of the young soldier. The girl gives a willing consent, and a joining of hands by the parent sanctions the union of two loving souls.

MASSENA EVACUATES POMBAL, PORTUGAL, MARCH 10, 1811.

[illegible]

This was at the beginning of the [illegible] retreat [illegible] French from [illegible] lines of Torres Vedras, where they had [illegible] Wellington [illegible] for nearly six months. Massena drew off cleverly, and was [illegible]

CHAPTER VI.

Massena holds on for six months with extraordinary tenacity before the lines of Torres Vedras, but in Ma[illegible] 1811 [illegible] Ney commands the rear [illegible] Wellington's pursuit with great skill and [illegible]. At Sabugal one brigade [illegible] Division [illegible] whole French [illegible] in the unequal struggle. About this time Sir Thomas Graham [illegible] won by the [illegible] and gallant [illegible] Lord [illegible]. Massena, believing Wellington to be [illegible] British at Fuentes d'Onoro. Wellington is on the spot, but holding too extended a position, is [illegible] Marshal [illegible] who had [illegible] the Portuguese Army, also fights an independent battle, that of Albuera, against Soult, [illegible] but the victory was gained by the indomitable courage of the British troops. Now Wellington finds himself op[illegible] Marmont, who has replaced Massena, and comes to blows with him in the [illegible] combat of El Bodon. After this, Wellington runs great danger by being exposed with a small force to the whole of Marmont's army at Fuente Guinaldo, but escapes.

MASSENA was not yet an old man, but he had lived his life, and this campaign in Portugal, with its disappointments and defeats, was not much to his taste. His invasion had failed [illegible] although he had great means, and was expected to perform great [illegible]. N[illegible] lashed him forward, as will be seen from an intercepted despatch [illegible] dated September, containing the following:—

"Lord Wellington has only 18,000 men, Hill no more than 6,000. It would be ridiculous to suppose that 25,000 English can balance 60,000, if the latter do not trifle. But fall boldly on, having well observed where the blow may be given."

The first blow had not made much impression, and no second was possible except by st[illegible] against [illegible] wall. Napoleon, when he wrote, knew nothing of Torres Vedras, an ignorance shared by many [illegible]. It was almost universally declared that the embarkation of the English army was inevitable; that the [illegible] frontier and the battle of Busaco were devised as "a decent cloak to cover the shame" of it.

Wellington and Waterloo.

So strong was the feeling that in England the Opposition openly proclaimed the withdrawal from Portugal. The Ministry, too, which gave Wellington no support, but plainly told him he must rely upon his own resources, anticipated it, and a letter of instructions, issued to an engineer officer proceeding to Portugal, began with the words, "As it is probable the army will embark in September — —." New arrivals, landing in Lisbon about this time, did not conceal their surprise at finding their comrades still there.

COIMBRA.

After a Drawing by Major St. Clair.

An important point on the line of Massena's retreat, and a thriving cathedral city, the seat of a University, has an observatory and a fine old aqueduct.

Wellington was, nevertheless, "all there," and there to stay. But now, once ensconced within his marvellous lines, he had to face another enemy—the traitors inside his camp. As soon as it was realised that nothing more was to be done that year, or even the next, that the war had practically become a blockade, then many self-sufficient, ignorant critics were unchained. He was assailed with bitter invective at home, chiefly on the strength of fault-finding letters from the army in Portugal, which denounced this wise inaction, and inveighed against the supposed incompetence of the General-in-Chief. This was not the way to shake Wellington from his firm purpose. He would not be drawn into playing the enemy's game, who would have been too pleased to see him issue forth from his safe citadel and offer battle in the open. He cared little for the most scathing attacks, but yet he could not pass them over entirely unnoticed. In one case he traced a very hostile epistle back to one of his own staff, General Charles Stewart, the Adjutant-General of the army. So he called him up, and, having convicted him of the treachery, said: "Charles Stewart, you are Castlereagh's brother, and he is one of my dearest friends. But unless you promise never to write in this strain again, I will deprive you of your appointment, and send you straight home."

GRENADIERS OF THE 42nd and 92nd HIGHLANDERS.

[illegible]

Two [illegible] Army, now the Black Watch [illegible] have been engaged in campaigns of the [illegible]

There was no reason why the army should be discontented. They were comfortably housed and sufficiently fed; there was little duty to be

MARQUIS OF WELLESLEY.

After a Painting by Home [illegible]

Lord Wellesley in 1809 accepted a special mission to Spain, as Envoy to the Spanish Government in Cadiz. He sought to strengthen his brother in his dealings with the difficult allies, and afterwards, when Foreign Secretary in the Perceval Cabinet [illegible] lords, strongly insisted on proper support being rendered Wellington in [illegible] done beyond routine work, guards, and pickets, with the constant drills needed to develop military efficiency. Officers had plenty of their favourite sports and amusements, both hunting and shooting, and they organised private theatricals and balls. There was nothing to grumble at but the one great grievance of not being led against the enemy.

The condition of Massena's army meanwhile grew worse and worse. He held his ground stoutly before the lines, and yet with unmeasured difficulty. He dispersed his foraging parties far and wide to beat up supplies in this terribly exhausted country. His efforts were boundless, and show up finely his energetic, resourceful character. The bulk of the food he gathered was maize; and he forthwith had ovens built to bake the bread made by the soldier bakers he hunted up in the ranks. There was plenty of skilled labour in his army, and he was able to organise artisans' shops to mend his disabled carts, shoe his horses, make gun-carriages, and even manufacture powder. How marvellous was the work he did is shown by the existence of his troops for five months in a country that could not have fed the British as many weeks. What the French suffered in that terrible time, and in the subsequent retreat, may be gleaned from the story told of a French soldier, who, at the first Spanish town he reached on leaving Portugal, bought all the white bread he could lay hands upon. He ate it voraciously, 17lb. of bread, without a pause, and Spanish bread is close, stodgy food besides.

INFANTRY OFFICER, PENINSULA.

From Ham[illegible] of the British Army, 1811-14

This was the [illegible] of regimental officers in marching; the overcoat was of blue "pepper and salt" colour.

DRUM-MAJOR AND PIONEER OF AN INFANTRY REGIMENT

From Ham[illegible] Costumes, [illegible]

The drum major heads the regiment, and was always distinctively and gorgeously dressed. The pioneers, now only one per company, are the survival of the artificers who once accompanied an army to throw up entrenchments.

Massena's splendid tenacity broke down at last. He might have held out longer had Soult come up to his support; but he had no means of communicating with his colleagues, for the Spanish irregulars intercepted all despatches passing between the French generals; and for months Napoleon had no news of Massena, except what he read in the English newspapers based on their reports from Portugal. Soult was, as a matter of fact, approaching, and could have co-operated had Massena stood firm for another ten days. But now in the early days of March, 1811, reinforcements had reached Wellington, and he felt strong enough to attack. His plan was to fall upon Massena in front, while Beresford, crossing higher up at Abrantes, turned his left. Massena very skilfully held his ground with his fighting men, as though he meant to take the offensive himself, and behind this screen sent his sick and baggage to the rear. Then his divisions filed off quickly, one after the other, and, when Wellington began to move on the 6th of March, Massena was gone. He had drawn off towards the Mondego, having gained four clear days, his aim being to reach Northern Portugal *via* Coimbra, and the rich unexhausted district of Oporto and the Douro. So cleverly was the retreat accomplished, that the Rifles, when ordered to advance, on the morning of the 6th, were checked by the bold stand still made by some of the French. A sharp fire was opened on them, and the wall held was "rushed," only to find that these last defenders were literally men of straw, lay figures in uniform, [illegible].

The retreating French moved in two columns, one direct on Coimbra, the other by [illegible] on Espinhal and Murcella. Ney, with his accustomed intrepidity, covered the retreat, and Wellington came up with them on the night of the 10th at Pombal. Massena barely got through the narrow streets of the town with the main body, but Ney formed up his rear-guard on the heights, and held the pursuers at bay till night fell and Massena could [illegible].

Next day Wellington, whose object was to operate continually against the inner flank, and turn the French away from Portugal, came up with Ney at Redinha. The Marshal was well posted, making the most of his meagre force, and he stood firm till the English developed their attack, with 30,000 men deployed in the plain. Then, firing a general volley, he escaped behind the smoke, but narrowly; and the skilful handling of the British troops made him more cautious in future, although it did not check his daring. As Napier says, "The country was full of strong positions, every village was a defile, the weather was moderate, and Ney, with a happy mixture of courage and skill, illustrated every league of ground by some signal combination."

Again and again Massena, covered by Ney, faced Wellington. Again and again the British General briskly attacked or skilfully turned every position taken up by the French; there were many sharp fights, as at Cazal Nova and Foz d'Aronce, in which the allies were always superior. Massena at last gained Moita, where he was allowed a brief respite, and finally, on reaching Celorico and Guarda, he was in comparative safety. Wellington

MASSENA'S RETREAT, 1811.

[illegible]

In the last phase of this retreat, Wellington, anxious to [illegible] French from a strong position, threw the Light Division [illegible] by the [illegible] and gained his object.

paused in the pursuit; his supplies had run short, and he had to wait till more reached him. This retreat through a wasted country was one of the most terrible on record. Massena showed great military ability, but also a fierce and ruthless spirit. No doubt his starving soldiers were often cut down and massacred by the peasantry, but the French reprisals were horrible. Whole villages were given to the sword and burned to the ground; murder and rapine marked the army's track. Even dumb patient beasts were sacrificed, and at one point Massena

SABUGAL, ON THE COA.

[illegible]

This was the scene of the fine action fought by [illegible] in March, 1811. Through the [illegible] staff officer, he found himself engaged [illegible] the Light Division against a whole French corps and yet held his own.

ordered some 5,000 asses to be hamstrung, and the British, coming upon the scene of butchery, were goaded to such fury that they would have given no quarter to the enemy if they had been engaged just then. "The conduct of the enemy throughout the whole retreat," wrote Wellington, "was marked by acts of barbarity which have seldom been equalled and never surpassed." The retreat put the crown, indeed, upon the cruelties practised before Torres Vedras. When the French foraging parties traversed the country, if they caught a Portuguese peasant, they would seize him, and put him to the torture till he confessed where he had hidden his provisions and goods. The rule was, first to hang him till he grew red in the face; if he still held out he hanged till he was black, after which, continued contumacy was punished by death.

Still Massena's manœuvring was masterly, and, in spite of his heavy losses, some 30,000 out of 75,000, he quickly recovered himself when once across the Spanish frontier, and would have resumed the initiative. His design was to work once more to the southward, and reach the valley of the Tagus through Sabugal and Penamacor. But he had to deal now with lieutenants who were mutinous; Ney defied

CAM[illegible] [illegible]VILLA, MAY 1[illegible], 1811.

[illegible] St. C[illegible]

Th[illegible] [illegible] by Wellington in this campaign of 1811, and [illegible] troops when bivouacking are here shown.

Wellington and Waterloo.

his orders, other marshals and generals neglected them, the combinations that would have forced the army to the Tagus were delayed, until at length they were foiled by Wellington. The French were now posted at Sabugal, where they could both hold on to Portugal and aim at the Tagus. This brought on an action which was hardly a battle, for it was marred by mischance, but was yet a crowning triumph to the small portion of the British army engaged. This was mainly the three famous regiments of the Light Division, the 43rd, 52nd, and 95th, who never behaved with greater gallantry than at Sabugal, under Beckwith, their intrepid brigadier. The morning was thick with heavy rain; and, through the mistaken zeal of a staff officer who found Beckwith's brigade halted at a ford, it was hurried forward to the attack prematurely. Beckwith came upon the enemy with barely half his brigade, a regiment and a-half against 12,000 strong (Reynier's Corps), but his heart was too big to quail. The Rifleman, Edward Costello, who was present, bears witness to his chief's demeanour on that day. "No one could have observed our colonel during the heat of the action and not have admired his cool and soldier-like bearing. 'Steady, lads—show no hurry,' was his cheering exhortation, accompanied by a smile when we were obliged to retreat, the blood at the same time flowing copiously from a wound he had received across the forehead." "Never were troops more judiciously or more gallantly led. Never was a leader more devotedly followed," is the tribute of another Rifleman present, Captain, afterwards Sir John, Kincaid. Kincaid has preserved two curious incidents of this fight. One was that a man in the action fell dead at his feet, yet "although I heard a musket-ball strike him, I could neither find blood nor wound." The other is a story of a little spaniel belonging to one of the officers, which ran about all the time barking at the balls; and says Kincaid, "I once saw him smelling at a live shell, which exploded in his face without hurting him." Beckwith fought an unequal battle with such fierce resolve, making so much use of the ground, that he held his own till reinforced, having inflicted enormous losses on the French. Wellington ungrudgingly styled this as "one of the most glorious actions British troops were ever engaged in."

MARSHAL NEY, DUC D'ELCHINGEN AND PRINCE OF MOSKOWA
After a [illegible]

Ney, son of an old soldier, threw up a [illegible] to enlist as an hussar. He was one of the most intrepid and [illegible] of Napoleon's marshals, and was shot as a traitor to Louis XVIII. in 1815. He was [illegible] advance or rear guard, and [illegible] in the handling of large [illegible]. He was constantly engaged in the Peninsula, against Moore, [illegible] and Wellington, later, although he never had an independent command. He was [illegible] active lieutenant at Waterloo.

The defeat at Sabugal, although not so decisive as it deserved to be, still obliged Massena to surrender his projects and fall back upon Salamanca. Wellington, seemingly master of the situation, invested Almeida closely, and, believing now that a period of inaction was certain upon this side, hurried off to give his personal aid to Beresford, who was engaged upon the siege of Badajos. During his absence Massena, thinking to take advantage of it, gathered up his strength for a fresh onslaught, and fought the battle of Fuentes d'Onoro, of which

MAJOR-GENERAL [illegible] INFANTRY.

Full-dress uniform [illegible] of the Peninsular War. [illegible] Knight [illegible] Bath.

more directly. About this period another brilliant feat of arms was performed by a distant detached force, that under Sir Thomas Graham, who, on the 5th of March, had won the battle of Barrosa, not far from Cadiz. This maritime city, now the seat of Government and the headquarters of the Cortes, was closely blockaded by Marshal Victor with 20,000 men. Graham thought he could best relieve the pressure of the investment by transporting a force down the coast, and, landing at Tarifa, attack the French lines in reverse. A word here as to Graham, one of the most gallant military leaders of these times, who only took to war late in life; but the ready instinct of a born soldier amply replaced the want of early training and long experience. There was a pretty but sad romance about his adoption of a military career. His youth and manhood had been passed in the Highlands; he was a Scotch laird, happily married, and devoted to field sports. At forty-five, the death of his wife, to whom he was devotedly attached, blighted his life, and he turned to the Army to seek an anodyne for his grief in active service. This is the Mrs. Graham of Gainsborough's immortal portrait, one of the finest known to the British school. She was a daughter of Lord Cathcart, a lady of the sweetest nature, and of great personal charms, as will be plain from the illustrations. What [illegible] bereavement meant to Graham may be gathered from the fact that, at his wife's death he ordered the picture of [illegible] to be locked up in a wall of his ancestral home, from which it was not extracted for many years.

Graham [illegible] at Toulon in 1793; then he raised a regiment of his own, the famous 90th, or Perthshire Volunteers, now the 2nd Battalion of the Cameronians, or Scotch Rifles, a regiment which has given two Commanders-in-Chief to the British Army, Lord Wolseley and Lord Hill. He served with it constantly in the Mediterranean and in Egypt under Abercromby; and, when [illegible], he accompanied Moore to Spain as [illegible]. After Corunna he was given [illegible] long been denied [illegible] a dying [illegible] Sir John Moore. He was now commanding the British garrison at Cadiz, and in February, 1811, [illegible] away with him 4,310 sabres [illegible] bayonets, [illegible] hardy troops, their commander [illegible] of a ready temper for battle." [illegible] a Spanish force, but, like [illegible] Wellington, was doomed [illegible] risk of disaster from [illegible] allies. The [illegible] supreme command, [illegible] by Graham, [illegible] certain [illegible] fresh.

AIDE-DE-CAMP TO GENERAL OFFICER.

An officer of the personal staff of a general officer during the war was always well mounted, so as to carry despatches quickly.

THOMAS GRAHAM, LORD LYNEDOCH.

unharassed by long marches, and compactly together. As they proceeded along the coast they came upon the heights of Barrosa, upon which Graham was very anxious to make a firm stand. But La Peña was bent on, and with great want of tact peremptorily ordered Graham to follow. Graham obeyed, but left two regiments on Barrosa to guard his baggage, and then entering a thick wood, was altogether deserted by La Peña. Now Victor, who was near at hand, saw a great opportunity; his enemy was in three separate bodies widely apart—the Spaniards a long way ahead, Graham in the wood, his baggage and its guards on the Barrosa hill. The French were at once sent forward to attack vigorously. The blow first fell upon Barrosa, and Major Brown, outnumbered but defiant, sent to Graham asking what he should do. "Fight," was the stout answer of the intrepid veteran, and, facing round, Graham, with great promptitude and determination, prepared to do the same. Retreat at that moment, although perhaps prescribed by the strict rules of the military art, would have been quite ruinous. Graham's only hope was in a prompt initiative. The order was to attack forthwith, without waiting for regular formation; every corps, every detachment, was to go straight at what was in front of it. But the British troops drew together in two great masses, which charged in a great shock with no decisive results on either side. Now the 87th, led by Major Hugh Gough, rushed forward in such a fierce and prolonged charge, "that they overthrew the first line of French, drove it on to the second, and the whole, being broken, went off in confusion, carrying away the reserves at the same time." Brown, on Barrosa, charged down, and was soon backed by Dilke's column, one of the two above mentioned; and there, too, the French were overborne. The discomfited enemy tried hard to reform as their columns converged in retreat, but the fine play of the British artillery forbade it, and the battle could not be restored.

MRS. GRAHAM.

[illegible] by her gallant husband, [illegible] of General Earl Cathcart. [illegible] and Mr. Graham, although [illegible] the Army and served as a [illegible] stated elsewhere. At the [illegible] locked up in a wall at his [illegible] many years. It is one of the

The chief glory of Barrosa fell, of course, on Graham. But Gough and his gallant Irishmen deserve especial credit, for they struck in at the most critical moment and captured a French eagle, that seen in the woodcut. This was one of the first occasions on which Hugh Gough showed those [illegible] place among English soldiers. He was the same forward, intrepid [illegible] the forefront, throughout the Peninsular War, and afterwards in India when Commander [illegible]

He is represented on another page as he appeared at Chillianwallah. It is a familiar [illegible] knows the famous white overcoat. There are two or more of these portraits [illegible] the mess [illegible] 87th [illegible] the Royal Irish Fusiliers; and once a sergeant of the corps, whose father had fought at Barrosa, [illegible] heard explaining the portrait to a less well-informed comrade: "That's old Gough, grand old man, and that's his famous coat. After the battle he took that coat off, and just shook the bullets out of it." A pretty story of canine attachment belongs to this battle of Barrosa. Among the French killed was General Rousseau. He had owned a white poodle dog, which had been left in quarters when the general went out to fight, but which, finding his master did not return, wandered in search of him. He found him where he lay stricken to death, and remained constantly by the general's side, licking his hand and moaning piteously till his master died. For some time he could not be persuaded to leave the body, and for three days refused food. After the burial he still lay there upon the grave, utterly disconsolate, until Sir Thomas Graham, who was crossing the field, came upon the faithful beast. The general was ever a great lover of dogs, and he had no doubt at command much of that subtle sympathetic influence that wins at once upon canine nature. The poodle took to this other veteran, suffered himself to be drawn away from the grave, and presently transferred the whole wealth of his affection to Sir Thomas Graham, becoming his constant companion. Eventually the white poodle went to Perthshire, and lived at Balgowan till he died. Massena, as has been said, was prompt to take advantage

MRS. GRAHAM.

Wellington's absence at Badajos, and that the English General had gone was immediately known, for spies came and went between the two armies, and all important news was carried across the lines. [illegible] Massena made a push to relieve Almeida. With this [illegible] he drew [illegible] Salamanca [illegible] His army, so lately shattered, was now reconstituted and reorganised. He [illegible] allies as two to one in infantry, and three to one in cavalry. Wellington [illegible] of whom 10,000 were Portuguese and 1,000 cavalry. At the news of Massena's approach [illegible] in the British lines, and all ranks were eager for Wellington's return. As Kincaid says, "[illegible] long nose in the fight than a reinforcement of 10,000 men any day." This is not so [illegible] Welmade of the name of Napoleon's presence with an army, which he placed at 80,000 men. But it is pleasant to record how Wellington's men trusted him. "There was a charm, not only about himself but all connected with him, for which no odds could compensate," goes on Kincaid. "... I'll venture to say that there was not a heart in the army that did not beat more lightly when we heard the joyful news of his arrival the day before the enemy's advance."

TRIUMPH OF THE BRITISH FLAG AT BARROSA, 1811.

The victory of Barrosa was gained against great odds, and was the subject of great rejoicing in England.

Wellington did not hold much by the siege of Almeida, and need not have waited for Massena's attack. Nevertheless, as Napier put it, "his warlike spirit would not let him go back"; he was outnumbered, the position he occupied at Fuentes d'Onoro was vicious, for Massena, marching straight from Ciudad Rodrigo, could place himself with all his strength on the weak right flank of the English line; he had an enemy's fortress in his rear, and the river Coa with its rocky bed would have been difficult of passage in retreat.

There was a preliminary combat, but the real battle of Fuentes d'Onoro began on the 5th. Wellington took up a position unduly extended for his numbers, reaching from in front of Almeida on his left, through Fuentes d'Onoro in the centre, to the plateau of Nava d'Aver on his far right, which was held by one division, the 7th, and the cavalry. The French struck at this flank and turned it, their cavalry being so much more powerful than ours, and Ramsay's battery of Horse Artillery was quite cut off. This gave rise to the great historical incident of Ramsay's escape by his splendid charge.

THE LINES OF TORRES VEDRAS.

River T... ...

The famous lines of Torres Vedras where they ... river.

The story has been told and re-told, painted and re-painted. The main body of the French was suddenly seen to be heaving as though torn with some internal convulsion, which was focussed "at a point where a thick dust and loud cries, and the sparkling of blades, and flashing of pistols, indicated some extraordinary [illegible]. Suddenly the multitude became violently agitated. [illegible] the mass was rent asunder, and Norman Ramsay burst forth, sword in hand, at [illegible] fire, streamed like greyhounds along the plain, the guns bounded behind them like things of no weight, and the mounted gunners followed close with heads bent low and pointed weapons in desperate career [illegible] the finest and proudest episodes in war.

But now the French were fast gaining ground, the British [illegible] nearly compromised; the battle would surely be lost unless Wellington quickly closed in his line. He was never better than in the tactics of the battlefield, and now he skilfully drew back his right, forming a new front at an angle with the 5th. This change was not completed a moment too soon; while it was in progress, the plain was covered with baggage, and commissariat, and broken detachments all in wild, long confusion. [illegible] the British [illegible] could not make daylight. Had the French pressed their advantage with a vigorous attack, the battle would have been lost to Wellington. But the British got into their new place safely; while the delay in Drouet's assault on the village of Fuentes, which he might have taken easily enough, would have made this new position untenable.

One of the [illegible] barracks (Kincaid) gives a graphic picture of this change of front. He describes the movements as "a magnificent military spectacle [illegible] the plain between us and the right of the army was [illegible] [illegible] in the p[illegible] sion of the French cavalry, and while [illegible] with the order and [illegible] [illegible] dimensions of this, made [illegible] instantly [illegible] [illegible] carrying [illegible]." [illegible] was hot, and fiercely contested, [illegible] on both sides, [illegible] [illegible] evening. The village was then abandoned by the defenders, and [illegible] was claimed as our charge [illegible]. The French also claimed it on the ground that they had [illegible] and forced Wellington [illegible] miles of ground. Massena, [illegible] was the victim [illegible] the [illegible] of Fuentes [illegible] were discredited, [illegible] and incompletely [illegible] was the [illegible] Massena

GENERAL VISCOUNT GOUGH.

He commanded [illegible] 1812, when [illegible]

[illegible] GENERAL MACDONALD.

[illegible]

retired without relieving Almeida. He had, however, communicated with its Governor, General Brennier, desiring him to cut his way out if he could. Some rumour that an attempt of this kind would be made, and by the road to Barba del Puerco, had reached Wellington, and he had warned Brennier not to try.

"I had some intimation of Brennier's purpose to blow up the place and retire," the Duke told Lord Stanhope in 1836, "and I sent him word that, if he did, he and every man we should catch should have no quarter. It is contrary to the law of nations, and troops so conducting themselves are not entitled to be considered prisoners of war." The Duke sent orders to a Colonel Bevan to occupy the bridge at this Barba del Puerco and so intercept the fugitive garrison. Bevan got these instructions at 5 p.m., but postponed moving till next morning, when, of course, he was too late. Brennier blew up his works, which had been mined, and started at midnight. Some cavalry tried to stop him and were beaten off, then the infantry, having got rid of their knapsacks so as to march light, pursued and overtook Brennier's men near the bridge, where some 300 were made prisoners, but Wellington did not execute any of his threats upon them. General Brennier had another strong reason for wishing to get away. He owed Wellington £500, and feared that if taken he would have been obliged to pay. He had been made prisoner at Vimiera, and in London, before he was exchanged, he had borrowed this money. The authority for this is Wellington himself, who in telling the story said he had never heard of or from Brennier since.

ROYAL HORSE ARTILLERY, 1811.

Norman Ramsay's troop of Horse Artillery greatly distinguished itself at the battle of Fuentes d'Onoro, where, being surrounded by French cavalry, the gunners cut their way through with their swords, dragging out their guns at a gallop.

The delay over the blowing up of Almeida and the escape of its garrison lost Wellington the chance of being present at the battle of Albuera. He had fully meant to rejoin Beresford and to take command against Soult, who was now hurrying up from Seville to raise the siege of Badajos. "Had I been there" (at Albuera), Wellington said, "we should have made a great thing of it," which Beresford scarcely did, although he won the battle. Wellington had the highest opinion of Beresford nevertheless, and always pointed to him as the man who should succeed him if he became

II. ARTILLERY DRIVERS.

In early days ... were taken ... who were not soldiers; now the drivers are soldiers, but ... could be taken off their horses.

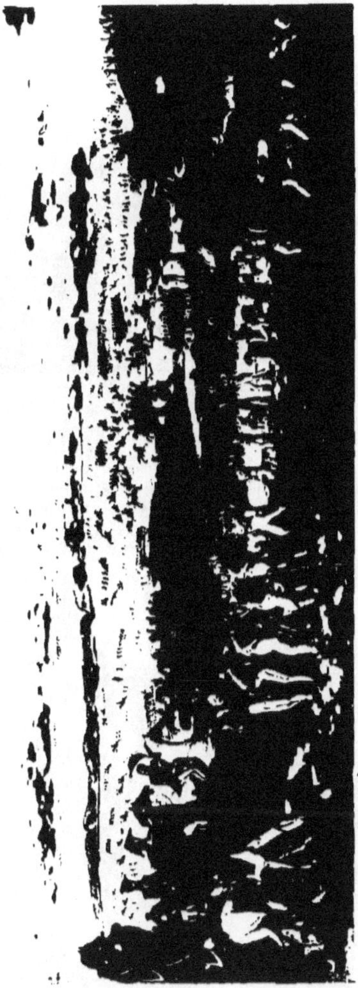

BATTLE OF FUENTES D'ONORO, MAY 1811.

hors de combat. "He is the ablest man I have yet seen with the army," was the Chief's opinion as expressed to the Government, "the one having the largest views . . . they tell me that when I am not present he wants decision, . . . but I am quite certain he is the only person capable of conducting a large concern." Once when the qualifications of the various generals in the Peninsula were openly canvassed at the dinner table, and Wellington was asked to name the best, his choice fell on Beresford. "I see what you mean by your looks," he went on, noticing general surprise. "If it was a question of handling troops, some of you fellows might do as well, nay, better than he, but what we want now is someone to feed our troops, and I know of no one fitter for the purpose than Beresford." This is rather negative praise, but Wellington expressed himself more strongly on other occasions. He never decided on any course without consulting Beresford, and often said that there was "no one like the marshal for seeing the weak point in a plan." He also always took the marshal with him if he could on his reconnaissances, for he relied greatly on Beresford's sagacity and quick eye for country. In the early phases of the war, Beresford had been very usefully employed in building up the Portuguese Army. During his previous service he had captured Madeira, and while there made good use of his time by mastering the Portuguese language. He had already seen much service at Toulon, in India, with Baird in the desert march from the Red Sea to the Nile, again with Baird in the capture of the Cape of Good Hope, and he was concerned in, but in no way blamed for, the defeat and surrender of General Whitelocke at Buenos Ayres. The wisdom of his selection to command the Portuguese was amply justified by the result. His was a strong, firm hand, yet he used large powers with great tact and judgment. There was no honesty, no spirit among the Portuguese troops; the regiments were without organisation; officers were mostly absent in civil

BATTLE OF FUENTES D'ONORO.

From B[illegible] Campaigns of We[illegible]

This battle was closely contested, with varying fortunes, from morning till night. Both parties abandoned the town of Fuentes during the night.

FALL OF ALMEIDA.

[illegible]

[illegible] blown up [illegible] commandant, General Brennier, who escaped with the [illegible] few hundreds [illegible] being made prisoners. Had Wellington's orders been [illegible] escape [illegible] flight.

situations; one officer borne on the cadre, but necessarily absent, was its patron saint, whose pay was regularly drawn by the monks of some convent. The rank and file were not without military aptitudes, but they were only imperfectly drilled and greatly in want of all military necessaries—clothing, arms, equipment.

Beresford's first move was to import a number of English officers into the Portuguese service. Every unit, every squadron, battery, and battalion was, as far as possible, put under their command. British staff and commissariat officers were also given to the army, and among these were many who rose to great distinction. Colonel Hardinge in particular, to whose prompt action, as we shall see, the victory at Albuera was largely due.

Well led, and disciplined by officers they could respect, the Portuguese soon developed into excellent soldiers, men who took their turn stanchly in fighting and never turned from it. In the early times they had been known by our soldiery as the "Vamoses," from a common catch cry, "Vamus, let us be off," which they shouted before they ran away. But after Busaco, where they behaved so well, they gained a more honourable sobriquet, the "Valerosas," or courageous. They hugged and cheered each other after the fight, and cried "Mucha Valerosa," to the admiration and delight of all who saw them. To return to Albuera, Soult left Seville on the 10th May, and on the 15th he was at Santa Marta, within thirty miles of Badajos. Beresford, hearing of his near approach, raised the siege, and crossing the Guadiana, concentrated at Albuera, prepared to give Soult battle there. It was the best position he could

VIEW OF CIUDAD RODRIGO.

[illegible]

In 1812, as a preliminary to [illegible] operations, Wellington swooped [illegible] unexpectedly upon Ciudad Rodrigo, and captured it after a brief siege of eleven days. The assault [illegible]

[illegible], as he afterwards reported to Wellington, and stood directly in the road between the enemy and Badajos. He was joined here, but very tardily, by a Spanish army under Blake. This dilatory general did not move till his posts had been driven in by Soult's cavalry, and he only arrived on the ground about midnight before the battle.

The strength of the opposing armies was as follows:— Beresford, 32,000 infantry, 2,000 cavalry, and 38 guns; but of these only 7,000 were British, and the balance, Spaniards, were very inferior troops. Soult, on the other hand, had 40 guns, 4,000 splendid horsemen, and 19,000 [illegible] infantry, [illegible] spirit," amply compensating for their inferiority in numbers by their fine organisation and their leader's capacity, which was "immeasurably greater than his adversary's." The quotation is from the historian Napier, who was always a little hard on Beresford. Yet the dispositions of the British general were undoubtedly weak. He held his main strength about a high hill in the centre which covered the road to Badajos, and which he deemed the key of the position, as it was, if the enemy attacked in front. But Soult, who had closely reconnoitred the ground, saw at once that his left might [illegible] get very near the English right by using a long ridge that acted as a screen to hide his concentration. Beresford had neglected this ridge, and [illegible] know what was in progress behind it. Hence his right was [illegible] being turned, for Soult resolved to make his [illegible]. Success here would take the whole British [illegible] the Badajos road Beresford would be [illegible] front. When the battle began on [illegible], moving upon the bridge at Albuera, [illegible] British centre, but now Beresford [illegible] would be on his right, and he [illegible] in the centre to show a front [illegible] to reinforce it, and

COLONEL HARDINGE.

[illegible] Field-Marshal Viscount Hardinge. [illegible] Portuguese Army. [illegible]

H.R.H. THE [illegible] OF ORANGE.

[illegible] Waterloo [illegible]

GENERAL THE HON. LOWRY COLE

General Cole was [illegible] Commanded the [illegible] Division all through the Peninsula. He saved the battle of Albuera.

bringing thither the cavalry, also backed it with his 4th Division. Now Blau, the Spanish general, refused to move, declaring that the real attack was on the bridge. Beresford galloped over to insist in person, but the change of front was still delayed, and "thus half-an-hour had sufficed to render Beresford's position nearly desperate. Two-thirds of the French were in compact order of battle perpendicular to his right, and his army, composed of different nations, was making a disorderly change of front." Soult believed that the day was already his own. He pushed his columns forward to crown the hills, while his guns swept all the approaches. Moreover, the 1st Brigade of the 2nd Division came up under General Stewart, who could not form line before he charged, and was, therefore, discomfited; the French cavalry swooped down and captured six British guns, and in this melée a Polish lancer was rash enough to measure swords with Beresford himself. The marshal, who was a man of undaunted courage and great personal strength, fought splendidly. Gripping his adversary by the throat, he threw him out of his saddle, a fine exploit, characteristic of his race and name. Nor was this the marshal's only personal effort. For when the Spaniards still obstinately hung back, Beresford caught up an ensign bodily and carried him with his colours by main force to the front. "Yet the troops would not follow, and the coward ran back when released from the marshal's iron grip."

MARSHAL MARMONT, DUC DE RAGUSE.

After a Painting by [illegible].

Marmont, an artillery officer, was a devoted adherent and prominent soldier of Napoleon's, who was with him in Egypt as a Brigadier, and was made a Marshal after Wagram. He was sent to replace Massena in Spain, but was no more successful. Although he had out-manœuvred Wellington before Salamanca, he committed a grievous blunder, was caught, and utterly defeated in the battle of that name. He fought with the Army in Germany at Lutzen, Bautzen, and Dresden. He was always blamed for having been a chief agent in bringing about Napoleon's abdication in 1814.

Fortunately at the critical moment the weather became thick, and Soult did not put forth all his strength, or the fight must have ended disastrously for us. A 2nd Brigade (Houghton's) of Stewart's Division came up, and maintained the fight. Houghton was killed (he had commenced the action in plain clothes, but his servant bringing up his uniform, he donned the scarlet coat in the thick of the battle), his regiments were decimated, the 29th suffered terribly, the 57th too, gaining them their immortal title of the "Die Hards" from the noble words of their indomitable Colonel Inglis, who, though stricken to death, still cried "Die hard, men, die hard!"

In this the darkest hour Beresford began to despond. He had already contemplated retreat and was placing troops to cover it, when Colonel Hardinge, one of his staff, boldly apostrophised him, telling him he must now choose between a peerage and a court-martial. "I will go for the peerage," cried the sturdy Irishman, ashamed, no doubt, of his temporary weakness, and from that moment fortune changed. The 4th Division (Cole's), still quite fresh, came into the battle, and with a resistless purpose that nothing could stay. No wonder that Wellington in speaking of this battle considered the "action one of the most glorious and honourable to the character of the troops of any that has been fought during the war." It was no doubt a soldier's victory ranking with Inkerman and Rorke's Drift. The general in command earned no credit except of personal intrepidity. Some say that Hardinge of his own accord gave the order that brought Cole up with the 4th Division. It is on record certainly in his journal that he sent Abercromby forward, but he says nothing about Cole. How bloodthirsty was the battle may be judged from the statement that after it the débris of five whole regiments were formed into one provisional battalion. This was formed of one company of the 3rd Buffs, one

Wellington and Waterloo.

On the sick list.

MILITARY ADVENTURES OF JOHNNY NEWCOME.

After a Caricature by Rowlandson.

At this period the army in the Peninsula was exceedingly sickly.

of the 66th, two of the 29th, three of the 57th, and three of the 31st, all under the command of Lieutenant-Colonel L'Estrange of the 31st. The 29th, a grand regiment, so famous for its steadiness and discipline that it was known as the "Guards of the Line," had suffered so terribly that its wounded almost filled the hospital at Elvas "Why, old 29th, I am sorry to see so many of you here!" said Lord Wellington a few days after, when visiting the hospital, and the touching answer he got bears witness to the implicit confidence his men had in him. "Ah, my lord, there would have been fewer if you had only been with us." As has been said, it was Wellington's most earnest wish to be there, frustrated by adverse luck. No decisive engagements marked the remainder of the year 1811. Wellington twice again essayed to capture Badajos; but he was foiled by the enemy's superior strength. Napoleon was not yet content to let go his hold of Spain. On the contrary, he continually poured in fresh troops; and now, in the August of this year, the French in Spain reached the tremendous total of 352,000 men and 52,000 horses. At one time, too, it was strongly rumoured that Napoleon was coming in person to direct the war, a host always in himself, and a master of the science before whom even Wellington might quail. At this time, indeed, with barely 40,000 British under his command, the thoughts of the great Englishman once more returned to Torres Vedras and a strictly defensive game. Now in his immediate front Marmont had replaced Massena,

MAJOR-GEN. OF CAVALRY IN THE PENINSULA.

From Hamilton Smith's Costumes.

A fancy portrait of a General commanding a Cavalry Brigade.

LIEUT.-GENERAL OF CAVALRY IN THE PENINSULA.

A fancy portrait of a General commanding [illegible] By [illegible]

who had been recalled in disgrace, and who never again entered the field for a master who seldom forgave failure. Marmont had a high reputation, especially as a tactical leader, and he proved it. Now, in September, he advanced with a large force, and, covered by it, he succeeded in throwing supplies into Ciudad Rodrigo, on which fortress Wellington had long cast covetous eyes, having in July brought his battering train up the river Douro as far as Larnego. Marmont's operations brought on the fight at El Bodon, a fierce combat that shed imperishable renown upon the British cavalry and two five-year-old infantry regiments, the 5th Fusiliers and the 77th, under their gallant brigadier, Colville. With one regiment of Portuguese, Colville held his regiments on a rough height, threaded by the main road, and was repeatedly

GENERAL SIR STAPLETON COTTON, AFTERWARDS FIELD-MARSHAL LORD COMBERMERE.

After a Painting by Mrs. C. Pe[illegible]

A dashing cavalry officer, who commanded the 25th Light Dragoons at twenty-[illegible]. Gained rapid promotion, and commanded a brigade of cavalry under Wellington at the Douro and Talavera; later, all the British cavalry in the Peninsula. He was highly commended for the gallantry of his charges at Salamanca. He was an excellent officer, skilled in detail, a fine forward rider, smart in appearance, [illegible] cavalry officer. His fondness for brave apparel gained him the sobriquet in Spain of the "Lion d'Or." It was said that in Spain, when [illegible]tred, man and horse, he was worth £500.

[illegible] [illegible] by three [illegible] and General [illegible]. The French cavalry gained ground, and captured six guns, when the gallant "[illegible] 5th," [illegible] Ridge, a "daring men," charged, infantry against cavalry, generally a rash proceeding [illegible] guns, while the 77th and Portuguese drove back the French horse on the other flank. But [illegible], and Wellington, who was now on the ground, ordered a retreat. The Portuguese got safely to the rear [illegible] 5th and 77th re- [illegible] formed in one square, [illegible] brunt of the whole French [illegible]. But [illegible] could make no impression [illegible] who [illegible] destructive volleys, and then showed the same steadfast hedge of glittering bayonets.

At last, after [illegible] fruitless charges, finding the square could not be broken, the enemy drew off. Lord Wellington warmly thanked the troops for this "memorable example of what [illegible] effected by steadiness, discipline, and confidence."

"It is impossible," he went on to say, "at any time to be exposed to the attacks of numbers relatively greater [illegible]"; and he commended [illegible] as an example to be followed by officers and soldiers in all such circumstances. This occasion, or rather the situation that followed it, was one in which Wellington was so [illegible] favoured by fortune that Marmont, when he heard what had happened, declared that Wellington's star was as much in the ascendant as Napoleon's. Wellington now retired, with the troops he had [illegible] Guinaldo, a good position [illegible].

But [illegible] more than 14,000 men [illegible] army was still separated from him by long distances: the [illegible], under Graham, [illegible] Nava d'Aver; the 5th Division [illegible] Payo; the right [illegible] and it was to secure [illegible] made so bold a show. Marmont, on the other hand, was close with 60,000 men. He knew nothing of Wellington's weakness, who lay thus almost at his mercy [illegible] actually retreating when his scouts brought him news of the chance he had [illegible] quoted as one of the finest evidences of his great mind. Although [illegible] was begged urgently to retire, he still stood fast, meaning to extricate [illegible] jeopardised, probably lost, had the rest of the army retreated. His [illegible] one of those daring impulses of fine genius which rules were

SIR CHARLES COLVILLE.

[illegible]

He was gazetted Ensign [illegible] and joined [illegible]. He was [illegible] Brigadier in the [illegible]. His first [illegible] of arms was in the fight at El Bodon, when he formed square with two battalions, and repelled the repeated charges of the French cavalry. Wellington said it was "an example to be followed by all officers and soldiers."

Wellington and Waterloo.

RETREAT OF THE FRENCH FROM ARROYO DE LOS MOLINOS.

After a Drawing in Maxwell's "Life of Wellington."

A French division, carelessly commanded, on the south side of the Tagus was surprised by General Hill, after a rapid march through the hills, at Arroyo de los Molinos, a mountain town. The French were mostly destroyed or dispersed.

CHAPTER VII.

Wellington contemplates great movements in 1812. Hill is employed to surprise an exposed French force at Arroyo de los Molinos. Then Wellington swoops down on Ciudad Rodrigo, having secretly prepared for the siege of that important fortress, which he captures almost by a *coup de main*. He turns next on Badajoz, a second and stronger place of arms, which is besieged in due form and carried by assault with great daring but severe losses. He now prepares to attack Marmont; Hill having taken Almaraz, on the Tagus, on which river the French have now no bridges. Wellington crosses the Tormes and takes Salamanca. Marmont retires and again advances. A series of masterly movements on both sides. At last, when Wellington proposes to retreat finally, Marmont makes a flagrant mistake, which Wellington seizes upon, and wins the great battle of Salamanca, "beating 40,000 men in forty minutes." After this victory the French withdraw behind the Ebro, and leave the road open to Madrid.

AS the year 1811 drew to its close, Wellington was still revolving great projects, but waiting for time and opportunity to essay them. Meanwhile, his principal lieutenant, Hill, carried out a brilliant feat of arms on his own account. The raid, as it may be called, upon Arroyo de los Molinos, a sudden descent upon a French division carelessly commanded, redounded greatly to Hill's credit and that of the troops engaged. General Rowland Hill was an especial favourite with his chief. Wellington, who liked implicit obedience—to whom, indeed, anything less was intolerable—always called Hill his best subordinate, because he "always did exactly what he was told." From the first there was the closest confidence between them. "I rejoice extremely at the prospect I have before me of serving again with you," Wellington wrote Hill when first embarking for Portugal. Again, after Talavera, when Wellington constituted a second, practically independent, command for the valley of the Tagus, he gave it to Hill.

"I will not make any arrangements," he wrote, "either as to the troops that are to comprise it, or as to the officer who is to command it, without offering the command to you." Hill accepted, modestly deprecating his appointment, but promising to do his best, as he did on every occasion during the war.

Hill was one of four soldier brothers, who were all in the Peninsula with Wellington. He himself had been a delicate, sensitive child, who fainted at the sight of blood, who could not bear to look at a prize fight, and hated every form of cruelty. He was greatly beloved throughout his career for his sweet, gentle disposition, and was known to his men by such endearing epithets as "Father Hill," "Daddy Hill," and "Farmer Hill," the last-named because of his round cheery face with its apple cheeks. He was the very picture of an English country gentleman, and in far-off Spain spoke of home to the exiled soldiery. His thoughts were ever for his men, whom he spared on every occasion; he was generous and humane to the people of the country, kind and chivalrous to the enemy.

Hill had seen much service. He was aide-de-camp to General O'Hara at the siege of Toulon, where he worked side by side with Graham; he was in Egypt with Abercromby, and wounded at the battle of Aboukir; he was in the expedition against Copenhagen, where he was first thrown with his illustrious chief. Landing one of the first at the Mondego, he saw all the fighting; was at Roleia and Vimiera, with Sir John Moore in the retreat on Corunna, again with Wellington at the passage of the Douro, where the lion's share of the work was laid on his shoulders. It was the same at Talavera, where he held the key of the position; and at Busaco he came in advance of his leader's call to throw his weight into the scale at a critical moment. Lastly, in the long defence of Torres Vedras, it was Hill who held the right flank, the weakest part of the wide entrenchments.

After a visit to England on sick leave he returns to Spain, and goes again to the front.

He is now an officer of the Guards, and is well received by Lord Wellington, who appoints him a member of his staff.

MILITARY ADVENTURES OF JOHNNY NEWCOME.

After Caricatures by Rowlandson

Now Hill was again in command south of the Tagus, and as the main body of the French had withdrawn further south across the Guadiana, Wellington desired Hill to fall upon the few left between those rivers. This was a division commanded by Girard, who, retiring slowly, had reached the mountain village of Arroyo de los Molinos on the 26th October, a place where many roads met, and where Hill, marching rapidly at his heels, fell upon him and smote him grievously. Girard knew that Hill was after him, yet took no precautions. Fortunately one of his brigades had got off, but Hill poured upon the rest without warning. The French cavalry were unbridled, the infantry only gathering on parade; Girard was inside a house waiting for his horse when the British advance charged down the street, the guns opened fire, and the cavalry cut off all retreat. There seemed nothing for it but surrender, yet Girard would not yield; his men, all hardy veterans, were desired to disperse and escape as best they could. They took to the mountains by twos and threes, and in the end some 600 were saved out of 3,000. For his success at Arroyo de los Molinos, and at Wellington's earnest request, General Hill was made a K.C.B. But so unpretending and modest was his nature, that it was long before he [illegible] himself to accept his new title, and he blushed, shyly, whenever he was addressed as "Sir Rowland."

[illegible] with no very brilliant prospects, as it seemed. Beyond the fact, now positively known, that Napoleon [illegible] engaged in a colossal struggle with Russia, and would therefore neither come to Spain nor reinforce his army [illegible] Wellington had but little reason to rejoice. The British army was in poor case, ill-[illegible] prolonged [illegible] Sickness had struck down thousands, many of the regiments recently come out still suffered from Walcheren [illegible] could not bear even exposure to the night air. Food was scarce; half and [illegible] were often issued; [illegible] times the troops were without bread for three consecutive days; they were

LORD HILL.

in rags, their uniforms so patched that one regiment could not be distinguished from another; country boots had been given out to many, and being coarse, and worn without socks, only produced sore feet. All animals were fed scantily upon chopped straw; horses in the cavalry and artillery were half starved, and the transport mules could hardly work. Yet Wellington, with surprising astuteness, turned these drawbacks to good account. He encouraged his enemy in the belief that he was too weak to undertake any great enterprise, and when at last he got his battering train up to Almeida, through eighty miles of rugged mountain country, it was supposed he only meant to re-arm that fortress. Great secrecy was also kept in making other preparations for a siege. For now, at the moment when Marmont thought him at a standstill, was his time to attack Ciudad Rodrigo. A bold movement might give him that fortress before the French, all greatly dispersed and at great distances, could collect a sufficient force to interrupt the siege operations.

TAKING OF CIUDAD RODRIGO, ON 19th JANUARY, 1812.

From Bertrand's "Campaigns of Wellington."

The whole business did not take twenty minutes, from the starting of the forlorn-hope to the capture of the place, but the assault cost many valuable lives.

A sudden change of weather had improved the general health of the army; many thousands had returned to duty, and Wellington could dispose of 35,000 men, including cavalry, for any enterprise. He had diligently collected the materials for a siege at places within easy range of Rodrigo; his guns and ammunition were at Almeida, where also some 8,000 round shot had been

ANOTHER VIEW OF THE STORMING OF CIUDAD RODRIGO.

From Maxwell's "Life of Wellington."

The news that Marmont was approaching to relieve the besieged fortress drove Wellington to hasten the attack. "Ciudad Rodrigo must be taken to-night," was the order he issued; and it was done by the 3rd and Light Divisions, with [illegible]

picked up out of the ruined fortifications. Great bodies of infantry had been trained in military engineering, and they could turn out fascines and gabions and all the appliances used in a siege.

Ciudad Rodrigo lies on the northeast bank of the Agueda, and the attack must, of course, be made on that side; but Wellington kept his force on the southern bank, and sent his divisions over the river daily, in turn, to carry on the trench duties. He had constructed a bridge six miles lower down for the passage of material, but the troops always forded the river, which was often encumbered with ice. The weather was very wintry, and snow lay on the ground. Wellington, on reconnoitring the place, found that it had been strengthened; guns had been placed in two large convent buildings, and an enclosed redoubt, called Fort Francisco, had been built on a long ridge known as the Greater Tesson, which covered the principal front of the fortifications. Wellington was resolved to attack from this side, because it offered him the best ground for establishing batteries, and then working forward he hoped to breach the main walls from the second ridge, or Lesser Tesson.

SIR JOHN COLBORNE,
Afterwards Field-Marshal Lord Seaton.
After a Portrait by [illegible]

Colonel of the 52nd Regiment, and esteemed as one of the best leaders in the Peninsula. Had true genius for war, and in many engagements, by his prompt instinct, saved the situation. He is said to have completed the overthrow of Napoleon's guard at Waterloo by taking them in flank, on his own initiative. Afterwards he was Governor-General of Canada and Lord High Commissioner in the Ionian Islands.

It was first essential to capture Fort Francisco, and this was entrusted to Colonel Colborne, of the 52nd, with his own regiment, and two companies from the other regiments of the Light Division. The attack was made with so much fury that "the assailants appeared to be in the ditch, mounting the parapets, fighting on top, and facing the gorge at one and the same time." The French were soon driven out, and Colborne was master of the fort with a loss of only twenty-four men. Now Elder's Portuguese caçadores broke ground, and worked with such a will that by daylight the first parallel, 600 yds. long, upon the Greater Tesson, was completed.

This gallant exploit gave a good start, and the siege was thereby advanced several days. Time was the very essence of the business. Wellington had calculated he would need twenty-four days to carry out the siege; as the result proved, he captured Ciudad Rodrigo in twelve.

News came on the 13th January that Marmont was on the move, and would soon succour the place. Increased activity was therefore shown in pushing on the siege, and that same day guns were placed in battery and began to break down the ramparts. There were two breaches, a great and a small, and the destructive work went on rapidly, although the defenders' fire in reply was very lively, and did much damage. Yet by the 19th both breaches were declared practicable, and the assault was at once ordered. "Ciudad Rodrigo must be stormed to-night," was the stirring preamble to Wellington's plan of attack. There were three columns of attack — right, centre, and left; the first against the castle on the east front, the second against the great breach, the third against the lesser breach. It will be simplest to describe them in turn.

1st.—This column was led by Colonel O'Toole, of the Portuguese caçadores, closely followed by the 5th and 94th Regiments, while the 77th, meant to be in reserve, soon joined in the attack. These

CIUDAD RODRIGO.
After a Contemporary Print.
The fighting at Ciudad Rodrigo was fierce and hand-to-hand while it lasted, and the French were driven back, inch by inch, from the ramparts through the streets.

were the first to go forward, and their movement was at once taken up by all the other assailants.

2nd.—The centre attack, that on the great breach, was the business of Picton's Division, the "Fighting 3rd," and they leapt out of the trenches, preceded by a forlorn-hope of a storming party of 500 volunteers. Without waiting for the hay-bags, which were to be thrown into the ditch, they jumped down, and pouring in at the great breach, got inside almost simultaneously with the men of the first column. Here the fight was very stubborn; the French, yielding at first, presently rallied, and held their assailants at bay.

3rd. But now the left column, furnished by the Light Division, and under the personal direction of their intrepid General, Robert Craufurd, who was unhappily soon killed, sent forward its stormers, headed by Major George Napier, who had refused to let his men load lest they might be tempted to forego the use of their bayonets. They entered the breach pell-mell, with the forlorn-hope. Although Napier was laid low, he still cheered on his men; all other officers rushed to the front, and by a tremendous effort the breach was carried.

At this moment three French magazines exploded, spreading death and confusion on both sides; but the 3rd Division, undismayed by their losses, broke into the gap thus made, and won the inner retrenchments. The assailants, converging from all sides, now filled the streets, and the place was soon ours.

A great prize fell to Wellington in this capture. The whole of Marmont's battering train, and a vast number of field guns,

MAJOR [illegible] MACKINNON.

He [illegible] the [illegible] [illegible] attacking [illegible] by [illegible]

GENERAL SIR GEORGE MURRAY.

After a Painting by Sir Thomas Lawrence.

He was Wellington's quartermaster-general throughout the Peninsular War, and was considered [illegible] renowned chief. He had served in Flanders as a captain of the Guards, and afterwards [illegible] staff in Egypt [illegible] the army which landed in Portugal, and saw almost all the fighting from Roleia to the Pyrenees.

Wellington and Waterloo.

9th, OR EAST NORFOLK, REGIMENT.

(From ... C ...)

This distinguished regiment was engaged in all the great actions of the Peninsular War, from Corunna to the fighting before Bayonne. It was Lord Clyde's first regiment.

— were taken; also great quantities of warlike stores, which were greedily seized to re-equip our troops. In one case a regimental commanding officer was able to complete his band of drummers with French brass drums, and, indeed, found more than he wanted.

Our losses were great—two generals, the gallant Craufurd and the brave Mackinnon, fell, and General Vandeleur was wounded. The first, by this time acknowledged as one of the most skilled and daring leaders of light troops in any army, was a grievous loss. The second, a fine soldier, was ever foremost in the fight; and Napier speaks of another death, deeply felt through the army, that of a captain of the 45th, of whom it was said that "three generals and seventy officers had fallen, yet the soldiers fresh from the strife only talked of Hardyman."

It would be well if the glory of this splendid capture had not been tarnished by the disgraceful excesses of the victorious troops. But those were days when a successful storm was always followed by a sack; and at Ciudad Rodrigo the soldiers broke loose in rapine and the worst disorder. The innocent inhabitants were outraged and plundered, the town was fired, men in their drunken fury shot each other and threatened their officers; but for the merest chance the chief magazine would have exploded and thousands must have been killed. Nor was this the only stain upon the character of our troops in Spain; the horrors of Rodrigo were afterwards outshone by those of Badajos and San Sebastian. This brilliant episode, which gained Wellington an earldom, was only the first part of the programme he hoped to perform. His eyes were ever fixed upon Badajos, the other fortress that was essential to his future operations; and now again, as with Ciudad Rodrigo, he used all his ingenuity, all his art, to prepare for its siege. It was a much harder nut to crack, stronger in every way, and held by a larger garrison—5,000 resolute veterans under a famous governor, Phillipon, one, at least, who has left a great name. Phillipon has been ever associated with the defence of Badajos as its Todleben, a skilled engineer, ready-witted, resourceful, indomitable—what Todleben was at Sebastopol. But yet Phillipon's ability has been denied by some of his contemporaries, and he certainly did not act up to his great reputation when advanced to high command in the field. By almost superhuman exertions Wellington got his battering train collected at Elvas in the beginning of March—fifty guns, some of them borrowed from the fleet; a pontoon bridge had been ... up, and great quantities of gabions and fascines. ... but rations were still scarce, and cassava ... in place of bread.

... on the 15th March, and the ... three divisions, the 3rd, 4th, ... in all 15,000 men. At the ... under Graham, watched ... doubt try to raise the

A FIELD OFFICER OF THE ROYAL ENGINEERS.

(... C ...)

This distinguished corps helped Wellington greatly in his sieges, and in forming the formidable entrenchments of Torres Vedras.

siege. For the moment little was feared from Marmont in the north; he had retired on Valladolid, and was not disposed to interfere.

It would be tedious to describe the siege operations, which were pressed forward with even more vigour than at Ciudad Rodrigo, and against a more enterprising and resolute garrison. Badajos proper, the main body of the fortress, was defended by strong outworks, and the chief of these, called the Picurina, was the first attacked. Torrents of rain retarded the work in the trenches, and the defenders constantly added to the strength of their works. Artifice was called in by the ingenious Frenchmen, and at one point, where cover was needed in stony ground, brown cloth was hung up, having the appearance of earth, and afforded protection that was respected. The Picurina fort was attacked on the 25th March, the eighth day after the opening of the siege. It showed no great strength outwardly, but it had a deep narrow ditch, and the stout ramparts were covered by thick palings, on the slant, that made an escalade impossible. At last the axemen hewed a way in by the gate, and the assailants rushed the fort. Still the French resisted till half the garrison were killed; of the rest, some surrendered, some sought escape and were drowned in the inundation that was out on this side.

NAPOLEON'S GUARD OF HONOUR.

[illegible]

The French peasantry in the Landes [illegible] walking, [illegible] when Napoleon passed through their [illegible]

This prompt capture advanced the siege by several days. Lodgments were now made, parallels traced, breaching batteries established against the eastern front, and all the guns brought into play. Now on the 30th news came that Soult was on the move from Cordova, rapidly approaching, and the bombardment was pressed

BADAJOS, FROM THE ALBUQUERQUE AND ELVAS ROAD.

[illegible]

This ancient place is best remembered in connection with the [illegible] this war. The [illegible] on the Guadiana, called the Puente de las Palmas [illegible] forward with all energy and despatch. The breaches were nearly practicable on the 3rd April, but Soult was very close and concentrated. On the 4th it was decided to hold the trenches without assault, but to give Soult battle on the old ground of Albuera if he still advanced.

The French, however, were no nearer than Llerena on the 5th, and that day the breaches were reported ready. But Wellington waited yet another day to complete a third breach, and then ordered the assault. Then his soldiers, as Napier tells us, "eagerly made ready for a combat so fiercely fought, so terribly won, so dreadful in all its circumstances that posterity can scarcely be expected to credit the tale."

The whole circuit of the fortress was included in the attacks, which were of all kinds, some feints, some subsidiary, the rest principal and really determined. The west front was to be assaulted by the 5th Division, the eastern and castle by the 3rd, and the 4th and Light Divisions were to be sent in full strength against the breaches at the bastions Trinidad and Santa Maria; 18,000 men in all were employed in this daring, bloodthirsty undertaking. Every column was furnished with scaling ladders and axes; at the head of each went its forlorn hope and its devoted band of stormers.

The attack of all was to have been simultaneous, but a fireball betrayed the 3rd Division, and they hurried forward in advance of the signal. The 4th and Light Divisions were also impelled to attack, reaching the glacis of the Santa Maria almost without accident; but there a terrible explosion caused frightful carnage among the Light Division. Phillipon, the French general, said afterwards that he had thought "this would finish the business," and he was fairly amazed at the courageous tenacity of the British troops, who still held on undismayed.

At the great breach at Trinidad, the 4th Division also crowded forward, "cheering vehemently," and reached the top of the rampart "as if driven by a whirlwind." But here they encountered that terrible obstacle, the world-famous chevaux-de-frise of sword blades fixed in ponderous beams, and all chained to the ground. This sharp-edged barrier was impassable, it could not be surmounted nor removed; the men in rear would have driven those in front upon the swords and made a bridge of their writhing bodies, but failed in the attempt, while defenders and

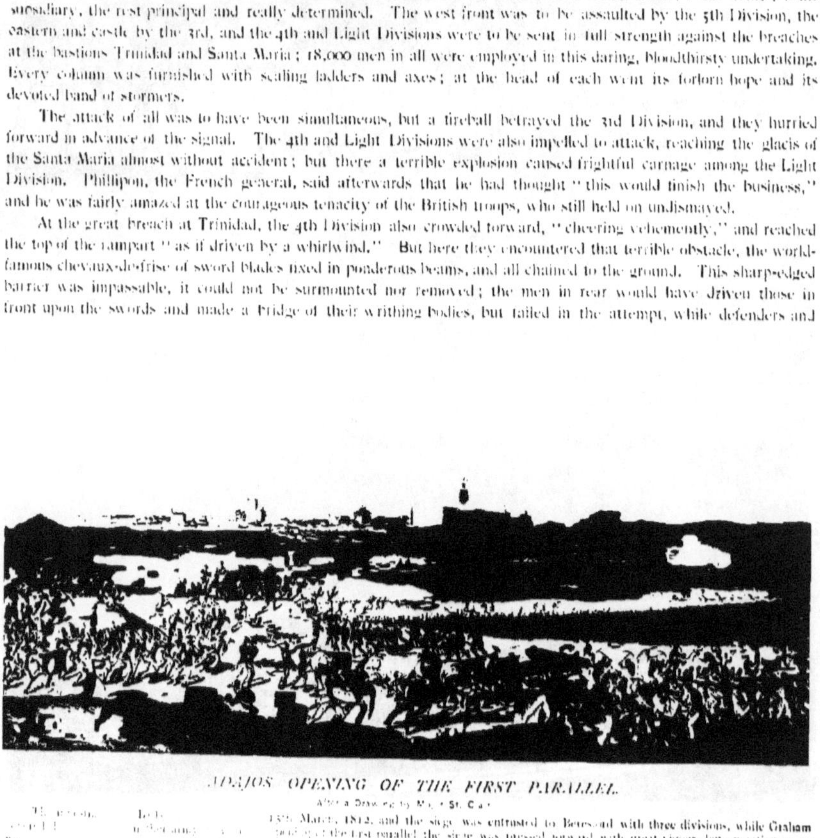

[B]ADAJOS: OPENING OF THE FIRST PARALLEL.

After a Drawing by Major St. Clair.

[illegible] 15th March, 1812, and the siege was entrusted to Beresford with three divisions, while Graham [illegible] the first parallel the siege was pressed forward with great vigour, but operations were [illegible] ...ay.

assailants blazed into each other at short range, and hundreds fell. For two fearful hours this murderous conflict went on; the eager men found many intrepid leaders, and essayed but vainly to storm this impregnable breach. Even after repeated failures they still collected in groups ready for fresh efforts, while the French plied them with fire, taunting them ever, and asking them "why they did not come and take Badajos?" It was now midnight: 2,000 men had fallen. This principal attack was clearly unsuccessful, but Wellington with unshaken constancy was prepared to organise another. They came to him with the details. "My Lord," said an officer, breathless, "I am come from the breaches; the troops cannot enter them. The men are without leaders, so many officers have fallen; unless strong reinforcements are sent the attack must be abandoned."

THE DUKE OF QUEENSBERRY

After a Contemporary Caricature.

He warmly espoused Picton's part when the latter was tried for cruelty, and would have paid the costs. At his death he left Picton a large sum.

GUNNERS, ROYAL ARTILLERY.

[illegible]

Descendants of the ancient H[illegible] and [illegible] Arms who date back to the days when [illegible] was [illegible] used.

Wellington's face was pale and full of deep anxiety, says one who stood near him. But he spoke with cool self-possession, and quietly ordered up fresh troops to support the main attack. His reward came presently with better news. The 3rd Division under Picton had made good their entrance into the castle. It had been carried by escalade, but not until many of the tall ladders reared against its [illegible] walls had been [illegible] back by the despe[illegible]

VILLA VELHA.

After a [illegible]

The River Tagus is here imprisoned between two high walls of rock, the stream is rapid, and the only means of passage was by [illegible] a bridge of [illegible] their living loads. At last Colonel Ridge of the 5th, and another of his officers, Ensign Canch, mounted safely, followed by a number of fusiliers, and they were strong enough to beat off all opposition.

Other ladders were quickly and effectually placed, the stormers climbed up fast as best they could. A lieutenant in the 88th Connaught Rangers, a survivor who got up with the rest, has left an account of how he found, when he had reached the top of his ladder, that it was too short by many feet. Someone above shouted to him, "Mr. ——, is that you? Och, murder! murder! how shall we get you up at all? Here, Bill, hould my leg"; and throwing himself flat on his face in the embrasure, he extended an arm, caught the lieutenant by his collar, and landed him "clever and clane" upon the ramparts. Five more comrades were lifted in the same manner.

By these tremendous efforts enough force was collected to drive the French back to an open space near the castle, where they stood for a time, but soon fell back, and the castle was won—at a terrible cost, for the gallant Ridge was killed and many more. General Picton had gone to the rear severely wounded, so had General Kempt, and the division remained under the command of Colonel Campbell, who wisely determined to lie low, but to firmly repel all attempts to dislodge him from the position.

This success at the castle, which was maintained, decided the fate of Badajos. Now, too, General Leith, with the 5th Division, penetrated the western defences and entered the town. When at last the breaches were abandoned

BADAJOS: ASSAULT OF LA TRINIDAD BY THE 4th AND LIGHT DIVISIONS.

After a [illegible] Engraving.

These [illegible] at a terrible expense of life. The breach was held with extraordinary tenacity by the garrison, [illegible] at the castle, the French would have beaten Wellington off.

GENERAL (SIR THOMAS) PICTON.

After a Paint[illegible]

Picton was in a way the hero of Badajos. The escalade [illegible] the castle [illegible] his division led [illegible] [illegible] hardy soldier, and a strenuous fighter. In his early service he had been arraigned before an English Court [illegible] Indies, and his temper had been soured, for the accusation, although never proved, laid heavy on him. [illegible] and took an active part in all the battles of the war.

SALAMANCA.

[illegible]

[illegible]

Philippon, who had withdrawn into Fort Christoval on the northern side of the river, surrendered; but not before he had despatched a messenger to inform Soult of the catastrophe and to warn him to retire.

Wellington was glad to admit all he owed to Picton and his "Fighting 3rd" Division. He wrote that general after the capture to thank him, assuring that "the 3rd Division has saved his honour and gained him Badajos." Of all who shared in the triumphs, none after Ridge was more conspicuous for personal courage than Picton himself.

Picton did not come out to the Peninsula until 1810. Wellington had applied for him when looking for new [illegible] generals, and he did not regret it, for Picton never disappointed him when there was stirring work to [illegible]. Yet up to the time of his arrival in Spain he was under a cloud. Indeed, the aspersions unjustly cast [illegible] to the very last, and the charges on which he had been tried in the British Courts of [illegible] legally set aside.

[illegible] Picton had acted as Governor of a West India Island, Trinidad, and it had [illegible] to authorise the infliction of torture—as it was called—upon an unwilling [illegible] witness. [illegible] was "picketed"—raised from the ground by her arms, while one foot rested on the point [illegible]. This seemingly inhuman treatment was in accordance with the insular law, and it was proved [illegible] little, if at all.

[illegible] travelled home, and in due course the public mind became hotly inflamed against [illegible]. He would no doubt have been acquitted had not a local witness [illegible] that the law of torture was not in force at the time in Trinidad. A fresh [illegible] the first finding was never actually reversed.

[illegible] among them the eccentric and well-known Duke of Queensberry, [illegible] his legal expenses. "Old Q.," as he was styled, called to see Picton [illegible] begged him to write occasionally from the seat of war. "Now we [illegible] when a letter arrived, so strong was his belief in Picton's straight- [illegible] a legacy of £10,000.

THE EARL OF LIVERPOOL.

Robert Banks Jenkinson, a college friend of [illegible] 1791 [illegible] negociated the Peace of Amiens in 1802 [illegible] War [illegible] 1809 [illegible] Secretary [illegible] communication with Lord Wellington [illegible] 1812 [illegible]

Wellington and Waterloo.

WELLINGTON AT SALAMANCA.

[illegible]

This [illegible] by Marmont [illegible] in extending his left flank too far. Wellington, fixing [illegible] on the error, won a brilliant victory.

Many stories are told of Picton. One of the best has become a "chestnut," and is now claimed for Crauford, but on no sufficient authority. It is the incident of the commissary who was negligent in bringing up supplies and whom Picton (or Crauford) threatened to hang. The commissary, it will be remembered, appealed to Wellington for protection, but got no more satisfaction than the famous reply, "Did he threaten that? Then you may depend upon it he will be as good as his word."

Picton was no doubt irascible and given to strong language, swearing freely on every occasion, as was the custom of the day. He roundly abused his men when they offended him, especially in marauding, but speedily forgave them when they supported him in some desperate undertaking. Badajos was won at a terrible cost; 5,000 men and officers fell in the siege and 3,500 during the assault, when 60 officers and more than 700 men were killed on the spot. Napier records that when Wellington heard the full extent of the havoc, "the firmness of his nature gave way [illegible] and the pride of conquest yielded to a passionate burst [of] grief for the loss of his gallant soldiers." It was the same after Waterloo, when he made the well-known remark, "One thing only is worse than losing a battle, and that is [illegible]."

Again, as at Ciudad Rodrigo, the soldier's heroism was tarnished by hideous excesses. The sack of Badajos was a scene of the most desperate wickedness, when every evil passion was in [illegible] "Shameless rapacity, [illegible] savage lust, [illegible] and piteous [illegible]

[illegible]

MOUNTAIN PASS, BETWEEN NISA AND VILLA VELHA.

After a Drawing by the Rev. Mr. Bradford.

[illegible] is on the Portuguese frontier, and was one of Wellington's lateral communications from north to south of the Tagus.

all been plundered. The actors in these excesses were attired in the habits of priests with broad-brimmed hats of monks and nuns; and in the dresses of grandees and soldiers of rank." Many officers were exposed to great personal danger from the licentious conduct of their men. One records that he found three soldiers in the Cathedral literally drowned in brandy. One of the vaults had been used as a spirit depôt; the casks had been pierced by musket balls, the brandy flowing out and forming great pools, into which the drunkards fell prone and were suffocated. Order was at last restored by the arrival of a brigade of Portuguese under General Power, who at once set up a gallows in the principal square. The effect was magical. It was unnecessary to proceed to extremities, for the rapine and disorder suddenly ceased.

GENERAL ALAVA.

[illegible]

The Count Alava was a Spanish officer attached to Wellington's headquarters, with whom he lived on most friendly intimate terms. Alava was at Trafalgar on the Spanish side, and, again, at Waterloo on ours.

Lord Wellington had intended that the capture of Badajos should be followed by bringing Soult to do battle for the possession of Andalusia. But now ominous news reached him from the north. Ciudad Rodrigo was in danger, the fortress so recently recovered might be again lost, for the Spaniards had failed to repair its shattered defences; and a new battering train, expected daily from France, would enable Marmont to lay fresh hands on the place. Wellington turned northwards therefore; he had now the advantage of a new position, and happily based on two rivers, the Agueda and the Guadiana, he could operate as he pleased. To attack Marmont was the most urgent and the most promising line, and accordingly he adopted it.

GENERAL LE MARCHANT.

[illegible]

He was killed at the head of the heavy cavalry in the battle of Salamanca after a magnificent charge. Le Marchant was the first to advocate the higher education of officers, and he helped to found the military colleges at High Wycombe and Marlow, which were afterwards concentrated at Sandhurst. He was a fine swordsman, and gave the Army an excellent system of sword exercise.

But first it was important to isolate the army of the South. To prevent ready communication between Marmont and Soult, south of the Tagus, Wellington planned the surprise of Almaraz, where the French had a bridge of boats covered by strong fortifications. General Hill was commissioned to do this, and he succeeded with his customary promptitude and vigour. But there was no surprise, for his column, checked by the rugged mountain roads, arrived after daylight, [illegible] met with an enemy alert in resistance.

Hill, nothing daunted, went straight in at the first fort at Almaraz, that of Fort Napoleon; and although his stormers found their ladders too short, the men climbed on the "berm," or space at the foot of the ramparts, dragged their ladders after them, and so got over the main wall. Pushing on with impetuous charge, the assailants drove the garrison out and followed them across the river into the second or larger fort, which they carried by sheer boldness. Many of the French jumped into the river, the rest were made prisoners. Only a detached fort in the mountains, Mirabele, held out; and Hill, being left in the lurch by a subordinate, was obliged to retreat without reducing it.

OFFICER OF FRENCH LIGHT CAVALRY LANCERS.
From Horace Vernet's French Uniforms.
Frequently engaged with our troops.

LEGION DE GENDARMERIE.
From Horace Vernet's French Uniforms.
The dangers of the line of communication with France perpetually harassed by Spanish partisans, led to the formation of a special corps for escorts.

Wellington now held the most important points on the Tagus, thus interposing a great river barrier between Soult and Marmont. Being thus able to deal with the latter alone, he moved against him with all his available strength, and began the famous campaign of Salamanca. His new opponent was another of Napoleon's famous marshals, "a man," as Napier says, "to be feared." He was a practised soldier, one who as an artillery officer had studied the science of war, naturally quick-witted, too, and in the full vigour of a healthy life; gifted with a fine courage, great ambition; and a noble tactician. He had restored discipline to an army that had been demoralised by Massena's disastrous retreat; and it was now a well-tried, perfected military machine, asking only to be wielded by able hands to accomplish great things.

VILLA FRANCA.
After a Drawing by the Rev. Mr. Bradford.
This Villa Franca, one of many so called in the Peninsula, is on the road from Seville to Badajos.

The early stages of this Salamanca Campaign have long been esteemed as containing excellent lessons for the student of military history. From the day that Wellington advanced and laid siege to Salamanca, driving Marmont before him, to the time of his retreat, when Marmont in his turn pursued him, it was a time of continual movement, of rapid marches on both sides, both pressing neck and neck for a common goal—the allies seeking some safe rallying point in rear, the French threatening ever to outflank, outstrip, and forestall them. Skirmish and combat went on perpetually, the cavalry riding between the opponents met often in conflicts, guns and muskets exchanged volleys, while French and [illegible] between the words of command saluted each other, "pointing forward with their swords and [illegible]."

In one of these daily collisions Wellington was for a moment in great danger. He and [illegible] Beresford [illegible] the day closed in order to examine the French position. Sir Stapleton Cotton was showing in front with the cavalry when a party of French horse swooped down in a furious charge, right into the fresh squadron accompanying Wellington. There was a general mêlée; his Lordship and Beresford both drew swords and had to fight their way out to safety. The French were presently beaten off with great loss, after showing incredible audacity.

Through all this the balance hung pretty evenly, or, if anything, inclined in favour of the French general. The two armies were handled with consummate skill by the first professors in the game, and manœuvred within musket shot, often full in sight of each other, wary and eager for the fight, yet giving no chances; so that the issue was in doubt until the very last. Then Marmont erred egregiously, and in the presence of an opponent who would let no such opportunity pass, and paid the penalty in a disastrous defeat. This great occasion came on the 21st July, 1812, and brought on the battle of Salamanca. Hitherto, Marmont's generalship had been on the whole superior to Wellington's. He had evaded battles when at a disadvantage, but was ready to attack when he held [illegible]. It was seemingly so the night before Salamanca. By clever management he had placed his [illegible] to

SIR STAPLETON COTTON (LORD COMBERMERE) [illegible]

[illegible]

He was at this time in command of the whole of the British cavalry [illegible] great danger. He was still quite young, and taken [illegible] Marmont [illegible] great fondness for dress, and wore the most brilliant uniforms [illegible] although having the character of a fashionable lounger, Combermere was [illegible] by the Duke of Wellington to command in the siege of Bhurtpore, which he captured.

strike at Wellington's line of retreat, and to make that retreat imperative on the English, lest worse should befal them. He was in touch with other French armies; King Joseph with the army of the centre was within easy reach from Madrid, other reinforcements were coming up from the northern provinces. Wellington could only stand his ground at risk of being overwhelmed by greatly superior numbers. Retreat was his only wise course—retreat more or less humiliating after a campaign barren of all decisive results; retreat that might be impeded, and secured only by facing serious danger, incurring heavy losses, and that must probably be continued far back right into Portugal. But on the day of battle, the 22nd July, he was happily permitted to profit by a mistake of his enemy. Various changes of front had become necessary through Marmont's obvious desire to force on a battle; and the march of troops, the columns of dust raised by the commissariat and baggage already prudently sent to the rear, seemed to indicate a general retreat. Marmont, misled, over-eager, and fearing only that the English might escape, lunged forward, throwing a couple of divisions with all his light cavalry and fifty guns far ahead to strike at the Ciudad Rodrigo road.

NAPOLEON.

After a Drawing by [illegible] B. [illegible].

[illegible] Napoleon was at the pinna[illegible] greatness, and contem-[illegible] of Russia, that [illegible] and disastrous mistake.

It was a flagrant error, because it divided the French into two widely distinct parts, and exposed that now rashly advancing to a murderous flank attack. When they brought Wellington the news he rejoiced exceedingly. It was a sudden reaction against the crushing anxieties of the last few days; fortune suddenly reversed the relative positions of the French and English, and put the advantage altogether into Wellington's hands, provided only he would stretch out and take the gift.

We can see him throwing away unfinished the first morsel of food he had tasted that day, and it was already the afternoon, hurriedly mounting his horse, and galloping to high ground where he could verify the fact, and where he soon realised what had happened. He was filled with "stern contentment, for the French left wing was then entirely separated from the centre; the fault was flagrant, and he fixed it with the stroke of a thunderbolt." He issued his orders promptly and clearly, setting all his divisions in motion; then as time was needed for their march, as well as for the development of the French attack, he quietly laid down to sleep.

No better proof is on record of Wellington's iron nerves, of his power to sleep at will, like his great antagonist Napoleon and other great commanders, than this Salamanca case. No doubt he was much fatigued, for he had been in the saddle since daylight, not this day only, but on many previous days; and his anxieties, his fears, his responsibilities, had been immense. But now when the die was cast, and in his favour as he saw, he could take his much-needed rest. Giving brief instructions to his staff that he was to be called directly the advancing French columns reached a particular spot which he pointed out, he wrapped himself up in his cloak, lay down behind a bush, and was instantly sound asleep. When he was roused all was ready for attack in this the first great Peninsular battle where Wellington was the assailant. The cautious policy hitherto imposed on him by lack of means had persuaded the French generals he was only good on the defensive. And even this was untrue, for he attacked at Roleia and at the Douro, and at the recent capture of the two fortresses he was ready enough to take the initiative. Certainly he was the aggressor now, and his own brother-in-law, General Pakenham, temporarily in command of Picton's "Fighting 3rd" Division, was the one to open the ball.

SKETCH PORTRAIT OF WELLINGTON, 1812.

Facsimile of a Sketch made ... [illegible]

Goya was a man of versatile talents, equally skilled with oil, water-colour, or graver. A man of short temper, and it is said that being displeased with some remark of Wellington's, he threw a plaster cast at the Duke's head.

The 3rd Division, being on the extreme right of the English line, was ordered to cross the march of the French columns.

"Do you see those fellows on the hill?" Wellington is reported to have said. "Throw your regiments into line, Ned, attack and beat them to the devil." And, as Pakenham promptly gave the necessary orders, Wellington turned with the complacent remark, "How well the fellow knows his business."

The forward movement of the 3rd was followed by the rest of the first line, which included the bulk of the cavalry, at the same time, so as to cover the flank and occupy the rest of the enemy. The English left was directed to attack the centre of the French line. "*Mon cher Alava, Marmont est perdu,*" had been Wellington's confident forecast to General Alava, the Spanish representative, at his headquarters always a close friend and crony, a remark uttered when the French mistake was first observed. And the prophecy proved true, for 40,000 men "were soundly beaten in forty minutes," to use the words of one who took part in the action. The attack took Marmont altogether unawares at a critical moment, when his whole army was split up into three separate parts at too great a distance to support each other. Pakenham smote his advance, vigorously carrying all before him, and within half-an-hour Marmont was struck down with a severe wound. Two other generals had been carried off the field, and the French left was in utter confusion. Now Clausel, who succeeded Marmont, sought to restore the unequal fight; the centre was coming through the woods, and a new but weak line of battle was formed. Now Wellington, in his turn, launched forth all his cavalry, light and heavy, in that famous charge under its gallant leader Le Marchant, who fell at the head of his men. These splendid horsemen swept away the French infantry like

BATTLE OF SALAMANCA.
From [illegible]
One of the chief incidents was the cavalry charge. The battle was so quickly decided that a French officer described it as "beating 40,000 men in forty minutes."

chaff, and "the dragoons, big men on big horses, rode onwards, smiting with their long glittering swords in uncontrollable power." This finished the French left, which no longer existed as a military body.

Yet Clausel was a resolute and capable soldier, and he had made a grand effort in the centre, Pack's Portuguese having failed at a high hill, one of the "Brothers," the "Arapiles," of which the French held one, the allies the other, there was just a chance of saving the day; but the victory was for the general who had the strongest reserves at hand. This was Wellington, who as ever directed the fight at the critical point: and now he brought up the second line.

The French still fought bravely, but only to cover withdrawal. Wellington manœuvred, constantly strengthening his left so as to force all the beaten masses towards the point called Alba de Tormes, where stood a castle garrisoned as he supposed by Spaniards. But they had been withdrawn, not without leave, but without due notice to Wellington, and the Castle of Alba was promptly occupied by the French. This fortunate accident gave them an outlet for escape, altogether unknown to the victorious general who was pressing them so hard.

When Wellington thought his [illegible] lives [illegible] his hands, they had for the most part disappeared.

Still Salamanca was a great and glorious victory, the most brilliant achievement of which Wellington could [illegible] boast, and the noise of it resounded [illegible]

[illegible] strategical com- [illegible]

AN OFFICER OF THE ROYAL WAGGON TRAIN.
From Hamilton Smith's Costume.
Wellington, in the later years of the war, organised a Land Transport Service of his own.

northward against a third fortress, Burgos, the possession of which would give him a new and shorter line of communications with the sea. This foreshadowed and was in effect the essence of his plan so successfully carried out the following year. Of the various courses open to the French, King Joseph chose the worst. Soult, who was in great strength in Andalusia, holding all the resources of that rich province at command, urgently advised the King to come south and join him.

There strongly based, with ample stores, magazines and fortresses backed by 80,000 men, the theatre of war would be changed, Lisbon threatened closely, and Wellington would be forced to surrender Madrid and come back in all speed to Portugal. Soult's argument was that the loss of Andalusia would limit the French to the poor country north of and behind the Ebro, where he would eventually be starved out. Joseph had not the genius of his great lieutenant; he could only see safety in retreat for concentration, and he sent Soult peremptory orders to evacuate Andalusia forthwith and join him south of Madrid. His chief anxiety was to recover his lost capital, for Wellington had already entered it, as the first-fruits of his great victory of Salamanca. The pursuit of Clausel with his beaten army was somewhat slack, and the French retired behind the Douro without much molestation.

But then Wellington advanced towards the Guaderama mountain range, the passes of which Joseph did not attempt to defend. The King was fully occupied in clearing out of Madrid with his Court and non-combatant followers, an immense convoy of helpless folk, "crowds of weeping women and children, and despairing men." Horrible confusion arose in the hurried flight; the bonds of discipline were relaxed, [illegible] was [illegible], and the [illegible] sadly plundered and misused the weaker sex. "Countesses of the highest rank were to be seen in full dress, desp[illegible] striding with [illegible] [illegible] [illegible] rosaries than a[illegible]."

All these [illegible] to the one bridge available; but Wellington, whose cavalry advance was now well up, was too humane to molest them.

SIR JOHN BURGOYNE.

[illegible]

WELLINGTON ENTERS MADRID.

From a Collection of Historical Prints.

When Joseph fled from his capital in 1812, Wellington occupied and held it for some months.

BATTLE OF VITTORIA.

Third phase, the centre and left attacks combined, breaking the [illegible] driving the French [illegible] their position [illegible] Vittoria.

CHAPTER VIII.

Wellington enters Madrid, [illegible] position [illegible] his road to a new base on the Bay of Biscay. [illegible] compelled to raise the siege and retreat [illegible] suffer much hardship, but Wellington saved [illegible] 1812-13 large reinforcements arrive, and [illegible] W[illegible] masterly plan, by which he turns the [illegible] towards France. Joseph [illegible] the Vittoria [illegible] assault and with great loss of men and means.

OUR troops made a triumphal progress through the country. They [illegible] as the best of friends. Every night [illegible] the [illegible] wine, and [illegible] full of light-hearted rejoicing, singing, laughing, and [illegible]. [illegible] were organised for the officers, balls, banquets, and entertainments.

Although master of Madrid, Wellington's position was precarious. He [illegible] through the neglect and apathy of the home Government. The pay of his troops was many months in arrear; those quartered in the capital committed many thefts and excesses; those outside [illegible] comrades, and discipline generally was much relaxed. [illegible] strength. Clausel had reorganised and reformed [illegible] threatened the long line of English communications with Portugal and [illegible].

Wellington was resolved, therefore, to change [illegible] he actually carried out the following year. [illegible] Burgos, a stronghold in the hands of the French, and with this [illegible] Madrid, with four divisions and all his cavalry. Hill was left [illegible] capital against King Joseph and Soult combined, who were coming up to attack [illegible].

Clausel made a good show before Wellington [illegible] But on the 18th September he was driven out of [illegible] Burgos [illegible] confusion. The famous castle stood high on a hill [illegible] able to resist all Wellington's efforts. It was [illegible]

Wellington and Waterloo.

the intrepid Dubreton, an engineer of much skill and Serchance, who won a well-deserved success by his courageous defence.

Wellington began the seizure of a detached work on a small hill; it was stormed and [illegible] the first night, mainly through the gallantry of Major Somers Cocks, who led the attack. Then followed a close examination of the works. The castle was but feebly fortified, and Wellington hoped much from this. He heard also that [illegible] and that water was scarce within. His own means of attack were meagre [illegible] and [illegible] siege, and pushed it on with great vigour. [illegible] with [illegible] success. When the first [illegible] subordinate leader's disobedience of orders, [illegible] on his body, and it greatly assisted in [illegible] operations.

[illegible] preceded the second assault, but [illegible] in the walls, and w[illegible] [illegible] was effected by the batt[illegible] [illegible] and a lodgment made [illegible] assailants. The attack [illegible] and [illegible] In this sanguinary engage[illegible] [illegible] lost his life. [illegible] went forward [illegible] armed, fresh [illegible] [illegible] and [illegible] the 18th [illegible] A fourth and [illegible] [illegible] cessful than the others. [illegible] steadfastness to duty [illegible] the possession of other [illegible]

[illegible] the first [illegible] 12,000. Thus [illegible] with great

THE STAFF OF THE ARMY.

[illegible] the Army next to that of the Commander-in-Chief [illegible] the Sovereign.

[illegible] GRENADIER GUARDS.

[illegible]

MAJOR THE HONOURABLE CHARLES SOMERS COCKS, OF THE 16th LIGHT DRAGOONS.

This was one of the most gallant and promising officers [illegible] the fighting squadron. He was killed in a sortie [illegible] the Service at large. Had he [illegible]

SIR ROWLAND HILL.

1814 ... [illegible]

effect; they could at pleasure fall upon Hill, who still held Madrid, or they could dangerously interfere with Wellington, vex his rear, perhaps cut off his retreat.

Hill rose promptly to the occasion, and at once sent Wellington news of the impending evil. His despatch reached Burgos on the 20th October, two days after the last disastrous assault. Full instantaneous retreat was inevitable. Wellington's position before Burgos was critical,

A TROOPER OF THE ROYAL HORSE GUARDS (BLUES).

The Household Cavalry were sent out to Spain in the winter of 1812. The Blues took part in Graham's ... march through Galicia.

and he decided to withdraw the very next night. The retrograde movement was yet perilous, for the road to the rear lay right under ... the fortress, ... could inflict terrible losses on the retreating troops if the march was betrayed. W... the ... of the artillery were muffled, straw was laid deep in the streets, then the troops ... across the bridge. At the last moment the retreat was discovered and the guns opened fire, but they ... lost ... [illegible]

BURGOS.

[illegible] ... one of the finest specimens of Gothic ... The city lies below the ... in Wellington's ... [illegible]

and overwhelming [illegible] seemed imminent. But Wellington controlled events with a firm, strong hand; he retired behind the Carrion, and, being joined there by a reinforcement of fresh and newly raised troops, he awaited the enemy with calm fortitude, having sent his baggage and hospitals to the rear. Thus he forced Souham to show his whole strength, and finding, when the French were deployed, that he had to do with a superior force, he swiftly decided on further retreat. He fell back now to the Douro, and having ensured safety by destroying the bridges at Valladolid, Simancas, and Tordesillas, he quietly awaited Hill.

MARSHAL SOULT, DUC DE DALMATIE.

[illegible] enlisted [illegible] the Bar [illegible] in 1785. [illegible] general of brigade. He took part in [illegible] Andalusia.

That general was now coming up in hot haste from Madrid. He had had *carte-blanche*, and it was for him to choose between retreat along the valley of the Tagus and an advance to Wellington's support. He took the latter course, the wisest and now the most urgent, evacuating Madrid on the 30th October. The hasty departure of their English friends was a great grief to the people of Madrid, and the whole city turned out to accompany the troops some miles along the road with affectionate farewells. A true and deep regard had sprung up between the population and the British. Many romantic stories are told of friends who could not be torn asunder. In one case "a beautiful girl lightly clad refused to leave her lover, an English officer in the Portuguese cacadores, who dismounted and tied a silk pocket-handkerchief around her neck and placed her sideways on his horse. Towards evening the wind blew keenly, and I saw her," says the narrator, "enveloped in a soldier's great coat."

"Many females," we are told by the same authority, "left their homes in a similar manner with the French officers, and travelled about with them on horseback and astride, clad in the uniform of the Polish lancers or hussars, splendidly embroidered, with crimson [illegible] The ladies of Spain frequently ride astride, with pantaloons and Hessian [illegible] behind, and when they are on horseback it is unfastened, and hangs down [illegible]

[illegible] orders; he was obliged to countermarch and retreat on Salamanca,

Wellington had been unable to hold the line of the Douro, for the French had repaired the bridge [illegible] Toro and jeopardised his left; he had gone back to Salamanca himself with all speed, where he occupied the position [illegible] San Christobal on the 6th November, and was presently joined by Hill.

It has been said of Von Moltke, the great German strategist, that he would never allow himself to be compared with Napoleon or Wellington, because, unlike them, he had never commanded or directed a retreat. Certainly this from Burgos was enough to try a great soul; the dangers, the sufferings, the privations of the allies were terrible. They had nearly lost the semblance of an army. "Such a set of scarecrows never was seen," is the testimony of an eye-witness. "It was difficult to say what they were, as the men's coats were patched with grey; some had blankets over them, and most were barefooted; every step they took was up to the knees in mud; women and sick men were actually sticking in it. . . . A brigade of cavalry, however, which was covering the rear, had left Lisbon but a short time before, and was in high order. The clothing of the men scarcely soiled, and the horses sleek and fat, made a strange contrast with the others, especially the company of artillery that had served in the batteries before Burgos. We at first took the latter for prisoners, as they were mostly in French clothing, many of them riding in the carriages with the sick and wounded, drawn, some by oxen, and some by mules and horses. I never saw British soldiers in such a state."

KING JOSEPH BONAPARTE.

[illegible]

The eldest of the Bonaparte family. [illegible] at one time intended for the Church, he became a [illegible] [illegible] but [illegible] [illegible] escape after Waterloo [illegible]

While Wellington halted on the Tormes, the French came up with three great armies—Joseph's, Soult's, and Souham's—a vast force, when combined, of 100,000 men. But there were divided counsels among them: the leaders argued and quarrelled, after the custom of Napoleon's lieutenants in the Peninsula. Marshal Jourdan, who was the King's chief [illegible] principal adviser, was for moving up to an immediate attack; Soult wanted to take ground to the left [illegible] Tormes, which would have obliged Wellington to relinquish the advantages of his well-chosen [illegible] a previous victory. Soult prevailed, and a prolongation of the left, the same strategy as [illegible]

Salamanca, was repeated, but on a wider scale. It was executed very slowly, and Wellington, now too weak for the offensive, cleverly drew off his whole army under the very touch of the French. With amazing boldness and no little good fortune, for the weather was so thick and misty that his movement was unseen, his army circled in one great mass around the advancing columns of the French. That night he bivouacked to the rear of an army which in the morning had menaced him dangerously in front. This delicate operation, it must be remembered, was performed in the presence of the largest French force ever collected together in one place and at one time during the Peninsular War.

PORTUGUESE CART.

After a Drawing by the Rev. Mr. Bradford.

The transport of supplies was one of Wellington's chief difficulties in the Peninsula, and in 1812, when advancing on Salamanca, he got together as many Portuguese carts of this description as could be met with.

After this the retreat was continued towards Ciudad Rodrigo, the French in full pursuit now seeking to outmarch and outflank the retreating columns. The allied army was in miserable plight; the rain fell in torrents; the men marched ankle deep in tenacious mud, and at night time, soaked to the skin, they were unable to light fires or cook food, if, indeed, there had been food to cook. Sometimes the famished soldiers left their ranks to chase and kill the herds of swine, and the battue became so general that the firing was taken for a French attack. All the time the enemy's cavalry was close at their heels, or pressing hard upon their flanks, at times "almost mixing in our ranks," writes one who was there; "near enough," says another, "to bandy wit in the Spanish tongue with the English soldiers." Now and again they charged, sweeping up any baggage and all stragglers, [illegible]

TORO.

After a Drawing by the Rev. Mr. Bradford.

Toro was a point on the Upper Douro where Wellington's forces combined for the general advance on the Ebro. The bridge had been destroyed, but Hill forded the river with his command.

[illegible] On the 20th November, after lasting just a month, this trying retreat [illegible] amounting to some 9,000, including those in the siege of Burgos, while the

MRS. FITZ HERBERT.

After a Portrait by Cosway.

Mrs. Fitz Herbert, a lady of great beauty, is generally believed to have been married to George IV. when Prince of Wales. She lived to a great age at Brighton, and was much admired and esteemed.

OFFICER OF THE FOOT GUARDS.

[illegible]

In full dress uniform carrying the King's [illegible] home service in St. James's Park. In the Peninsula the officers of the Guards were [illegible] "Gentlemen's Sons." They were [illegible] and although [illegible] campaigning [illegible]

moral discomfiture was great. For this disaster, at the close of a year full of victories, Wellington was bitterly attacked. His reputation, although based on many great deeds, was acrimoniously assailed. He accepted all the blame of besieging Burgos. "It was entirely my own act," he said afterwards. "The Government had nothing to say to it." It was his own fault that he brought such insufficient means to bear upon the siege. He had guns enough at Madrid and Santander, but transport was lacking to convey them to the trenches. Again, he worked with the worst and least experienced of his troops; the 3rd, 4th, and Light Divisions he had left at Madrid with Hill.

The men he had with him soon grew dispirited, and then insubordinate. They were no doubt much harassed by the mistakes and negligence of the staff and commissariat. The first by wrong orders often put them to much unnecessary fatigue and useless marching to and fro; the latter was laggard and ineffective; there was often great carelessness in the distribution of rations, and frequently cowardly muleteers and conductors ran off to the rear upon false alarms of the near approach of the French.

Wellington's first act when the army went into winter quarters was to publish a general order reproving his troops for their misconduct. He declared that "discipline had deteriorated during the campaign in a greater degree than he had ever witnessed or read of in any army," and his scathing remarks were not taken in the best part, being deemed exaggerated and too sweeping. It was contended that he made no allowance for the privations endured, nor did he exempt from his severe strictures the Guards and Light Division, which had behaved uniformly well.

In the winter that now followed a very marked improvement was seen. The regiments in their cantonments recovered discipline, were newly clothed and regularly fed. Fresh reinforcements arrived continually [illegible] The cavalry was greatly strengthened; two whole brigades arrived, one of which was composed of the Household Cavalry, the 1st and 2nd Life Guards, and the Blues; the second, of the 10th, 15th, and 18th Hussars. Great pains were taken to complete equipment; new cooking utensils were issued, blankets, billhooks and tents; every foot soldier was given three [illegible] with an extra [illegible]

BATTLE OF VITTORIA.

After a Drawing by Heath.

Beginning of the action in the centre, where Wellington commanded in person.

a pontoon train, completed at every point, was attached to the army. Wellington, in short, laboured incessantly to perfect his army and prepare it for the new and more ambitious flight he contemplated in 1813. From henceforth he was to meet no check in his forward progress. The tide had turned and was setting strongly in his favour. His fine army outnumbered that of the French; English and Portuguese were veteran troops; the Spaniards placed under his orders as generalissimo were rapidly improving in soldierly qualities. The French, on the other hand, were much disheartened by almost continuous reverses, and the growing conviction that they were fighting a losing game. Wellington's masterly plan for the coming campaign entitles him to take rank with the first exponents in the military art. He saw that the river Douro could not be attacked without a great and costly effort; he decided, therefore, to avoid the difficulty in front by turning the right. By operating by his own left he could place a portion of his army behind the Douro; all the strong places on that river would be useless, the French position would be taken in reverse, and the whole country south of the Douro, including Madrid, would become untenable.

BATTLE OF VITTORIA.

After a French Drawing by [illegible]

The second phase of the attack in the centre. The 3rd and 7th Divisions forcing a passage across the bridges on the Zadorra.

LORD WELLINGTON, ENTOURÉ DE SON ÉTAT-MAJOR.

After a Caricature [illegible]

A fanciful picture of British military uniforms in 1813-14 as they appeared to French eyes.

Two things were essential to the success of this bold undertaking. Secrecy in the first place was indispensable, and the enemy's suspicions must be lulled by demonstrations against the front. In the second it would be necessary to traverse the wild district of the Tras os Montes with men and material—a wild mountainous region hitherto thought impracticable for wheels. Careful surveys made during the winter satisfied Wellington to the contrary, and he gradually drew his left wing towards the Douro to be ready for an advance on that side. By the middle of May the cavalry and five divisions had crossed the river, and the advance began. That fine old veteran, Graham, was in independent command of the left wing, and as soon as he was well forward in the difficult march through the mountains, Wellington set the rest of his army in motion by Salamanca towards the Douro, reaching it at Toro and Zamora on the 27th and 28th May. Graham, by this date, should have crossed the Esla, a northern tributary of the Douro, but he was still to the rear, and Wellington, uneasy, hurried round to him to direct the operation in person.

AFTER VITTORIA.

After a Caricature by Cruikshank

The plunder taken from the French included many trophies, eagles, artillery, and the bâton of Marshal Jourdan, which in the print is being presented to Wellington. He sent it to the Prince Regent, who in return created him a Field Marshal.

Graham had been delayed by many obstacles, and he was still on the wrong side of the Esla on the 30th May, when Wellington joined him. But on the 31st, the passage of both rivers, the Esla and the Douro, was effected, and the whole allied army was united at Zamora, north of the Douro. Here Wellington waited three days for the Spanish army of Galicia, a delay that alone saved the French from losing their line of retreat. As it was, they immediately evacuated Madrid, and hurried back to Valladolid, the very point indicated by Napoleon months before as the proper place for the King's headquarters, and where the bulk of the French army should be concentrated.

BATTLE OF VITTORIA.

[illegible]

[illegible] generalship of Joseph.

Now, with an inferior army, Valladolid was untenable by the French, and Joseph continued his retreat on Burgos, where he could be joined by the armies of "Portugal" and "the North," commanded respectively by Drouet and Clausel. But even Burgos he deemed unsafe, for Wellington, constantly operating by his left and turning Joseph's right, threatened the French communications with the frontier and Bayonne. So Burgos was blown up hastily with a tremendous explosion, and Joseph fell back behind the Ebro, [illegible]

Wellington had thus gained a supreme advantage by the mere direction of his [illegible] force. He intended, in his own words, "to hustle the French out of Spain before [illegible] his turning movement through the upper waters of the Ebro, he overtook [illegible] of Vittoria, and then smote them with a crack and overwhelming blow.

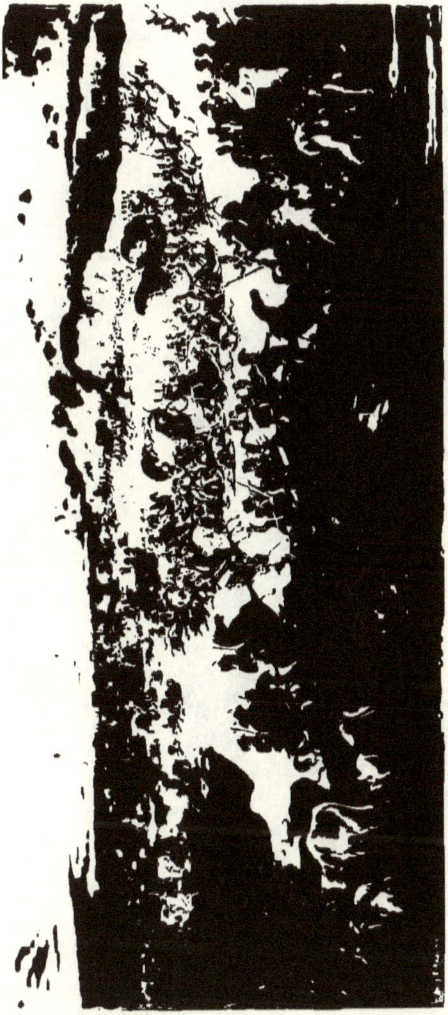

BATTLE OF VITTORIA.

Although the contest was to be stubbornly prolonged, this battle practically sealed the fate of the French in Spain. He had shown himself an admirable strategist; his undoubted powers as a tactician were now to be seen. He at once detected the cardinal error of Joseph's position that a great part of it was parallel to the main line of French retreat along the great royal road to Bayonne. This mistake was emphasised by the excessive length of the French front, some seven or eight miles in all, so that neither centre nor left could easily or quickly be brought to the help of the right, which, being astride of the above-mentioned royal road, was the key to the whole position. These faulty dispositions were the more felt in the battle because this line of retreat was choked and crowded with baggage—with vehicles innumerable laden with the accumulated plunder of years, which the French of all ranks and classes, from King to conscript, were trying at all hazards to carry out of the country.

HER GRACE THE DUCHESS OF RICHMOND.

After Engraving in 'La Belle Assemblée,' 1807.

Charlotte, Duchess of Richmond, wife of the fourth Duke, and mother of the Earl of March (afterwards fifth Duke), who was on Wellington's personal staff in the Peninsula until he rejoined the 52nd, and was badly wounded at Orthez. This is the Duchess of the famous Waterloo ball

Some of the force being still in rear, on the 20th June the English army halted to concentrate. Wellington used that day in minute reconnaissance, and thus became intimately acquainted with every detail of the enemy's position. It followed the course of a small river, the Zadorra, and occupied two fronts. Wellington, who had the advantage in numbers, resolved to attack in three separate and distinct columns. Hill commanded that on the right, Wellington in person the centre, Graham the left.

The first was to deal with the French posted among the rocky fastnesses of the mountain of Puebla, and he was the first in collision, having a stiff job in hand demanding all the energies of his troops. But he gained and held a forward position from which he could lend a helping hand to the central attack. Here Wellington met with, and was much delayed by, very rugged country. On reaching the Zadorra, he found all its bridges raked by well-placed artillery. Fortunately a brave peasant gave information that one bridge, Tres Puentes, was unguarded, and volunteered to guide a column to it. He lost his life in the task, but the column crossed, and the central attack was soon developed. Now Joseph, believing this the chief point of danger, withdrew from his right, that which he should have most jealously guarded, to reinforce his left.

About this time, [illegible] guns were heard on the [illegible] left of the English line, the vital flank of the French. They were Graham's. He had been earliest on the move, having the longest road to travel. His attack drew the attention of the French to his side, and they might have seen the imminence of their danger; but now Wellington in the centre began a furious battle with the 3rd and 7th Divisions. Their point was the village of Arinéz, which

A SPANISH GENTLEMAN.

[illegible]

The whole of King Joseph's personal baggage was captured at Vittoria, and with it a number of fine paintings [illegible] Madrid Galleries. Wellington [illegible] these to their rightful owner, Ferdinand VII. of Spain, who generously sent them [illegible] victorious general, and they are now hanging in Apsley H[illegible] of the finest, by Velasquez, [illegible]

POPE INNOCENT X.

[illegible]

the French held tenaciously, until at last Picton carried it at the run and with the point of the bayonet. With Arinéz the French lost their centre and left, and their last hope was to fall back upon the heights immediately before Vittoria.

In that city and in the plain beyond, panic [illegible] supreme amidst a fugitive and [illegible] multitude. Thousands of carriages and animals, [illegible], men, women, and children, were crowding [illegible] madness of terror. The [illegible] and at the close of the day, [illegible] retreat, flight rather, became general, and [illegible] road. Graham's successful [illegible] had quite cut the French from the main line. He had, however, fought hard for success, being faced by Reille, a capable and resolute soldier, who knew the vital importance of his task. As it was, Reille's stubborn resistance alone preserved Joseph's forces from annihilation. Victory every move in the game, the practised professional soldier, against whom the poor amateur, who could not even handle men, had but little chance. Never was army so hardly used as the French by its incompetent commander. A rear-guard under proper leadership might at least have stayed the British advance until the withdrawal was accomplished. The loss was incalculable, not alone in prestige, but in gear, substance, and material. As the Comte de Gazan, one of the generals, wrote, the French "lost all their equipages, all their guns, all their treasure, all their stores, all their papers, so that no man could prove how much pay was due to him. Generals and subordinate officers alike were reduced to the clothes on their backs, and most of them were barefooted."

LIEUTENANT-COLONEL GOMM, [illegible]

[illegible] Family

One of the victors draws another picture. "The road to Pampeluna," he records, "was choked up with many carriages filled with imploring ladies, waggons laden with specie, powder and ball, wounded soldiers, intermixed with droves of oxen, sheep, goats, mules, horses, and asses, milch cows, filles de chambre, and officers. In fact, such a jumble was never witnessed before; it seemed as if all the domestic animals in the world had been brought to this spot, with the utensils of husbandry and all the finery of palaces."

GENERAL SIR JAMES LEITH, K.B.

After a Portrait by [illegible]

General Sir James Leith commanded the 5th Division during the greater part of the war.

Vast and heterogeneous as was the spoil, the army was little enriched. The specie, estimated at about $5,000,000, fell into the wrong hands; not a fiftieth part came into the military chest. "The trophies were innumerable," says Napier. "The number of guns taken was fourteen, for the French only removed two. A stand of colours and great quantities of ammunition (400 waggon loads) . . . . Marshal Jourdan lost his baton, and Wellington sent it to the Prince Regent, who, in exchange, [illegible] the rank [illegible] Field-Marshal on the victorious general."

FIELD MARSHAL SIR WM. GOMM, G.C.B., [illegible]

After a Family Portrait

This distinguished officer served on the staff through the Peninsular War and at Waterloo, and rose to be a Field Marshal and Commander-in-Chief in India.

[illegible] narrowly escaped, and only got off by leaving his [illegible] first horse he could find. Vittoria ended his [illegible] career, for Nap[illegible] promptly dismissed him from command, and appointed Marshal Soult. He [illegible] with his crown the whole of his gathered loot, chief among [illegible] many fine works of art, removed from the Royal Gallery of Madrid. They were found in rolls, having been cut out of their frames for convenience of carriage. When recovered, Wellington restored them to the rightful owner, but Ferdinand VII., with kingly generosity, would not accept them, and sent them back to Wellington. They formed the nucleus of the Apsley House collection, and are, indeed, among its principal treasures. Two of these notable pictures have been reproduced in the text.

Immediately after Vittoria, Wellington set himself to reduce San Sebastian, the possession of which was of the utmost importance as a new base and useful seaport. The siege which was now undertaken was not crowned with great or even moderate success, and before it fell several severe engagements were fought in the neighbouring mountains, mainly to relieve that fortress and Pampeluna. These various battles I propose to leave for later description, as falling within the scope of the campaign in the Pyrenees and South of France, dealing now with the siege of San Sebastian, from first to last, although this is not exactly and chronologically correct.

KING JOSEPH'S FLIGHT AFTER VITTORIA.

After a Contemporary Print

The stampede was so sudden that Joseph abandoned his carriage, and mounting his horse escaped at a gallop. He lost everything but what he stood in.

SAN SEBASTIAN.

After a Drawing made by an Officer on the spot

An excellent view of the fortress which, under the gallant Rey, so long defied Wellington. The sketch shows the fortifications and the besiegers' lines of approach.

As the French fell back from Vittoria, General Rey, passing San Sebastian, occupied it; being a strong, resourceful soldier he resolved to defend it to the last gasp. It was but a poor place of arms at that time. Its fortifications were all but dismantled, many guns had been removed to other fortresses. "It had no bomb-proof, no palisades, no outworks, and was hardly fitted to make an hour's defence." More, it was filled to overflowing with helpless fugitives from King Joseph's scattered Court, which doubled the ordinary population.

Rey soon drove out all useless mouths, transporting the non-combatants to France; he gathered up the means

STORMING OF SAN SEBASTIAN.

[illegible]

The last and finally successful attack, showing the storm from the Chofre Hills to cross the sands and assault the second or side breach.

NAPOLEON.

[illegible]

of resistance, drew into the garrison all wandering detachments of troops, and laboured hard on the fortifications. Although nominally blockaded by one frigate and some small craft, for England, Queen of the Seas, could spare no larger naval force in Wellington's support, San Sebastian throughout the siege kept open its communications with France.

Wellington put the siege operations under Sir Thomas Graham, giving him 10,000 men, a new battering train, and the services of several excellent engineers, Sir Richard Fletcher at their head, who lost his life under the walls. The siege was not a brilliant success, and it is urged that the strict rules of scientific warfare were never closely followed. Wellington has been blamed for this; but his instructions were to take the place with all reasonable despatch, not to neglect the proper forms of engineering. In any case, there was a lamentable loss of life, and the first great assault failed.

The fortress stands on a narrow promontory jutting out into the sea; on one side the river Urumea, the harbour on the other. The approaches were made on two fronts—along the narrow isthmus and from the sand-hills beyond the river. The capture of a ridge which barred the isthmus was a preliminary to the attack on this side; this ridge (the San Bartholomew) the indefatigable Rey had crowned with a new redoubt. It was at once assaulted and captured, the conduct of the 9th Regiment under their intrepid Colonel Cameron being very conspicuous. Trenches were now opened, breaching batteries

SIR THOMAS GRAHAM (LORD LYNEDOCH)

Grahe [illegible]

[illegible], and [illegible] artillery [illegible] allowed, with the advantage [illegible] the [illegible] of the place seemed [illegible] confidently to the [illegible] up to the attack, but [illegible] Wellington's positive injunctions "[illegible]," [illegible]. The trenches [illegible] slippery rocks along the shore, and though [illegible], no officer of high rank [illegible], and [illegible] under regimental officers commanding only their own men.

HARRY [illegible]

Nothing could be [illegible] than the devotion of the troops of all ranks, and the slaughter was terrible, especially in engineer officers. Sir Richard Fletcher was killed, so was Major Frazer; Harry Jones was one of the first in at the great breach, and was made prisoner; 44 other officers and 500 men were killed or wounded. Wellington was much vexed at this untoward result, and hastened to San Sebastian to put the siege on a better basis, [illegible] was [illegible] Soult's offensive movement, which will be presently [illegible] [illegible] army in the field, and [illegible] [illegible] have been impossible [illegible] Admiralty [illegible] Naval [illegible] supplies of ammunition [illegible] [illegible] and war material [illegible] better stage than [illegible] shot and shell [illegible] consumption. [illegible] the end of August,

LIGHT DRAGOONS.

[illegible]

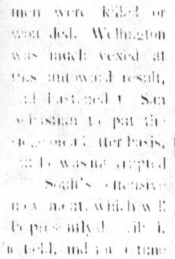

COLONEL SIR RICHARD FLETCHER, R.E.

[illegible]

[illegible] the Chief Engineer in the Peninsula, who [illegible] Torres Vedras, but was killed in the [illegible] assault [illegible] San Sebastian.

and now the fortress was ever so much stronger. Fifty days had elapsed since the commencement, and all the time the garrison had laboured most industriously in improving the defences. They used such surprising diligence that when a fresh bombardment was begun, breaches were repaired and retrenched almost as soon as they were made. Still the brave defenders were being gradually wasted under the incessant deadly fire. There was no sure hope of relief from outside; Soult had made one great effort and failed, and he was not [illegible] until the day on which San Sebastian was again stormed and finally conquered.

ASSAULT ON SAN SEBASTIAN.

A [illegible] representation of the [illegible] San [illegible]

This last successful assault was delivered at broad daylight [illegible] from the Chofre Hills across the sands left in the bed of the river at low tide. W[illegible] previous attempt, now somewhat ungraciously call [illegible] volunteers from the [illegible] the brave 5th Division, which had borne all the previous toil and suf[illegible]

LESACA.

This was Wellington's headquarters during the [illegible]

GEORGE IV. WHEN PRINCE OF WALES.

[illegible] [illegible] Prince Regent [illegible] Wellington [illegible] Field-Marshal [illegible] Army.

misadventure. Some 70 volunteers at once responded to the call, but Sir James Leith, who commanded the 5th Division, would not at first give these outsiders permission to join in the attack or leave the trenches, storming the main breach with his own men.

This second assault was like to have also ended in failure. The first attack made no impression, nor could the volunteers, who were now let loose to sweep forward like a whirlwind, but it was impossible to penetrate into the town. The other attack across the river was in the hands of the Portuguese and the 24th Regiment, and was also repulsed, only the fortunate

FRENCH DRAGOONS BROUGHT TO A CHECK BY A [illegible]

[illegible] Septe[illegible] 1813.

The [illegible] [illegible] ditch. The [illegible] when they [illegible]

accident of a fire among a great heap of stored combustibles which [illegible]. The French were obliged at last to give way, and, after five hours of [illegible] battle at the [illegible] stream of [illegible] into [illegible]. San S[illegible] was won in the [illegible] and torrents of [illegible] kindlier than the storm [illegible] victory. The [illegible] of this [illegible] Rodrigo and Badajos, and [illegible] the soldiery.

The victory at Vittoria [illegible] Wellington [illegible] pinnacle; he could look back [illegible] travelled, and [illegible] the [illegible] lose. He had won [illegible] everywhere, [illegible] [illegible] cities, and [illegible] Ministries. [illegible] tell [illegible] [illegible] W[illegible]

ENTRANCE TO THE HARBOUR OF PASSAGES.

[illegible]

The little land-locked harbour of Passages was Wellington's principal port of supply after leaving Portugal and the fall of San Sebastian in 1813.

Every Englishman, taking the expression in its widest sense, every true son of Great or Greater Britain, must learn something from the lesson so well and so steadfastly inculcated by Wellington. The whole Empire owes him a debt of gratitude, and we shall thrive and prosper the more closely his example is followed. Complete, unhesitating, the most single-minded devotion to public duty was the governing principle of his life. With him, duty stood first and before everything. The consciousness of duty seen, sought out, and unswervingly performed, supported him through every trial and in the darkest hours stimulating him to renewed efforts, giving him greater courage, a firmer self-reliance, and increased self-respect. The seed sown by Wellington and by his illustrious comrade in the sister Service, Nelson, has come up with an abundant harvest to be garnered as the backbone of our ever-increasing Empire.

FONTARABIA.

[illegible]

... the Bidassoa, which ... between Spain and France. The mountains in the distance are the Jaysquibel, in Spain.

DINNER TO CELEBRATE PEACE, 1814.

[illegible]

This is a [illegible] picture of the feast given in the Market Place of Lyme Regis to celebrate the Peace in 1814.

CHAPTER IX.

Soult replaces Joseph in the south, and promptly organises a new army to resist Wellington. Makes a great attack on the British right, which is in much danger till Wellington, hurrying from San Sebastian, gathers together his strength, and defeats the French at [illegible]. Wellington [illegible] the passage of the Bidassoa, captures the entrenchments, and prepares to invade France. Soult [illegible] on the Nivelle which is also forced; then a third upon the Nive at Bayonne, [illegible] on which he manoeuvres against Wellington's flanks, [illegible] is defeated [illegible] on the right and left. Finally, Wellington crosses the Adour by a bridge of boats, and leaving Hope to invest Bayonne, throws his right [illegible] into France. Again defeats Soult first at Orthez, then at Toulouse, the last action in the war. Napoleon [illegible] and [illegible] leaves his army. Wellington's reception in Paris and at home. He proceeds to the Congress assembled at Vienna [illegible] which is interrupted by the startling news of Napoleon's return from Elba. The nations prepare [illegible] war. Napoleon strains every effort to get an army together, and the allies occupy Belgium.

AFTER Vitoria, the war in the Peninsula entered on its last stage. Now the great [illegible] frontier was reached, and further successes must pave the way to an invasion of France. But Napoleon, although sore beset, had no thought of throwing up the sponge. The war was going against him in Central Europe, and worse would happen if Wellington's progress was not stayed. The best means of doing this was to organise new armies under a leader he could trust, and he forthwith despatched Soult to command in northern Spain. "The best military head we have," was Napoleon's opinion of this general, although in capacity Wellington placed Soult after Massena. At any rate, the choice was judicious, the best possible in those days of Imperial decadence, when constant warfare had grievously thinned the ranks of Napoleon's [illegible]. It is impossible to pay too high a tribute to the fine military qualities of Marshal Soult—his [illegible] his daring strategy, and masterly combinations; above all, the unwearied and unflinching constancy [illegible] he maintained a losing game to the very last, is deserving of the greatest praise.

He arrived at Bayonne within a fortnight after Joseph's collapse, and set himself to his task with such splendid spirit that he gathered together a fresh army almost by magic. On the 12th July (Vitoria was fought on the 21st June) he was at the head of 100,000 men, mostly new reinforcements, and the *débris* of the defeated corps, a well-organised and effective force henceforth known as the "Army of Spain."

At this date the siege of San Sebastian had but just begun; Pampeluna was also beleaguered, and Soult was resolved to strike an immediate blow to relieve one or both of these fortresses. He assumed the offensive at once, and fought the first series of the many battles and combats that illustrated the warfare in the Pyrenees

The movements in this first campaign are highly instructive to the military student, but too intricate to be described here in detail. Wellington occupied a great part of the western Pyrenees, from Roncesvalles to the sea, and held his army in three principal portions, each isolated and separated from the others, so that there was no inter-communication or mutual support. He was, therefore, at this disadvantage: that Soult, having made up his mind, could attack in force on either flank before he (Wellington) could concentrate at the menaced point. In other words, Soult could bring his whole force against one or other of his enemy's fractions, the great object held in view by every astute commander. Soult decided to strike at

MARSHAL SOULT IN 1838.

After a [illegible] G. B. [illegible]

Soult went over to Louis XVIII. at Napoleon's abdication in 1813, but rejoined his old master for Waterloo. He went into exile, but returned, and was War Minister to Louis Philippe, and for a time French Ambassador in London.

MARSHAL SOULT, DUC DE DALMATIE.

After a Portrait by Rouillard.

After Vittoria, Soult was sent to Spain by Napoleon to supersede King Joseph. He was given full powers, and soon organised a gallant resistance to the advancing allies. He nobly maintained a losing fight to the last, and although constantly worsted, never yielded until peace was signed.

Wellington's extreme right, that nearest Pampeluna and furthest from San Sebastian. He began his advance on the 21st July, meeting with many delays from storms and floods, but by the 24th he had concentrated 60,000 men with 66 guns in front of the small force holding the passes of Maya and Roncesvalles.

Wellington was thus outmanœuvred and outnumbered at the critical point, and had Soult's subordinate generals pushed forward with more enterprise and intention, or the British defence been less tenacious, the French must have won an easy and great triumph. There were hotly-contested, long-protracted combats at Maya and Roncesvalles, and the British right was presently forced back. These two fights took place on the same day, that also of the first unsuccessful attack of San Sebastian which had drawn Wellington thither.

Wellington and Waterloo.

The French advance had not been unexpected. Spies brought in news of some great movement in preparation, but Wellington looked for Soult on his other flank. Now, hearing the attack was on his right, he rose quickly to the emergency, and acted with his customary promptitude and self-possession. He mounted his horse and rode post-haste towards the threatened point; and as he galloped on he gathered in his wake all the troops he passed, and directed everyone to make for Pampeluna. He was in hopes, but not too sanguine, that he might be in time to succour his hardly-pressed right wing.

Meanwhile, Soult in person was driving back Picton, who now commanded on this side. The fiery British general could not stomach continuous retreats. He faced round, so did General Cole, the two taking up a strong position on the heights of Sauroren, where the French found them as they came on exultant. Soult was not to be checked, and he made dispositions for immediate attack, when a fresh and to him mysterious incident interposed, and induced him to pause. This delay was fatal to his plans.

On that day, the 27th July, Wellington was reaching the end of his rapid ride, and approaching Sauroren just as Soult arrived in front of it. He realised that a conflict was imminent, and despatched the only staff-officer who accompanied him to bring up all the reinforcements he could find. Then he rode alone along the steep hillside, and was recognised by some Portuguese troops. The loud and joyous shouts they raised were taken up by the British troops, whose ringing cheers were heard far and wide.

It was one of the most dramatic and at the same time most critical episodes in the war. For across the valley, and so near that his features could be plainly distinguished, rode Soult, and a spy, who passed freely between the two armies, pointed him out to Wellington. "Yonder," said the British leader, who by this time had summed up the character of his formidable opponent, "yonder is a great but cautious general; he will delay his attack to know the reason of those cheers; that will give time for my reinforcements to come up, and I shall beat him." And he did so "handsomely," to use an expression of his own, the very next day, Soult having made no serious move until then.

The first battle of Sauroren was a terribly

THREE VIEWS ON THE LOWER BIDASSOA.
From sketches made on the spot by Captain Batty, of the 1st Grenadier Guards, showing scenes and incidents in the operations in the Pyrenees and South of France.
(1) The frontier town of Irun. (2) The heights of San Marcial, held by the Spaniards against Soult when he sought to relieve San Sebastian. (3) Fuentarabia, a small town at the mouth of the Bidassoa River.

fierce struggle. Wellington himself described it as "bludgeon work." The French made repeated and determined attacks, and they must have succeeded had not the English reserves come up, after which they were well able to hold their own. Indeed, after this day's fighting, the more serious crisis was over for Wellington. But Soult received reinforcements, and on the 29th July fought a second battle on the same ground. He again encountered defeat, and saw now that there could be no safety but in retreat, for he was being gradually hemmed in on all sides; whereupon, having already sent back his wounded and his sick, he accepted the inevitable, and began to withdraw on the 30th, believing he was strong enough to fight his way round by San Sebastian, so as to regain France by the Bidassoa.

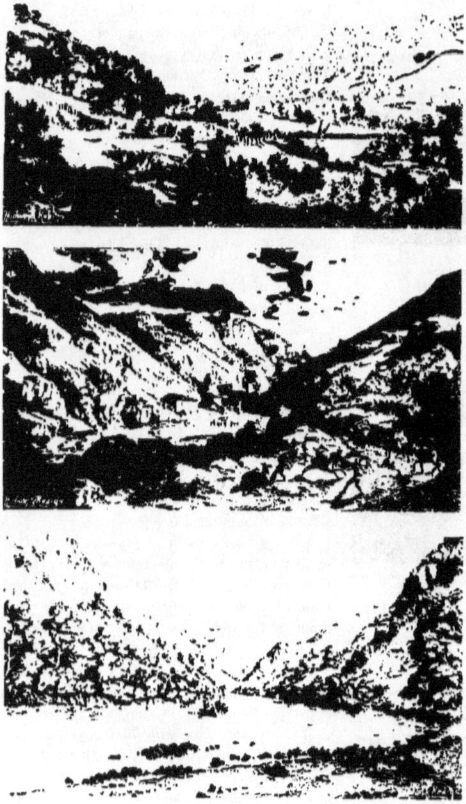

PASSAGE OF THE BIDASSOA FORCED BY WELLINGTON

From sketches made on the spot by Captain B[illegible], of the 1st Grenadier Guards, showing [illegible] and incidents in [illegible] operations in the Pyrenees and South of France.

(4) Shows the Guards cro[illegible] the Bidassoa, a wide, rapid river forming the frontier between Spain and France. (5) Shows [illegible] about Lesderlacha. (6) Gives a good idea of the [illegible] banks of the river.

Wellington, with consummate skill, directed converging columns on the retreating foe, and, but for one strange, unexpected *contretemps*, Soult must have been cut off. But the best military combinations will be marred by errors in execution. At the supreme moment, when the French had been caught in a narrow mountain valley, and were surrounded by the English army, Soult learnt the imminence of his danger by the rash appearance of three marauding red-coats wandering in search of plunder. Alarmed in the nick of time, the French made off through one unclosed issue in the mountains. Throughout this brief campaign their losses had been enormous. They had fought ten actions in nine days, at a total cost of from 12,000 to 15,000 men.

Soult made a second attempt to relieve San Sebastian in the latter end of September. He was now in force behind the Bidassoa, a river that marks the frontier line between Spain and France. He thought to take the royal road, and, cutting in between the sea and Wellington's left, get behind the besiegers. The bulk of his attack fell upon the Spaniards, who were well posted in earthworks upon the hill of San Marcial, and who fought with great courage, better than on any previous occasion. Three British divisions were near at hand, but Wellington left them to do their work alone, so that they might have all the credit. At the same time, penetrating his enemy's motive to hold the right in check by demonstrations while he fell heavily on the left, Wellington made a counter-move, threatening Soult's communications with Bayonne. Soult, alarmed and foiled, soon fell back. Next day San Sebastian was captured, and for the rest of the war the French remained on the defensive, making no further attacks.

It was now strongly urged upon Wellington from home that he should carry the war into France. The war in Germany was going all against Napoleon, and his overthrow was believed to be near at hand. Invasion in the south would surely hasten his downfall, and Wellington was promised every assistance by the Royalist party, troops, risings, and the support of the people. So many wild projects were put before him that he declared in one despatch he would long since have got to the moon if he had done what was expected of him. As for France, he long hesitated to enter the country; indeed, as a military operation, he would have preferred to act against Suchet in Catalonia, whose presence on his flank might have jeopardised his advance. Soult, too, was now strongly entrenched, holding works beyond the river that were reported impregnable.

At last the news of Napoleon's fresh disasters in Germany encouraged him to force the passage of the Lower Bidassoa, and establish one part of his army in the fertile plains of France, while by throwing forward his right he could occupy the mountains piercing the French centre, obtaining thus a commanding position on this side. The passage of the Bidassoa has been characterised by Napier as an enterprise more daring and dangerous than any undertaken by him during the war.

The enemy's line extended from the sea on their right to the left, strongly entrenched upon the hill of the Great Rhune. The interval was filled with entrenchments, forts, redoubts armed with much artillery, and the swift deep river was a formidable barrier, like a wet ditch to a fortification. The frontal attack of such a position was certain to be attended with terrible loss of life, and even then might fail.

PASSAGE OF THE BIDASSOA.

From sketches made on the spot by Captain Batty, of the 1st (Grenadier) Guards, showing scenes and incidents in the operations in the Pyrenees and South of France.

(7) The Spaniards, in the fording of the Bidassoa, took the right of the Guards, and are here seen marching to assail the French posted on the heights of Mandale. (8) Another view of the Bidassoa, from the road to Vera, with a train of wounded being carried to the rear. (9) Represents the town of St. Jean de Luz at the mouth of the Nivelle River, the scene of the next series of battles.

OPERATIONS IN THE SOUTH OF FRANCE.

From sketches made on the spot by Captain Batty, of the 1st (Grenadier) Guards, showing scenes and incidents in the operations in the Pyrenees and South of France.

(10) A small fortified harbour at the mouth of the Bay of St. Jean de Luz. (11) Bayonne was invested by Sir John Hope, but to effect this he constructed (12) a magnificent bridge of boats across the mouth of the Adour—"one of the prodigies of war."

But Wellington relied upon secret information he had received from the Spanish fishermen, and meant to cross by the sands near the mouth of the river. He had heard that they were passable at low tide, and yet the fact was not known to Soult. Wellington based his plan of battle upon it.

Taking his dispositions from right to left, from the mountains to the mouth of the river, he used Giron's Spaniards with the Light and 7th Divisions to attack the mountains, while the 6th Division made a demonstration beyond their right. Next, Freyre's Spaniards were to cross by fords in the centre. Lastly, the 1st and 5th Divisions, with Wilson's and Aylmer's independent brigades, took to the sands by the passage above-mentioned. These troops, on whom the success of this momentous operation mainly depended, were concealed to the last behind high ground near the mouth. To deceive the French further, the British tents were left standing; and they were the readier deceived, because Wellington's right seemingly promised to be the most suitable line for attack.

The columns for the sands started at daylight on the 7th October, silently filing across. When once upon the far bank, a rocket sent up gave the signal to the rest, and now seven more columns went forward in a general attack embracing a front of five miles.

Those that had crossed first (by the sands) were the first successful. Being entirely unexpected, they carried all before them; redoubt after redoubt, all feebly defended, fell into their hands. The whole of the French right was rapidly defeated, and fell back towards the second line of entrenchments on the Nivelle. Next, the centre attack made good progress, and here also the French soon retreated in disorder, almost approaching a rout. Higher up the river, on the right, the conflict was stiffer, although the surprise had been as great as elsewhere. The French were posted in strong works built upon the slopes of stupendous mountains. Much weary climbing of stiff country in places inaccessible impeded the attack, and the ascent occupied five hours

SIR JOHN HOPE, AFTERWARDS EARL OF HOPETOUN.

After a Portrait by Raeburn

This gallant officer, whose daring courage led Wellington to say he feared he should lose him some day, returned to the Peninsula in 1813 to serve under Wellington, to whom he had hitherto been senior. Hope replaced Graham, and was given the third Army Corps in the invasion of France.

The [illegible] was stubborn, the French fire devastating, but the assailants prevailed, and gained all the French strongholds but the H[illegible], on the very summit of the Great Rhune. This, too, Giron's Spaniards eventually secured. They long hesitated, but a young English officer, Havelock, one of General Alten's aides-de-camp, came up with a message, and stayed to give a lead. His fiery impulse quickly appealed to the spirit of the Spaniards, and with tumultuous shouts for "*el chico blanco*" (the fair-haired boy), they charged and carried all before them.

The Spaniards had greatly improved in courage, but they were still a th[illegible] the flesh to Wellington. The intrigues of the Spanish Government were unceasing. Many of its members hated Wellington as only those who are under deep obligations to another can hate him. They opposed and thwarted him, aspersed his character, evaded their obligations and distinct promises. They would not feed their own troops, who, directly they entered France, began plundering and marauding, so that Wellington threatened to send them back across the frontier, and, indeed, kept only a small contingent with him during the closing episodes of the war.

SIR ROWLAND HILL.

THE MARQUIS OF ANGLESEA.

[illegible]

The Por[illegible] [illegible] less troublesome. Foolish people [illegible] the Portuguese troops from Wellington's army and organise them in a separate command under a Portuguese general.

The ostensible excuse was that, being mixed up with the British, they got no individual credit; but the real reason was [illegible] wished to handle the subsidies provided for the support [illegible]

[illegible] frustrated Wellington that at one time [illegible] the country for ever. There [illegible] at this, the most triumphant [illegible] hostility behind him, worse [illegible] as the childish interference [illegible] still scarcely realised the

SIR WILLIAM BERESFORD.

After the Engraving by Brown

Wellington formed his army for the invasion of the South of France into three grand corps, commanded respectively by Sir Rowland Hill, Sir William Beresford, and Sir Thomas Graham (Lord Lynedoch). The last-named, however, soon returned to England, and was replaced by Sir John Hope (Lord Hopetoun).

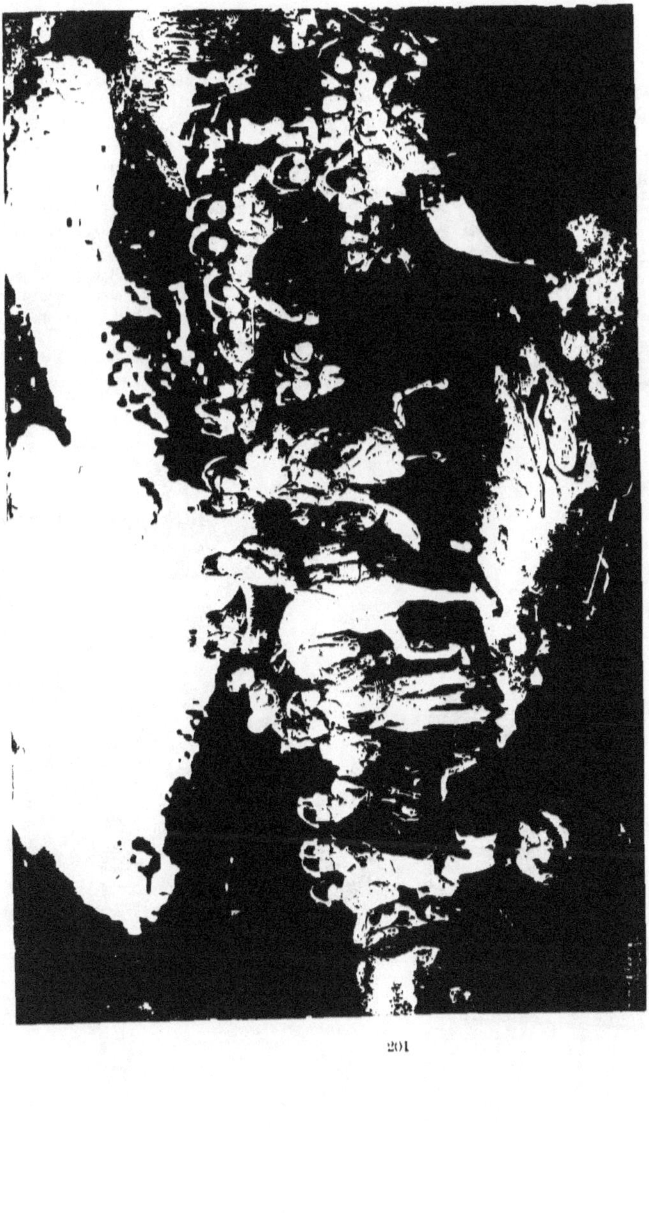

THE DUKE OF WELLINGTON AT THE BATTLE OF NIVELLE.

A BATTLE IN THE PYRENEES.

full value of the work he was doing, and proposed about this time to transfer him to Germany. He was to join the forces of the coalition as an auxiliary, not as supreme leader, and thus his genius would have been eclipsed. With his customary directness and common-sense he resisted the suggestion. While admitting that another general might do quite as well as he, whether in Spain or Germany, few, after his long experience, could enjoy the same advantages in the former country, and he pointed out that in Germany he would be no better than anyone else.

Throughout these early operations in the Pyrenees he was greatly hampered by the difficulties of supply. His troops were long stationed at high altitudes some distance from the coast, and to get food up to them was always a tedious business. The men suffered great hardships and were often on half rations; but yet so fine was their spirit, that when he appealed to them to bear these cheerfully, all murmurs, which had been loud and frequent in the camp, [illegible] lasted, desertions ceased, and the army exhibited great self-control. It was to improve their condition and simplify the supply of food and necessaries that Wellington had decided to enter [illegible].

A curious instance of his [illegible] may be quoted here: [illegible]

THE EMPERORS OF AUSTRIA AND RUSSIA AND THE KING OF PRUSSIA.

[illegible] Wellington [illegible]

Wellington and Waterloo.

BAYONNE.

After a Drawing by J. Vernet.

An old picture of this strongly fortified city, which was never captured, and still bears the title "Nunquam Polluta." The bayonet, [illegible] the British weapon, was invented in and takes its name from Bayonne.

of false money making were now utilised in transforming English guineas into French napoleons. It was an offence, no doubt, against the French mint, but no fraud, and the device exactly answered its purpose.

Soult, after the loss of the line of the Bidassoa, had constructed a new line of entrenchments, and on a scale to rival the famous lines of Torres Vedras, which had no doubt suggested the idea to him. He hoped to make up thus for the inferiority of his troops, but overlooked the probable injury to their morale by this admission. Another mistake was to imagine that he could create in three months anything like what had taken Wellington a whole year to perfect. Moreover, although Torres Vedras enjoyed the reputation of being impregnable, it must be remembered that these great lines were never actually attacked as were Soult's lines of the Nivelle, and in their weakest point.

PRESENTING TROPHIES TO THE PRINCE REGENT.

After a Caricature by Rowlandson.

This is the last phase in the military career of Johnny New…

Early in November, 1813, Wellington again moved forward. He had by this time given a new organisation to his forces, dividing them into three principal bodies, each very much on the plan of a modern Army Corps. The first was commanded by General Sir Rowland Hill, the second by Sir William Beresford, the third by Sir John Hope. The last-named had recently rejoined the Army under circumstances highly creditable to himself. He had been senior in rank to Wellington until the latter had been promoted Field-Marshal after Vittoria. Then Hope gladly offered his services to the distinguished officer who had now passed over him, and was

ADIEU MALMAISON.

After a Picture by Isabey.

1814 [illegible] the country seat, Malmaison, where he had resided constantly in the early da[illegible] [illegible] became Josephine's retreat after the divorce.

FIELD-MARSHAL THE DUKE OF WELLINGTON, 1814.

After a Portrait by Sir Thomas Lawrence.

The Duke is in full uniform, bearing the sword [illegible] State, as he [illegible] [illegible] in the grand procession to the City to return thanks for was gladly welcomed by Wellington, who called him "the ablest man in the Army." Sir John, it will be remembered, was with Moore in the retreat on Corunna, and succeeded to the command on the battle-field. His care that all should embark was so painstaking that he is said to have visited, personally, every street in Corunna, so as to satisfy himself that not one British soldier was left behind.

After the disastrous expedition to Walcheren, in which he commanded a division, Hope saw no service till he returned to the Peninsula in 1813. His gallantry was soon conspicuously shown at the battles of the Nivelle and Nive, where he was wounded, causing great uneasiness to Wellington. "Every day more convinces me of his (Hope's) worth. But we shall lose him if he continues to expose himself as he did during the last three days. Indeed, his escape was wonderful. His coat and hat were shot through in many places, besides the wound in his leg. He places himself among the sharpshooters without sheltering himself as they do." Hope, as we shall see, did yeoman's service right to the end of the campaign.

BATTLE OF ORTHEZ.

From [illegible]

The splendid charge of the 7th Hussars at a critical moment [illegible]

Of the three corps d'armée, Hill's and Beresford's on the right and in the centre were at first to take the more active part in the operations on the Nivelle, while Hope on the extreme left was to hold Soult's right in check. This right was so strongly entrenched that Wellington did not care to risk an attack; he decided rather to push in at a point in the centre which he deemed the weakest in Soult's line of defence, while a turning movement was made on his far right. Success in the centre would have the effect of taking both flanks in reverse and rendering Soult's position untenable.

BATTLE OF ORTHEZ, 1814.

From a Drawing by Martinet.

[illegible] in the war, and the only occasion on which Wellington was wounded.

The fighting that followed was of the most fierce and obstinate kind, lasting three whole days. The defenders, weakest in numbers, lost confidence at the persistent attacks of greater bodies, and yielded ground. Wellington broke in as he designed at

Wellington and Waterloo.

San Pé, but having too few troops in hand he failed to [illegible] Soult's right, which made good their retreat, but might with better fortune have been obliged to lay down their arms. Yet he told a friend that of all his victories he was best pleased with that on the Nivelle, and there can be no doubt that he directed his superior numbers with wonderful skill. His strategy was sound, his tactical movements skilful, and he was nobly supported by his troops.

When Soult had lost the line of the Nivelle he fell back upon the Nive, with his right occupying the strongly entrenched camp of Bayonne. But he would scarcely have held his new position had Wellington been able to promptly follow up his advantage. The broken weather and nearly impassable [illegible] much delayed his march. "On the byeroads the infantry sank to the mid-leg [illegible] cavalry above the horses' knees, and even to the saddle girths in some places." A still greater obstacle to [illegible] was the [illegible] conduct of the Spanish troops, who broke out into marauding and pillage. The bad example [illegible] some of the [illegible] Portuguese. The French peasantry fled terror-stricken, and had not Wellington [illegible]

BATTLE OF TOULOUSE, 181[illegible].

This was the last action in the campa[illegible]

excesses with a st[illegible] must have fell[illegible] France.

The st[illegible] were of the most [illegible] kind. All marauders [illegible] were incontinently [illegible] vent any retaliation [illegible] sent the Spanish [illegible] exception of Morillo's [illegible] across the frontier [illegible] days of December, the weather mended, and on the 9th he sent Hill's corps across the river Nive at Cambo, with Beresford's to follow in support, while Hope with the left occupied Soult, and pushed on, if possible, under the very walls of Bayonne. But during the night of the 9th Soult had drawn to himself every available man, and had fallen furiously upon Hope, now within three miles of Bayonne. A series of fierce engagements followed, extending over three days; but Hope's men stood their ground, and Soult's repeated attacks were always repulsed with immense loss. Then the French marshal, with that marvellous readiness that characterised him, entirely changed his plans, and believing Hill to be isolated upon the far bank of the Nive, retired before Hope, and threw all his weight upon Hill. The result was the battle of St. Pierre, fought with extraordinary tenacity by Hill, and with terrible carnage. Wellington said afterwards that he had never seen a field so thickly strewn with dead; the struggle must have been bloodthirsty in which 5,000 men were killed and wounded in three hours upon a space of one mile.

"VICTORY, PEACE, PLENTY."

[illegible]

An allegorical representation of Napoleon resigning his crown and sceptre to the British Lion.

There was a lull now till the beginning of the year 1814, a period spent in winter quarters, and devoted to preparation for a further advance. In February, Wellington resolved to throw forward his right into the heart of France to help the Bourbon faction, while with his left he invested Bayonne. To complete the circle of that investment it was essential to cross the river Adour, a seemingly impossible feat. Yet the work entrusted to Sir John Hope, under the impulse of Wellington's daring mind, was successfully accomplished. The great bridge of boats thrown across this wide river, with a current that ran seven miles an hour, and banks guarded by troops and earth-works and war-ships, has been well styled "a stupendous undertaking which must always rank among the prodigies of war."

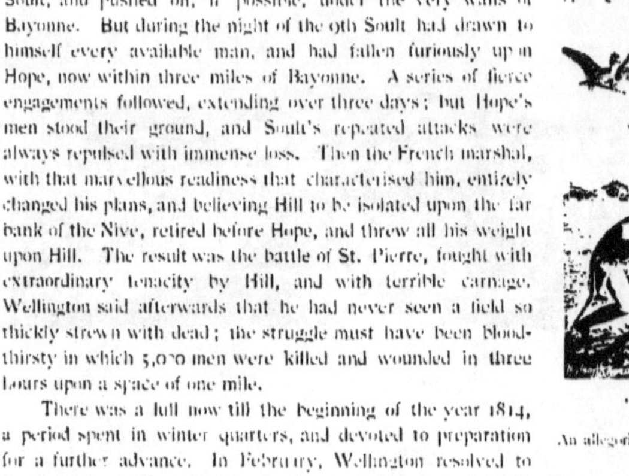

JUBILEE FAIR.

Engraved by J. Pitts.

Peace was celebrated with [illegible] which in London took the form of a great fair and sham fight on the water in Hyde Park.

Leaving Hope to besiege Bayonne, after he had made good his investment by a series of sharp actions, Wellington pushed on his right with great vigour. In little more than a fortnight he covered eighty miles, passed five large and several small rivers, and fought the battle of Orthez, another great victory, in which the French would have been dispersed but for the wound Wellington received. He was struck by a spent musket-ball just above the thigh; and, although he kept his saddle, he rode with

THE SOLDIER'S RETURN.

[illegible] George Morland [illegible] King's Bench Prison. [illegible]

difficulty, and could not maintain the vigour of the pursuit. The result of Orthes was to [illegible] Bayonne, which cut him off altogether from Bordeaux. But he was still [illegible] Although he had been defeated in twenty-four engagements within [illegible] as [illegible] first, and still remaining unconquered in mind." His last battle was at Toulouse [illegible] meet[illegible] of many roads, the chief storehouse of the South of France. The French [illegible] falsely, of fighting this battle with the full knowledge that Napoleon had [illegible] The messenger bringing him the news was detained on the road. Moreover, he w[illegible] attacked [illegible] W[illegible] was bound to defend himself.

While Wellington was thus driving Soult from position to position and winning repeated [illegible] forces of Austria, Prussia, and Russia had finally overcome Napoleon, and forced him to [illegible] succeeded easily, for at no period of his marvellous military career had the great soldier [illegible] master [illegible] of the science of war. It is universally admitted that Napoleon's campaign [illegible] finest examples of strategy known. By consummate skill in handling troops and moving them on "interior lines" he was able, although altogether inferior in numbers, to be constantly superior at the decisive points. No one has done more honour to Napoleon's conduct of this campaign than Wellington; and it is said that the English General believed the allies might have been kept out of Paris, probably forced to retreat, before any assistance could have come from the southern invasion. "Napoleon was ruined by his own impatience." The allies, on the other hand, were not unanimously keen to press him to the last extremity. The Emperor of Austria would have come to terms on the Rhine frontier, but Blucher and the Prussians were implacably hostile; they could not forget the humiliations of Jena. There is no doubt, however, that everyone in France, including his own chief supporters, was sick to death of fighting, and ready to come to any terms. Marmont has been blamed for being the first to surrender, but all the marshals had lost heart, and all opposed Napoleon's last desperate resolve of retiring behind the Seine and continuing the war *à l'outrance*.

OFFICERS, ENGLISH ARMY, 1814.
After a Drawing by Martinet.
Caricaturists made much capital out of the uniforms and characteristics of their enemies.

OFFICERS, PRUSSIAN ARMY, 1814.
After a Drawing by Martinet.
Exaggerated and grotesque drawings.

There is still some doubt whether the battle of Toulouse ought to have been fought, as peace had been already made. But the actual despatches announcing it only reached Wellington at a grand dinner the day after the battle, when he sent round champagne, and gave the toast "Louis XVIII.," with three times three. General Alava responded with "The Liberator of Spain!" and Wellington's health was drank amid wild enthusiasm. Then the whole party, wearing white cockades, went on to the theatre, where a fresh ovation awaited the victorious General, whose appearance, wearing the Bourbon emblem, was the plain announcement that the war was really over.

Wellington was the hero of the hour. When he arrived in Paris, to be present at the formal entry of the Bourbon King, the English General attracted more attention than the returning monarch. He had gone to Spain comparatively unknown, and after his second 1809, [illegible] been in the Peninsula without leaving it until the end of the war. The deepest [illegible] classes to have a glimpse of the simple soldier who had earned a Dukedom and [illegible] in five short years. As he rode through the streets of Paris, the allied Sovereigns [illegible] only of seeing Wellington; the crowds kicked and jostled and trampled on each [illegible] Strangers who had the good fortune to be introduced to him bowed low, [illegible] kiss [illegible] An eye-witness describes him as he appeared on this exciting occasion,

NAPOLEON IN 181[illegible]

BRITISH GRENADIER.

[illegible]

A soldier in marching [illegible] the period of the Peninsular War.

modestly dressed in plain clothes — a blue frock-coat, white neckcloth, and a round hat.

At home in England his reward was substantial. He received the thanks of Parliament and the universal plaudits of the nation at large, but he took his seat in the House of Peers as Baron, Viscount, Earl, Marquis, and Duke at one and the same time. The City of London, which once clamoured for his recall, now presented him with a magnificent service of plate. The great shield was emblazoned with designs of his victories, some of which will be reproduced in the text, and it is preserved at Apsley House with many other magnificent presentations, services of china, orders, and decorations enough to satisfy the hungriest ambition. Very soon he was summoned to assist in the councils of Europe. The nations' representatives were collected at Vienna, and were on the point of coming to blows in the distribution of Napoleon's estate. All had been despoiled in turn, and all looked for revindication and indemnity in various parts of the broken Empire. Thus Russia asked for Prussian Poland; Prussia would have satisfied her out of Saxon territories, and England, with France and Austria, strongly resisted the proposal. The political sky became [illegible] overcast; no nation would proceed with disbanding of troops; Austria, France, and England formed a triple alliance against Russia and Prussia, and war seemed imminent.

IN PARIS AFTER THE PEACE, 1814.

[illegible]

Caricatures of English visitors as presented on the French stage.

ENGLISH OFFICER ON HIS ROUNDS.

[illegible]

The [illegible] camp guards [illegible]

Meanwhile the French restoration was proving a pitiable failure. The Bourbon Princes had no hold upon the people; they were returned, bigoted, narrow-minded sticklers for divine right, and, with their fast-growing unpopularity, the ex-Emperor was more and more regretted. Already his old adherents were conspiring to bring him back; several military conspiracies were afoot under his devoted generals to secure his escape from Elba; and one day he easily quitted his island prison.

All Europe was startled, terrified indeed, with the news. Napoleon was once more at large. Where was he? What would he do?

Wellington and Waterloo.

LORD FITZROY SOMERSET.

After a Painting [illegible]

Lord Fitzroy Somerset was a devoted member of Wellington's staff, his military secretary all through the Peninsula and Waterloo. He lost his arm at Waterloo by one of the last shots.

Talleyrand, no doubt anxious to mislead his diplomatic colleagues at Vienna, declared he had taken refuge in Switzerland. Metternich was not to be so deceived. The best place to look for Napoleon, he said, was on the road that leads to Paris. And the fact was soon known that he had landed at Antibes, near Cannes, where the small garrison fell rapturously at his feet; and from thence, amid general acclamation, gaining strength with every mile, he hurried on to his former capital. It was a triumphal progress. The people cheered him, the troops went over to him, they who had sworn to bring him back a prisoner turned to follow in his suite, and the Bourbons fled post-haste from Paris. This period, the famous "hundred days" which now began, was perhaps the most remarkable in the whole of the Napoleonic legend. They were characterised by incessant feverish activity, for the administrative machinery, civil and military, was to be reconstituted, and an army organised and placed with all despatch in the field. Already the European nations had sunk their differences to combine against their common enemy. An offensive-defensive alliance was entered into by which England, Austria, Prussia, and Russia agreed to give Napoleon neither truce nor peace, but fight on till he was altogether overthrown. Their forces were at once set in motion, huge armies of 150,000 each: the Russians and Austrians towards the Upper Rhine; the Prussians marched on the Lower Rhine; Murat, in Italy, was menaced by another Austrian army; England, at the head of a mixed force of Anglo-Belgians, occupied the Low Countries—"the cockpit of Europe." Although Hill was sent on in advance to Belgium, Wellington was, of course, to command. All eyes were turned upon the English General, who alone had uniformly made successful head against the French. It is recorded that at Vienna, when the news came of the flight from Elba, the Emperor of Russia took Wellington by the arm, and with the fullest conviction said, "*C'est pour vous encore sauver le monde.*"

Meanwhile Napoleon by his gigantic exertions had got together a fine army, many of them veteran soldiers lately released from the German fortresses and war prisons. He was short of officers, especially in the higher ranks, and he missed many of his stoutest and staunchest supporters in the field. Berthier, his indefatigable chief of the staff, was replaced by Soult, who had no special training for the work;

NAPOLEON IN THE FIELD.

After an Etching by Dun[illegible] Berthault

This shows him at his best period, when he was young, active, and capable of prolonged fatigue.

Wellington and Waterloo.

CONGRESS OF VIENNA, 1814-15.

[illegible]

In the [illegible] 1814 [illegible] Congress [illegible] assemble[illegible] at Vienna to re-settle Europe. The D[illegible] of Wellingt[illegible]n and Lord Castlereagh [illegible] the British Government, Talleyrand the French.

[illegible]	[illegible]	[illegible]—Count Nesselrode	Russia.	[illegible]—Lord Clancarty	England.
[illegible]	[illegible]	[illegible] Count de Palmella	Portugal.	[illegible]—M. Wacken	—
[illegible]	[illegible]	[illegible] Viscount Castlereagh	England.	1[illegible].—M. Gentz	—
[illegible]	[illegible]	[illegible] Duc de Dalberg	France.	20.—Baron von Humboldt	Prussia.
[illegible]	Prussia.	13.—Baron Wessenberg	Austria.	21.—General Lord Cathcart	England.
[illegible]	[illegible]	1[illegible].—Prince Rasoumoffsky	Russia.	22.—Prince de Talleyrand	France.
[illegible]	[illegible]	1[illegible].—General Lord Stewart	England.	23.—Count Stackelberg	Russia.
[illegible]	[illegible]	16.—[illegible] Labrador	Spain.		

RETURN FROM ELBA.

PRESENTATION OF COLOURS.

[illegible]

[illegible] the Champ de Mars, when Napoleon presented [illegible] colours of his regiments.

and the story goes that when Napoleon asked him if he had ordered Grouchy to come up at the critical time during Waterloo, Soult replied that he had sent a messenger. "A messenger," he retorted, contemptuously; "my poor dear Berthier would have

Wellington and Waterloo.

WELLINGTON AND HIS CHIEF SUPPORTERS.

After [illegible]

The Duke is in the centre; next him, mounted, is Lord Hill, [illegible] Lord [illegible] [illegible] is the Prince of Orange, the rideman [illegible] is the Duke of Brunswick [illegible]

CHAPTER X.

Waterloo [illegible] campaign. [illegible] and character of the opposing armies. Napoleon [illegible] Wins Ligny, but not Quatre Bras. Wellington retires and takes up position at Waterloo. Blücher [illegible] English [illegible] him. Ground occupied by both opponents. Numbers of armies engaged. [illegible] on the field. The five phases of the battle: First, French attack on Hougoumont; [illegible] which is repulsed; third, the great cavalry charges, which cannot break the British squares; [illegible] La Haye Sainte, which is [illegible] the arrival of the Prussians on the eastern field; [illegible] the Imperial Guard. Final rout of the French and general advance [illegible] pursuit.

THE campaign of Waterloo, as it is generally called, after the principal action fought, was one of the briefest yet most momentous in history.

Early in June Napoleon's five army corps were stationed as follows:—1st and 2nd Corps, under D'Erlon and Reille, were close to the Belgian frontier; the 3rd, under Vandamme, was in the Ardennes; the 4th, under Gerard, was on the Moselle; the 6th, under Lobau, with the Imperial Guard and the Reserve cavalry, were on the march from Paris, and rapidly approaching. On the night of the 14th June the whole [illegible] the river Sambre. The right wing was at Solre-sur-Sambre; the centre about B[illegible] Philippeville. The direction of the whole was Charleroi, a town on the great road to Brussels, [illegible] capital. A general advance was ordered for next morning, the 15th June. [illegible] to Napoleon; his whole future depended upon it. It was a condition of success [illegible] with the English and Prussians before the Austrians and Russians could bring their overwhelming numbers to the eastern frontier; and in another month they might be expected to arrive. Early as Napoleon realised this important consideration at the outset of the campaign, there were many occasions subsequently when he neglected it to his own undoing.

Taking the Prussians next. Blücher had four army corps under his command; the 1st, Z[illegible] Charleroi; the 2nd, Pirch, at Namur; the 3rd, Thielmann, farther to the eastward at C[illegible] the 4th, Bülow, far to the rear at Liége.

Wellington's army was mixed in character, and only 30,000 were British troops. W[illegible] were young and inexperienced; only 6,000 of the 30,000 had ever seen a shot fired. The veteran Peninsular army had been broken up at the close of the late war, and the bulk of it sent across the Atlantic to serve against the United States. The Brunswick and Nassau contingents were untrustworthy; they had been in French ranks so recently, that their sympathies were with their old comrades; the Hanoverians and Dutch Belgians were largely made up of recruits. There were some grounds for Wellington's opinion that his was "an infamously bad army"; yet his cavalry was superb, and his artillery splendidly equipped and mounted. The batteries were so well horsed that Blucher, after inspecting Mercier's, exclaimed, "There is not one horse here not fit for a field-marshal to ride."

Incredible as it may sound, the General who stood at the very head of his profession was so far from master of his means that he could not choose his own subordinates. Some good soldiers could not be overlooked, men who

NAPOLEON OVERTHROWN.

[illegible]

One of the finest pictures in existence showing the Emperor as he [illegible] after his [illegible].

had won their laurels in the Peninsula and who were able to control family interest, such as Hill, Cole, Clinton, Colville, Byng, Vandeleur, Ponsonby, and Vivian; but others, with equal claims but less popular with the powers, who were denied fresh chance of distinction. This was especially the case with Sir Stapleton Cotton, now Lord Combermere, who was not selected for service, although Wellington had made a great point of asking for him. He had once given offence to an august personage, and it was always remembered against him. Lord Uxbridge, who as Lord Paget had commanded the rear guard in Moore's retreat on Corunna, was now put at the head of Wellington's cavalry—no bad appointment, it may be admitted, for he was undeniably a good cavalry leader; but Cotton had greater claims, and was the choice of the General-in-Chief. Picton, the famous fighting divisional leader, was not warned for service till the eleventh hour, and he proceeded to Belgium in such hot haste that he went ahead of his uniforms. It is not generally known that he

[illegible] "HUNDRED DAYS."

[illegible]

commanded at Quatre Bras, and fell at Waterloo, wearing plain clothes.

Favouritism had also filled most of the lesser staff appointments, and Wellington complained bitterly of the men he had to work with. Only a few were veterans of the Peninsula, such as the ill-fated Sir William de Lancey, the Deputy-Quartermaster-General, Sir William Gomm, and Shaw Kennedy, whose account of the great battle is one of the most graphic on record. The junior staff-officers were often blamed for their shortcomings; one of the most flagrant was the neglect to fortify Hougoumont, as ordered by Wellington, which became a decisive tactical point in the action.

NAPOLEON AT CHARLEROI, 1815.

[illegible]

The Emperor entering upon the campaign of Waterloo, the day before the battles of Ligny and Quatre Bras, directing the forward movement of his cavalry.

For convenience in quarters the allied army occupied widely-dispersed cantonments. They lay rather to his right, towards the flank by which, whether rightly or wrongly, Wellington always expected that the enemy would advance, and which was no doubt the most vital to him, as it covered his communications with Ostend. The result was that he was weakest on his left, at the point of junction with the Prussians, and when the time for concentration arrived, there was long a dangerous gap at this the most critical point. Nor was it very rapidly filled. Wellington, to the last, was loth to believe in the direction of the French advance. He continued till quite late on the 15th June to consider the movement along the Charleroi road as a feint, and still looked for them on his right coming towards Mons. By nightfall on that day complete rupture between Wellington and Blücher was imminent. Ney, to whom Napoleon had entrusted the advance on the left, was at Frasnes, on the high road to Brussels, and had in front of him only one [illegible] of Dutch-Belgians, commanded by Prince Bernard of Saxe-Weimar, who, [illegible], with commendable promptitude and true military instinct, had occupied Quatre Bras.

THE MARQUIS OF ANGLESEA.

[illegible]

An excellent cavalry officer, who, as Lord Paget, commanded Moore's cavalry in 1808, and Wellington's cavalry at Waterloo, where he lost a leg.

It was this positive and unlooked-for gain in time by the French that gave rise to the supposition that Wellington had been surprised. He always denied the charge, and it is told of him that, [illegible] years, when sitting for his portrait, Pickersgill, the painter, was bold enough to ask if the story was true. "I never was surprised—until this moment," was the Duke's testy retort.

Napoleon did not, however, benefit fully by his initial advantages.

by this rapid advance. He wasted many precious hours during the early morning of the 16th June, and was so strangely inactive that it can only be explained by failing health; he was no doubt already suffering from the malady that caused his death. Not till 9 a.m., having lost five hours' daylight, did he decide to operate upon two lines, dividing his whole army into two wings, the right commanded by Grouchy, the left by Ney. The first was to deal with the Prussians, who were at Ligny, but in no great strength it was thought, yet Blucher was there with every Prussian corps but one; the second was to push back whatever he found in front of him, then wheel round and support. Napoleon does not seem to have had any notion that the English and their allies would be in position at Quatre Bras.

WELLINGTON IN THE FIELD.

[illegible] Lawrence.

This was W[illegible] [illegible] ordinary distance. The frock-coat was dark [illegible] [illegible]. The telescope he carried all through Spain and [illegible] [illegible] Lord Stanhope.

Napoleon's new dispositions were not made until 2 p.m. By this time, however, Perponcher had reinforced Prince Bernard of Saxe-Weimar, and the 5th Division under Picton was approaching Quatre Bras from Brussels. Wellington himself reached this critical point about 10 a.m., having ridden out at daylight; but finding all quiet, he had gone across to Ligny, eight miles distant, to confer with Blucher. It was settled between the two commanders that the English should support the Prussians in the battle that seemed imminent. Wellington promised to come, provided he was not attacked himself. He was not pleased with Blucher's position, and predicted the Prussian defeat; their reserves were so badly posted upon a sloping hill as to be exposed to a destructive artillery fire.

Returning to Quatre Bras about 2 p.m., Wellington was soon seriously engaged. Our men fought with their customary dogged courage, and, although Ney attacked repeatedly, he made no impression. The French cavalry charged our squares with great determination, but could not break them. Ney, moreover, had lost the services of D'Erlon's corps, which by a series of unfortunate blunders had marched and counter-marched, taking part in neither action. But for this the French victory at Ligny, which was already assured, would have ended in the complete annihilation of the Prussians.

At the end of this first day's fighting the situation was as follows: The British were still firm at Quatre Bras; the Prussians [illegible] at Ligny, [illegible] full retreat. Now, again, Napoleon ruined his chances by wasting valuable time. He did not wake till late next morning, and no one dared disturb him. When he appeared, he gossiped, reviewed his troops, but gave no orders to put them in movement till about midday. Then he sent Grouchy with 33,000 men to pursue the Prussians and keep in close touch with them, especially noting the direction of their retreat, which he presently heard, and probably expected, was towards Namur, and away from Wellington. This was a mistake, for the Prussian generals had decided to abandon their real line of communication, and, bent only on keeping up connection with their allies, had retreated on Wavre.

Having sent off Grouchy on a mission which was destined to have very fatal results, Napoleon turned next on the British, thinking to crush them easily and march on Brussels in triumph. Ney was to attack Quatre Bras with all his strength; but he was too late. Wellington had disappeared. As soon as the news reached him of Blucher's defeat, he had gone back, withdrawing his whole force quietly but steadily, and in excellent order, making for Mont St. Jean, the position in front of the forest of Soignies, which he had already chosen as his battle-ground for the defence of Brussels. So little was he in a hurry that he let his men cook and eat their breakfasts before they marched, and in consequence his rear guard was overtaken by the French horse. A sharp fight occurred, in which Lord Uxbridge's cavalry was rather sharply handled.

GENERAL LORD HILL.

After a Painting [illegible]

Lord Hill was really second in command at Waterloo, and would have succeeded had anything happened to Wellington.

Wellington's resolve to face round at Waterloo was contingent on Blucher's support. This is expressly stated by Muffling, the Prussian attaché to the British headquarters, whom Wellington assured that he was ready to fight if he had the assistance of only one Prussian corps. There was seemingly some doubt of this. The Germans were not all of them cordial. Gneisenau distrusted Wellington, and, so it is said, scarcely believed that he meant to hold his ground. Blucher, on the other hand, was staunch and loyal, a devoted friend and admirer of Wellington's. But he had been wounded at Ligny, and it was possible that he might not be able to take the field in person, and that in his absence other counsels might prevail. This gives some colour to the story, not fully substantiated, that Wellington paid Blucher a visit late on the night of the 17th [illegible] to get a promise of support from his own lips. This story is told on the Duke's own authority, but only in later years, when his memory was beginning to fail; and it is hardly credible that, with such tremendous issues at stake, he would have [illegible] practically alone—as the story runs—fourteen miles [illegible] in the

MARSHAL BLUCHER'S PERIL AT LIGNY.

After a Drawing by [illegible]

The great Prussian general was thrown in a cavalry [illegible] that he was *hors de combat* for a couple of days, but he turned [illegible] still suffering, for Waterloo.

THE MARCHIONESS OF HUNTLEY.

After a Drawing by [illegible] B

[illegible] Lady Elizabeth Conyngham was present at the Waterloo ball. The Conynghams were the [illegible] companions of George IV. in his later life.

dead of night. The risk he ran is further shown, if we are to believe the story, by the accident that befell him on the road, when he fell into a deep dyke and was pulled out with difficulty [illegible] his orderly.

That he got some promise, however, one way or another is pretty certain, for without it he would not have fought, strongly as he was impressed with the necessity for a battle. To have continued to retreat before Napoleon would have been mischievous, arguing weakness, and greatly encouraging the partisans of Napoleon. As for the Emperor, his only fear was lest his enemy should escape him. He spent an anxious, restless night on the eve of Waterloo. At one in the morning he rode out to the outposts, accompanied by a single aide-de-camp, and was but half reassured at the sight of the allied watch-fires, which burnt badly under the incessant rain. When at daybreak he received the [illegible] reports to the effect that the English were still there he rejoiced exceedingly. "I never was so pleased," he said afterwards at St. Helena, "as when I saw that Wellington intended to fight. [illegible] I had [illegible] that I should annihilate his army. [illegible] When [illegible] was [illegible] the battle single-handed, I felt confident I should destroy him."

A picture has been preserved of him at [illegible], surrounded by his marshals and staff-officers. Ne[illegible] "They are retreating." "It is too late," exultingly cried Napoleon. "They cannot escape now." "Ah! sire," said General Foy, [illegible], "*Les Anglais en duel sont le diable*" ("These English [illegible] are the very mischief"). Foy had fought through the Peninsular War, and had learnt to respect the British troops in the field. When Soult added a few cautious words, the Emperor turned on him brutally, saying, "You think the English invincible because you have always been beaten by them."

The night had been wet, the ground was still [illegible] —too much so for the free movement of artillery. [illegible] the French.

THE DUKE OF RICHMOND [illegible]

This is the Duke at the Waterloo ball. He was Master-General of the Ordnance.

THE DUKE OF RICHMOND

As Colonel Lennox, M.P.

After a Caricature by Kay.

This is a caricature portrait of the Duke of Richmond at the time he fought his duel with H.R.H. the Duke of York, in 1789.

Wellington and Waterloo.

were strong and Napoleon would not begin the action, as he feared, prematurely. The same fatal dilatoriness told against him; for with the time gained in an early attack he might have won a victory before the Prussians could come upon the ground. To emphasise the error, he ordered his troops to move into their places with all possible pageantry: bands playing and colours flying, as though for a birthday parade; while he looked on with a soldier's delighted appreciation. "The earth seemed proud," as he put it, "to bear so many brave men." As soon as they had all taken their stations he passed down the lines, reviewing his regiments one by one; and at the end, with gladsome exultation, he stretched forth his arms towards his enemy, crying, "*Les Anglais! Enfin je les tiens.*"

By this time Wellington's troops were also in position. The great leader was in the saddle at daybreak, riding his famous charger, Copenhagen, which carried him without distress through the entire day. As it was this horse that Wellington is said to have ridden on the disputed expedition to Wavre the previous

HIGHLAND SOLDIERS.

After a French Drawing.

A fancy but faithful picture of the Scotch uniform as seen through French eyes. A covert sneer at our soldiers' tastes is conveyed by the bottle and basket.

night, not many hours before, and twenty-eight miles, this point must surely be taken as discrediting the story. Yet he was a horse of great mettle and endurance, for, according to another story, he lashed out when the Duke had dismounted and was seeing him fed at the end of this tremendously fatiguing day, and nearly killed the conqueror.

LADY AUGUSTA BARING.

[illegible]

This was a daughter of the [illegible] Countess of Cardigan. She was at the Waterloo ball, and afterwards married Mr. Baring, M.P.

The modern visitor to the field of Waterloo is at some difficulty in making out the positions occupied. There are now no very marked features, and the gentle slopes that once defined the battle-ground have been shaved down to provide earth for the memorial monument. But we know that the allied army was astride the high road from Charleroi to Brussels, occupying a low ridge of hills that ran east and west. On the flat narrow top was the road to Wavre; at each end the hills were slightly salient, in the centre they trended inward, forming a re-entering curve. In front of this, the main line, were three foreposts, advanced points that played an important part in the battle. These were the chateau and garden of Hougomont, the farm of La Haye Sainte, and the homesteads of Papelotte and La Haye. The whole position was to be

Wellington and Waterloo.

THE FOREST OF SOIGNIES.

[illegible]

This great wood was immediately in rear of Wellington's position at Waterloo, which it was thought to have imperilled.

commended as fulfilling the best conditions: a slope in front, a slope to the rear, concealing strength of reserves and general movements, free and complete communication with all parts. The right flank was strongly posted; if the left was less so, that was the side on which the Prussians were expected. This position being bisected by the Brussels high road, the army occupying it was divided, naturally, into a right and left wing. Lord Hill had general charge of the right, which was made up of (taking them from right to left) Clinton's 2nd Division, Cooke's 1st (Guards) and Alten's 3rd Division. Mitchell's brigade of Colville's Division was in rear of the Guards, and a portion of the latter held Hougomont, with a mixed detachment of Nassauers and Brunswickers, 1,500 in all. On the other side of the high road there were Cole's 6th Division and Picton's 5th Division, with Bylandt's Dutch brigade a little in advance. Baring commanded the garrison of La Haye Sainte, and Perponcher in La Haye. The reserves were in a second line. The Brunswickers, cavalry and infantry, were behind the right, also the cavalry of the King's German Legion; a Dutch-Belgian division was in the centre across the high road, and here were Somerset's brigade of Household Cavalry, and Ponsonby's Union Brigade, Royal Dragoons, Scots Greys, and Enniskillens. The extreme left was filled in with Vandeleur's and Vivian's brigades of Light Cavalry.

Th[illegible] of the allied troops upon [illegible] was 68,000 men—a very [illegible] inferior in [illegible] Napoleon [illegible] the [illegible] [illegible]

THE FOREST OF SOIGNIES.

After [illegible]

The [illegible] showing the paved road by which the troops arrived from Brussels.

Wellington and Waterloo.

Wellington, no doubt, was ever anxious for his right flank, and this must have been his best line of retreat if defeated; but he has been sharply criticised for depriving himself of so considerable a reinforcement on the day of battle. He had plenty of time—if he had thought fit—after Napoleon's attack was clearly developed, to bring Colville's Division over to Waterloo, where it would have been of inestimable value before the day was done. Another reason given, and on excellent authority, was that the Dutch troops under Colville were untrustworthy, and that his British regiments hourly expected to have to fire upon them.

GEORGE IV. AS COLONEL OF 10th HUSSARS.

The King was [illegible] corps, were the [illegible]

Napoleon had 72,000 men on the ground, and 240 guns. Grouchy, at a greater distance from Waterloo than Blucher, had 33,000 more; but they never came into action, a failure for which he was primarily responsible, although his defence is that he was strictly obeying his orders. In any case, he was misled in following a will-o'-the-wisp, and neglected the well-known axiom, "Work towards the guns." The noise of the conflict was distinctly heard and its direction known by him at a time when he might still have rendered assistance. Being resolved upon a vigorous offensive, Napoleon disposed his force in three lines on slopes towards his enemy, having his right flank at Frischermont, his centre at La Belle Alliance, his left on the Nivelles-Louvain road. D'Erlon's corps, [illegible] men, was on the right of the first line, and Reille's corps on the left, 18,000 strong; a cavalry division, about 1,800 sabres, was on each extreme flank. The second line was of cavalry on each flank—Milhaud's corps, 3,300, on the right; Kellerman's, about the same strength, on the left; with Lobau's infantry corps, 7,000, in the centre. The third line was the reserve, and formed of the far-famed Imperial Guard, three divisions—the old, middle, and young guard—the whole under Drouot, and 12,000 strong.

GEORGE IV.

After the Portrait by Sir T. Lawrence.

The King in his later days was persuaded that he had been present at the battle of Waterloo, and would appeal to Wellington in confirmation. "I have often heard your Majesty say so," was the Duke's ingenious reply.

His plan of battle was to throw his chief weight on the enemy's inner flank, Wellington's left and left centre [illegible] that success here would drive the [illegible] apart; the English would be rolled back towards the sea, and the road to Brussels exposed. With this in view he ordered D'Erlon's corps forward, preluding the movement with a determined attack upon Hougoumont to distract Wellington's attention. From that time forth Napoleon remained in one spot, a knoll named Rossomme, on the main road about a mile to the rear of La Belle Alliance, where he [illegible] reports, and whence he issued orders by his aides and messengers, leaving it only once in the afternoon to visit [illegible]

...LD-MARSHAL THE DUKE OF WELLINGTON.

[illegible]

when the Prussian advance began to tell. He left the executive work entirely to his lieutenants, and never personally supervised or controlled movements.

Wellington, on the other hand, was here, there, and everywhere during the fight. He was never better than on a battle-field, prompt and resourceful, galloping hither and thither as fortune varied, and making fresh dispositions with a quick eye for country and ready skill in handling troops. "Wherever there was a turning point in the battle there Wellington directed in person, judging for himself, and met the storm." He took no thought of danger, and was in the thick of the fight, freely adventuring his person, [illegible] was [illegible]. When the enemy's fire became hot and the shot came rather too near, he was heard to say to his staff: "[illegible] gentlemen; we are a little too thick here."

AMMUNITION WAGGON ON FIRE.

An incident in the battle when a shell exploded an ammunition [illegible]

"It is hardly possible," writes one of his aides-de-camp, Lord William Lennox, "to describe the [illegible] in which the hero gave his orders and watched the movements and attacks of the enemy. In the midst of [illegible], bullets whistling close about him, round shot ploughing the ground he occupied, and men and horses falling on every side, he sat upon his favourite charger, Copenhagen, as collectedly as if he had been [illegible] the [illegible] Troops in Hyde Park." No doubt he was at times reconnoitred, and [illegible]

WATERLOO.

[illegible]

A general view of the battle about the [illegible] picture is in the possession of the United Service Club.

staff. He was more chivalrous himself, and would not allow an artillery officer, who had made out Napoleon distinctly, to open fire upon the French Emperor. "No! no! on no account," was his remark. "It is not the business [illegible] commanders to fire at each other."

Another story illustrating his [illegible] character is told of him. At the close of the day, when the battle was practically won, but the French fire had not quite ceased,

LA HAYE SAINTE, 1815.

After a Drawing [illegible]

Another outpost about the centre of Wellington's position, constantly attacked, but [illegible] held by Colonel Baring until late in the afternoon, when it was taken by the French.

work is done." No one worked harder than the great leader in this "battle of giants," as he called it himself; a battle won, according to his opinion, in the playing fields

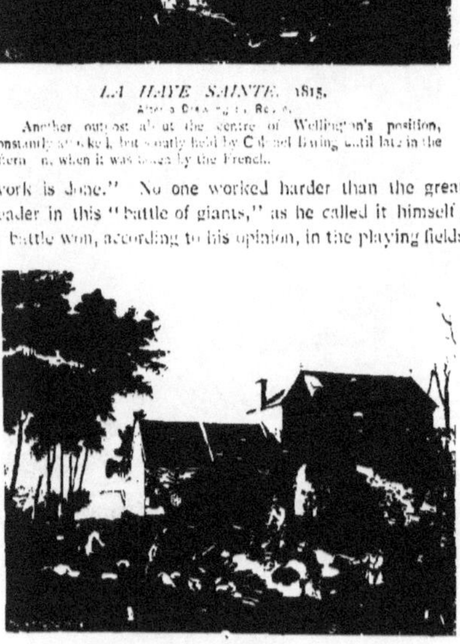

HOUGOMONT, 1815.

[illegible]

INTERIOR OF HOUGOMONT, 1815.

After a [illegible]

The bitterness of the struggle for the possession of this outpost is seen [illegible]

he ventured too far and nearly lost his life. When one of his staff protested, he [illegible] answered: "What does it matter now? My life is of no consequence, for the

HOUGOMONT TO-DAY.

The farm still stands [illegible] 1815. The great gateway is [illegible] in the foreground.

of Eton, when the young officers "ran as they did at cricket," and the men sturdily "pounded" on and on, till they "pounded" the hardest. He was in the saddle for sixteen or seventeen hours, riding the same horse, thus increasing the fatigue; in his ubiquitous movements he often distanced his staff and was seen alone on the field. Sometimes he had no one at hand to carry his orders, and took the first passer-by. Once it was a person in plain clothes, whom he had already met and advised to leave the field! a commercial traveller who, finding

APPROACH TO VILLAGE OF WATERLOO, 1815.

After [illegible] by [illegible]

Waterloo was two miles in rear of the field of battle [illegible] has been so named because Wellington [illegible] in the village.

said to a comrade, "That opens the ball." It was then 11.20 a.m. Soon after this began the attack on Hougoumont and the other villages, the prelude to the main

MONT ST. JEAN.

After a Drawing by [illegible]

Wellington's headquarters during the night. The French long named the battle Mont St. Jean.

principal episodes, each containing a distinct, separately delivered attack. Napoleon made no general or combined movements; each attack was an isolated, clearly-marked effort. These attacks, briefly stated, were: 1st, Reille's unsuccessful assault of Hougoumont; 2nd, [illegible] attack of the allied centre and left, repulsed [illegible] by a counter-charge of allied cavalry; 3rd,

himself at Brussels [illegible] 18th June, and [illegible]

[illegible]

An old Peninsular [illegible] look out for [illegible] at the [illegible] and

LA HAYE SAINTE.

[illegible]

advance of D'Erlon. It will be convenient for a better understanding of the great struggle to follow the method of General Shaw Kennedy, who divides the day into five

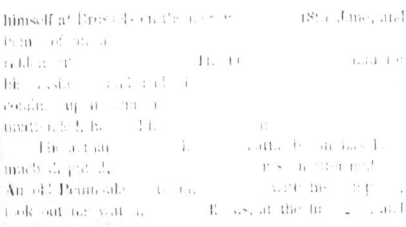

LA HAYE SAINTE [illegible].

[illegible]

attack, which failed to break the British squares; 4th, renewed attack of the centre, ending in the capture of La Haye Sainte; and 5th, the final magnificent attempt of the Imperial Guard, nobly withstood by the British Guards. During the third episode, and afterwards, Lobau's corps was fighting an independent battle at Planchenoit against the steadily advancing Prussians.

WELLINGTON'S HEADQUARTERS AT WATERLOO.

After a [illegible] Gerard of Brussels.

In this house the Duke slept the night before and the night of the battle. He also wrote his despatch from here, and here Sir Alexander Gordon died.

1st. Reille advanced without first shaking the buildings of Hougomont with artillery fire, and although his men went forward with great gallantry and in great numbers, they could make no permanent impression. They gained a footing in the gardens and orchard, but were presently driven out, and they never entered the chateau. One of the finest incidents of the day was the struggle at the great gate, which was closed by a stalwart Guardsman in the very teeth of the invading Frenchmen. Wellington had been near by when the attack on Hougomont was imminent, and he had had time to send in support; he continued to reinforce it during the day, but never to the extent of weakening his centre, as Napoleon had intended, and the real effect of the attack was to lock up Reille's corps in a desultory combat that was injurious to the general result.

CHARGE OF THE SCOTS GREYS AT WATERLOO.

The [illegible] charge of the [illegible] Dragoons, Scots Greys, and Enniskillens, was [illegible] in the second phase of the [illegible] [illegible]ing the havoc made by the Scots Greys, was [illegible]

2nd. Ney—"bravest of the brave"—had been put at the head of the main attack, and he formed D'Erlon's corps in columns of attack under cover of a tremendous battery of guns, and backed by Milhaud's and Kellerman's heavy cavalry. The French aim was to break through our line in the centre and gain Mont St. Jean to the rear, thus severing all connection with the Prussians, and obliging Wellington to show a new front, with his left thrown back to cover his communications

COLONEL GORDON MORTALLY WOUNDED.

Gordon, brother of the Earl of Aberdeen, was a favourite aide-de-camp, and his death caused Wellington the most poignant grief.

with the sea. The attack was met by Picton, whose most advanced brigade, Bylandt's Dutchmen, broke and fell back. Then Picton brought up Kempt's and Pack's Brigade at the run—3,000 men in a deployed line—to fall upon Donzelet's Frenchmen, who were all but masters of La Haye Sainte. A fierce combat ensued, in which the British bayonet told, and the French were discomfited; but the intrepid Picton was slain. Further to the right, Quiot and Marcognet's Frenchmen had been more successful; but now Wellington arrived at a hand-gallop from Hougomont, and with great promptitude ordered up the cavalry in support. These were the only near and available reserve for his left wing.

The charges made by the Household and Union Brigades were as splendid as anything recorded of cavalry encounters in the annals of war. The shock was tremendous, but the British overbore the French, and the whole mass swept down into the valley, pell-mell, a confused body of fighting men. Numberless desperate hand-to-hand combats took place, and many glorious deeds of heroism were performed. It was now that Shaw the Life Guardsman, a horseman of colossal strength who had once been a pugilist, slashed the life out of several opponents before he was himself killed; now Ewart of the Scots Greys won the Eagle of the French "Invincibles," a regiment proud of its great achievements at Austerlitz, Jena, Wagram, Eylau, and Friedland. Napoleon, who was watching the fight with breathless interest, was moved to admiration of the Scots Greys—"*Ces terribles chevaux gris!*"

Now bodies of fresh French cavalry came up and checked the progress of our impetuous dragoons, and who might otherwise have been cut to pieces. They had already suffered terribly. Barely half of the Union Brigade regained the British lines; the Life Guards and Blues were nearly decimated. But on the French side D'Erlon's corps was shattered, and the whole fell back to reform. This second great attack, like that on Hougomont, had also signally failed.

3rd. There was a lull now for a brief space while Ney was organising a new attack to be made by cavalry alone; by the corps of Milhaud and Lefèbvre Desnouettes and the Light Cavalry of the Guard—12,000 magnificent horsemen, cuirassiers, lancers, and chasseurs, in every variety of splendid uniform, filling all the space between Hougomont and the Charleroi road. As they advanced with deafening cries of "*Vive l'Empereur!*" the British infantry quietly formed squares to receive their terrible foes: small compact bodies awaiting with calm fortitude the cavalry

COL. JOHN CAMERON, 92nd HIGHLANDERS.

After a Portrait.

This fine soldier was killed at Waterloo at the head of his regiment. He will be known to English readers as the Fassiefern of Grant's novel, "The Romance of War."

attack. They were charged repeatedly, and with an impetuous gallantry that won the unqualified praise of Wellington, who said he had never seen anything finer than the courage of the French horsemen. We may accord still higher praise to the British infantry which sustained these attacks for nearly two hours, during which not a single square was broken. The withering fire of the [illegible] living fortresses [illegible] emptied saddles and shook the constancy of [illegible] soldiers. [illegible] Ney led on his cavalry;

SIR ROBERT GARDINER.

[illegible] This distinguished [illegible] commanded a horse battery through [illegible] Waterloo. He rose to the highest rank, was [illegible] Governor of Gibraltar.

[illegible] Guyot's Grenadiers, the Dragoons [illegible] Cavalry Corps; the whole of Napoleon's [illegible] were now engaged. It was an heroic [illegible] indomitable infantry. The French [illegible] again, cut at the bristling bayonets, thrust over [illegible] their long lances, but they could [illegible] defeat. Only a small [illegible], and the [illegible] disorganised, rode back,

A GENERAL OFFICER.

[illegible]

COLONEL SIR WILLIAM DE LANCEY.

[illegible]

An excellent staff officer, who was Deputy Quartermaster General at Waterloo, where he was mortally wounded.

AFTER THE BATTLE.

the hopeless victims of a grave military mistake. This attack by cavalry alone, at this early stage of the action, is condemned by critics. It was directed against infantry still unshaken, it was unsupported by infantry, and Napoleon is blamed for having permitted it. Some say he yielded to the urgent solicitations of Ney, who had a strong belief in the prowess of cavalry, and especially of such cavalry as this. Some say that Napoleon was too much occupied at the time with the significant news that had reached him that the Prussians were near at hand. An intercepted despatch had stated that they were approaching in strength 30,000, and he had desired Grouchy to deal them a crushing blow. But the message had not reached Grouchy in time, and now the Prussians, pressing steadily forward, were threatening to ruin his chances at Waterloo. The very direction of their march struck at a vital point; his right flank was imperilled, and to meet the danger it was imperative to show another front on that side. He sent first some of his reserve cavalry to ward off this unexpected peril; but as the increasing noise of battle showed the vigour of the Prussians' attack, he went to Planchenoit in person, and in due course moved thither the whole of Lobau's corps.

CAVALRY COMBATS AT WATERLOO.

From Kelly's "Waterloo."

A dismounted Life Guardsman in a hand-to-hand fight engages a French cuirassier, whom he kills, and then rides off on his horse.

4th. It was while he was thus absent on the eastern field that Ney's earnest appeal reached him for troops to renew the attack on Wellington. Ney asked now for more infantry. "Infantry?" retorted Napoleon angrily to Ney's messenger. "Where am I to get them? Does he think I can manufacture them?" But Ney was not yet disheartened. The day was drawing on, true, but it was as yet barely 5 p.m.; there were nearly four hours of daylight. Ney got together a sufficient force—a division of Reille's corps, the reformed commands of Quiot, Marcognet, and Donzelet, to make a new attack upon the allied centre; this was the only effort that almost met with success. Had he been backed by proper reserves at this critical period, the fate of the day might have been changed. La Haye Sainte was captured, and there was a dangerous gap in the British

SHAW, THE LIFE GUARDSMAN.

From Kelly's "Waterloo."

The personal prowess of this intrepid soldier, who attacked and slew two French cuirassiers before he lost his own life, is still remembered. He had been a prize fighter.

WATERLOO

line. Shaw Kennedy says that he pointed this out to Wellington, who appeared upon the scene at precisely the right moment, and was directed to gather up what detachments he could to fill it, while the chief brought up Kilmansegge's Hanoverians. From henceforth Wellington was sanguine of success. It was asserted afterwards that there were one or two periods in the battle when he was inclined to despair. This he denied to Croker, declaring that he was never seriously alarmed for the result. Mr. Croker adds that those among the Duke's entourage whom he asked were unanimous in saying that the Duke's confidence was never in the least shaken. As against this, we have the evidence of General Alava, to whom he remarked as the day drew on: "By G——, Alava, I believe we shall beat them yet!" There must, then, have been some doubt in his mind previous to this, and his anxiety is also shown by his constantly consulting his watch. His own subsequent explanation of this was that he knew the result depended upon the "staying power" of his troops. He must win if they could only hold out till dark. The story, however, that he prayed aloud "for night or Blucher" is altogether apocryphal.

[illegible] Napoleon [illegible] saw, equally plainly, that he must [illegible] now, if at all. Although he never [illegible] Prussians were more than a single corps, [illegible] persistent attack. Besides, he had the last reserve [illegible], the Imperial Guard. There were [illegible] and these he organised in two lines, [illegible], and they were to be sent against the allied right. A hot artillery fire from guns [illegible] the attack. Cavalry followed close to maintain the advantage. Wellington [illegible] this last great effort. No longer concerned for his left flank, through

GENERAL SIR WILLIAM PONSONBY.

[illegible] Brigade in its great charge.

H.R.H. THE PRINCE OF ORANGE.

[illegible] King of the Netherlands.

H.S.H. THE DUKE OF BRUNSWICK.

Frederick William, Duke of Brunswick, killed at Waterloo.

WELLINGTON AT WATERLOO.

[illegible]

The painter's idea [illegible] background [illegible]

NAPOLEON'S FLIGHT FROM WATERLOO.

After a Picture by John Gilbert.

After the discomfiture of the Imperial Guard, Napoleon rode away at full speed to Charleroi, *en route* for Paris.

the Prussian advance, he drew all his force towards the right, and massed his guns to play upon the approaching columns of the Imperial Guard. Besides other forces, he held Maitland's Brigade of Guards unseen behind the slope, and a brigade of light troops, including the 52nd, under that practised soldier, Colborne, prolonged the line on his right. The right column of the French, although swept and torn by our artillery fire, bore directly towards the spot occupied by the concealed Guards. Ney dismounted and led on foot; but as they crowned the ridge, Wellington, who was, of course, there, gave the order, "Up, Guards, and make ready." They sprang up, fired a volley, which told direfully on the dense column and halted it, paralysed. Then a voice cried "Now's the time, boys," and the Guards charged home, driving the enemy headlong before them. The second column of the Imperial Guard fared no better. While one brigade stopped them in front, Adam caught them in flank, and Colborne, with the 52nd, happily inspired, wheeled his regiment to the left in line and poured in a destructive fire upon the doomed column. From this moment the attack was over and the battle practically ended. Napoleon, who had been active in these encounters, essayed to rally his guard on the west of La Belle Alliance; but they could not show any front against the victorious foe. There was a brief combat between the remnant of the French cavalry and that of Wellington, but the former were soon included in the rout. The troops of Lobau also held their ground about Planchenoit for some time, but being at length outflanked and altogether outnumbered by the Prussians, they took to flight.

The Emperor himself escaped on horseback, but presently picked up a travelling carriage, in which he continued his journey without pause, and reached Paris on the third day after his defeat.

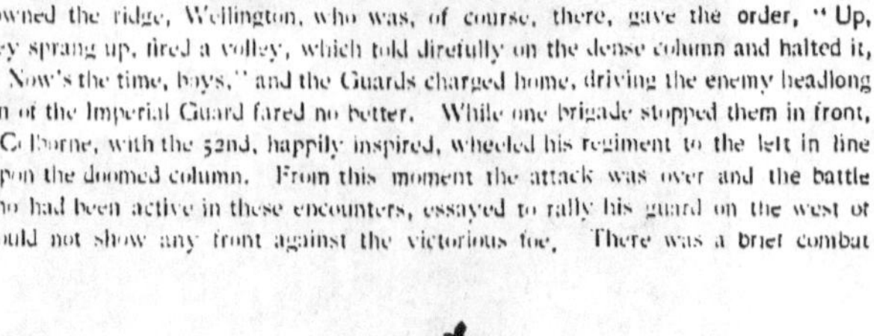

THE LION MOUND, WATERLOO.

From a Modern Photograph.

The creation of this trophy robbed the surrounding country of so much earth as to change its features.

THE ALLIES ENTER PARIS, 1815

After a Drawing by Martinet

The allied commanders, Wellington and Blucher, at the head of a brilliant staff, are crossing the great Square of [illegible] Paris.

CHAPTER XI.

After Waterloo. Friction between English and Prussians. Disposal of Napoleon. [illegible] in Paris. Wellington returns to England in 1818. Appointed Master-General of the Ordnance, and later Commander-in-Chief. Prime Minister, 1828. [illegible] Difficulties with the King's brother. Catholic emancipation. The Duke's duel with Lord Winchelsea. The Reform Bill. The Duke's strong opposition and consequent unpopularity. His windows broken at Apsley House. His life in danger. [illegible] Again in office, and for a time sole dictator. Accession of Queen Victoria.

THE occupation of Paris by the allied armies brought new and very vexatious anxieties upon Wellington. His chief trouble at first was the irrepressible rancour of the Prussians towards the French, and their keenness to avenge former defeats. Old Marshal Blucher had set his mind on two desires: the payment of an indemnity of a hundred million of francs by the City of Paris, and the demolition of the Bridge of Jena, across the Seine. To both of these Wellington was firmly and consistently opposed. He [illegible] the contribution on his own behalf, and he saw no reason, he said, why the Prussians should [illegible] principle was conceded, which it was not. As to the destruction of the bridge, it [illegible] the French Bourbon King and the body of the French people, with whom the [illegible] least necessary as a military measure, and was only demanded on sentimental [illegible] an objection that disappeared when the French offered to change the name of the [illegible]!

The Prussians were not to be easily shaken from their purpose, insisting [illegible] less offensive to the English than to the French. Although they actually mined two [illegible] the bridge, [illegible] done, their engineers being little practised in the work; and Wellington at last secured the postponement [illegible] retaliatory measure until the arrival of the allied Sovereigns, among whom was the King of Prussia [illegible] safe he stationed a British sentry on the bridge at all hours. The Duke was heard to say that the P[illegible] have been bold enough to blow up the bridge, but they would not have dared to take the [illegible] Their conduct in France was all of a piece; they were a terror to the peasantry, [illegible] perpetrated by Napoleon's army when it ravaged Prussia.

ENGLISH UNIFORMS.
After [illegible] "Le Bon Genre."
Cavalry officer, Highlander, and staff officer in great coat form the last group.

Another difference between the allied commanders might have bred still more serious trouble. This was as to the disposal of Napoleon when captured. He had been declared an outlaw by the Congress of Vienna *hors la loi*, beyond the pale of civil and social rights; it was decreed that he had forfeited them by leaving Elba, and was amenable to public justice. Wellington had signed this decree, and was much blamed for doing so, but he strenuously resisted the interpretation Blucher would have put upon the word "justice." The old Field-Marshal would have shot Napoleon out of hand had he caught him on the flight from Waterloo. Afterwards he was for shooting him in the ditch of Vincennes, on the very spot where the Duc d'Enghien had been executed. The Duke of Wellington, while admitting Napoleon's culpability, would not tolerate any such summary proceeding. Public justice could not mean assassination.

The Prussians still pressed their point, and Gneisenau wrote suggesting that as the English shrank from these stern proposals, Napoleon should be handed over to the Prussians, who claimed to be "the tools of Providence, who has given us such a victory for the ends of eternal justice." But Wellington promptly and plainly spoke his mind. He would not be a party to the transaction, and reminded Blucher that since winning so important a battle they had become conspicuous personages in the eyes of Europe. "Such an act would hand down our names to history stained by a crime, and posterity would say of us that we did not deserve to be the conquerors of Napoleon, the more so [illegible] is now quite useless, and can have no [illegible]."

[illegible] Wellington's [illegible] concerning the [illegible] his friends. He had [illegible] still in France those who wished Napoleon well, although secretly. Talleyrand and [illegible] The [illegible] dallying [illegible] America, for [illegible] [illegible]

FRENCH COSTUMES AND ENGLISH UNIFORMS.
After [illegible] "Le Bon Genre."
[illegible] hussars, heavy dragoons, and [illegible] officer, with the ladies in the latest Parisian fashion.

was no safety if he again became an independent agent; none, indeed, while he remained on French soil. His sympathisers were still numerous, and one held on to the Castle of Vincennes, in the environs of Paris.

It had been agreed by the Convention that all fortresses north of the Loire should be handed over to the allies, but Vincennes was not given up, although its governor had hoisted the white flag. Wellington told Fouché, whom he suspected of complicity, that he would wait no longer. "But what can I do?" protested the wily policeman. "It's not my business to tell you, but I can tell you what I shall do, and that is capture the fortress by force of arms. Do you understand?" Fouché still hummed and hawed, hoping that the matter might soon be settled amicably. The Duke, with whose iron will he had hardly yet come in contact, was not to be put off any longer. "I have said my last word, and," he repeated, "either the fortress shall be surrendered to-morrow at 10 a.m., or it will be taken at 12."

To show how clearly his mind was made up, it may be added that he invited his friend Croker, then in Paris, to be present at the assault. "You have never been at a fight, Croker," he said; "come and breakfast with me at 9 a.m. to-morrow, and I will give you a mount to see me take Vincennes." There were French Ministers present who protested, and begged Lord Castlereagh to interfere. But his old

ENGLISH OFFICERS.

A light cavalry officer and Highlander.

friend knew Wellington, and that he meant what he said. "It is a military question, of which the Duke is sole judge." The orders were actually issued for the attack, but the necessity was avoided by the hasty surrender of Vincennes.

Wellington was [illegible]

[illegible]

especially the necessity [illegible] [illegible] their [illegible] were serving Louis XVIII. [illegible] [illegible] in particular was [illegible] [illegible] the Duke [illegible] marshal of F[illegible] King [illegible] [illegible]

BIVOUAC OF PRUSSIANS IN PARIS.

Some of the Prussian [illegible] in 1815 [illegible] gardens of the Luxembourg.

NAPOLEON GOING ON BOARD H.M.S. "BELLEROPHON," IN 1815.

After a Picture by [illegible].

Napoleon, having been foiled in his desire to escape to the United States, took a small craft from Bordeaux and voluntarily surrendered to the English.

encounters. "It is their custom to show me their backs."

The ill-feeling exhibited by the French officers was very general, and not to be wondered at. It was enough to rouse their bitterness to see Paris invaded by foreign uniforms, and for the second time within twelve months to meet English, Russians, Prussians, and Austrians parading the streets and public places, in the cafés and gambling saloons, holding their heads high with an air that was galling, although not necessarily meant to offend. The French are not a patient nation, and they retaliated according to their means: the military used their weapons; duels were incessant, the result of open insult or any trifling provocation; the civil community took their revenge in the ridicule that, with all the exuberance of French wit, was heaped on everything foreign.

Yet France at large had reason to bless Wellington. It was by his exertions mainly that the country escaped partition or serious mutilation. The policy of the Vienna Congress was revived, and "all Gaul" would have been once again "divided into three parts," or more, but for Wellington. But the permanent [illegible] of France by loss of territory [illegible] short-sighted [illegible] new wars.

The Duke [illegible] remained in France [illegible] Generalissimo of [illegible]. When [illegible]

NAPOLEON ON THE DECK OF H.M.S. "BELLEROPHON."

After an Original Drawing by L. M. Skene.

This is an authentic water-colour sketch, made from life by Dr. Skene, the assistant surgeon of the ship.

Wellington and Waterloo.

1818, he returned home, and never again drew his sword. His wars were over, but he was still the servant of his Sovereign and country, ever ready to act in any capacity. Even in his extreme old age he was prepared to take the field, and it will always be remembered how, when pressing Sir Charles Napier to take the command in India after Chillianwallah, he said, "If you don't go, I must." But his services during the remaining years of his long life were mainly political, and although he was ever upright and straightforward in dealing with public affairs, his reputation as a statesman was far below that as a soldier. He held office and directed the Government in a troubled epoch, when party passion ran high, and burning questions distracted the country. He became identified with unpopular measures, resisted others on which the nation was bent, and if he yielded at length, it was only because he thought concession a lesser evil than revolution.

ENGLISH OFFICERS IN THE STREET.

The French artists ... portraying the most grotesque ...

In the earlier years, however, he took no more prominent place than as Master-General of the Ordnance, which gave him *ex officio* a seat in the Cabinet. The post, one of great antiquity and importance, was in this way superior to that of Commander-in-Chief, and quite independent of it. The Master-General controlled, alone and entirely, the two scientific corps, the artillery and engineers, which enjoyed a distinct existence from the rest of the Army—one of those curious and anomalous conditions that complicated our military administration till the days of the Crimea. Until then, it must be remembered, four several and separate departments were concerned with Army matters. There was no Secretary of State for War with general control as nowadays. A secretary "*at* war and for the colonies" dealt with the military Estimates in Parliament, and during active operations was the channel of communication with the General in the field. The Home Office managed the Militia, the commissariat was under the Treasury, and the distinct functions of the Board of Ordnance were as stated above. As Master-General, the Duke was chiefly engaged in matters of promotion and patronage. He maintained the privileges of the two corps, although he never heartily approved the system.

THE AMIABLE PRUSSIAN.

A ... ing Parisian

It was not until the death of the Duke of York that Wellington took his proper place as head of the Army, and held for a time the two offices of Commander-in-Chief and Master-General of the Ordnance combined. He used the word "proper place" himself, "the place for which he was destined by his trade," as he told Croker. "I am a soldier, and my place is at the head of the Army, as the Chancellor, who is a

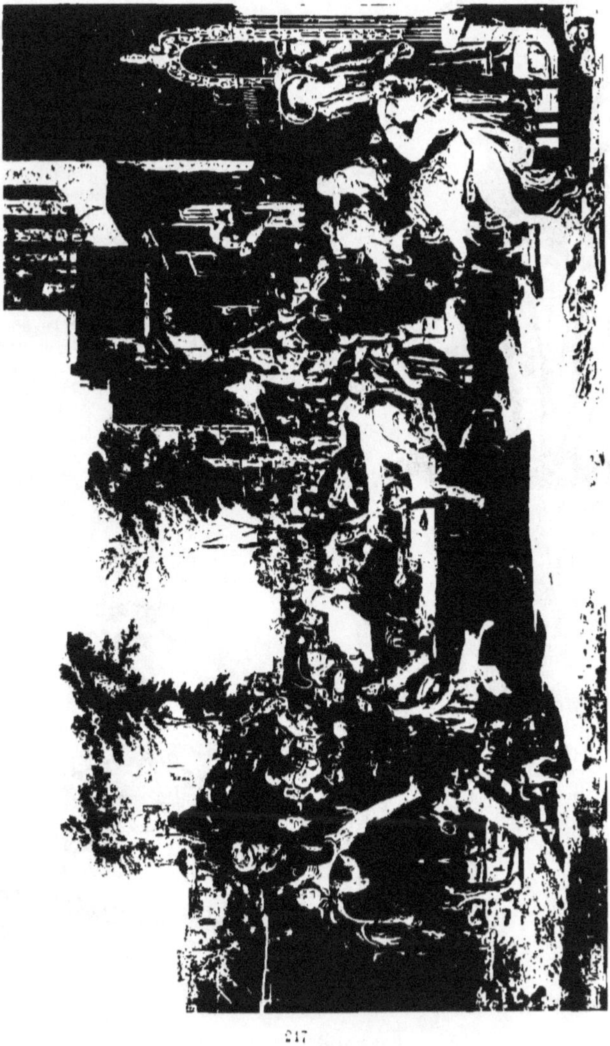

READING THE WATERLOO GAZETTE

ENGLISH OFFICERS OFF DUTY

Another caricature ridiculing the dress of English officers.

lawyer, is in his on the Woolsack. We each of us have a trade, and are in the proper position when exercising it."

He gladly accepted the offer which was made him by George IV. in the most complimentary terms. The King wrote: "I must tell you that I feel a pride . . . . in showing not only the affection I have for you, but the gratitude which this country owes you. The glory of my reign is so identified with *you* that the one cannot be separated from the other." The King's language to the Duke was generally couched in this same tone of somewhat extravagant eulogy. He began his letters always, "My dear friend," and ended them with, "Ever your sincere friend." In the differences with the Duke of Clarence, brought on by the latter's unconstitutional desire to run the Board of Admiralty as his own private concern, the King took Wellington's side. But he was much vexed with his "dear friend" when the Duke took umbrage at Mr. Canning's treatment and insisted on resigning his offices when that statesman formed a new Administration. Canning had seen fit to rebuke him in an unprovoked fashion, to which Wellington would not submit.

The King was very anxious that he should withdraw these resignations, which had aroused a strong feeling in the country, but the Duke was firm. There was, indeed, no reason why he should not retain the office of Commander-in-Chief, which, unlike that of Master-General of the Ordnance, was entirely unpolitical. But without a full apology from Canning he would not return to the Horse Guards, and the deadlock was only ended by the Minister's sudden death. Then the King reminded Wellington that the post of Commander-in-Chief was still open, and "if you choose to recall that resignation, which," as he said, "it grieved me so much to receive, you may have my sincere permission to do so." This second tenure of the command was but brief, however. A few months later he again resigned on being entrusted with the formation of a Cabinet; for although he had thought of holding it in conjunction with the Premiership, the Opposition, indeed many of his own colleagues, disapproved. Lord Hill now succeeded as General Commander-in-Chief, and held the post until [illegible] 1842, when the Duke finally went to the Horse Guards for the rest of his life.

It has been [illegible] that the Duke of Wellington [illegible] very [illegible] the British Army; he has been much and often blamed for his want of sympathy with his old comrades in arms,

AN ENGLISH "GALLOPER."

After a Drawing by C. Carl Vernet.

An aide-de-camp carrying a message on the field. The intention to caricature is obvious, yet there is little fault to be found with the rider's seat and horse's action.

for suffering the strength of forces to be sadly diminished, and for failing to secure adequate rewards for the gallant services of those who had won him his great renown. As a matter of fact, the periods for which he held the chief command between Waterloo and his death were really brief, and although as head of the Government he might have done more for the Army, he no doubt felt that it was beyond his province to interfere. As to the reductions in numbers he was nearly powerless, but he protested, and at last devised the plan of keeping the troops as much as possible out of sight, lest they should still further irritate economists. This led to that utter want of training of mixed or large bodies that tended to diminish the knowledge and usefulness of officers. In the matter of rewards the Duke was old-fashioned; he took what was given him because it was given, not because he asked for it, and he strongly reprobated self-seeking in any shape or form.

The King's fondness for Wellington was equalled by the confidence he reposed in him, which prompted him to send for the Duke at the fall of the Goderich Ministry, in 1828. This was Wellington's entry into the arena of party politics, and he hesitated to undertake the formation of a Government, which presented many difficulties. He took council, however, with Peel, and got together a good working team which held office for a couple of years. It had to deal with many intricate questions: a war between Russia and Turkey was at one time imminent; the agitation to abolish the slave trade came to a head; the desire for Parliamentary reform was growing rapidly throughout the country; the unsatisfied claims of the Roman Catholics for emancipation were threatening serious disturbance in Ireland; and Daniel O'Connell's recent election to a seat in

READING THE NEWS.

After a Caricature by H B

The caricatures of "H. B.," the pseudonym of Richard Doyle, were very caustic and severe during these long years of political strife. This represents George IV., with his chosen intimates, privately receiving a statement from the Duke of Wellington

A HORSE MARINE.

After a Caricature by H B

This unsparing caricature ridicules the deficient horsemanship of the sailor King, William IV.

the House of Commons. The Duke did not really enter the arena of political strife until 1828, when on the collapse of the Goderich Cabinet the King sent for "his dear friend" and entrusted him with the formation of a Ministry. The intimacy continued nearly to the last, but the relations were at times much strained. The pleasure-loving monarch was now a poor broken creature without judgment or insight, and he clung obstinately to views quite unsuited to the times. He was in the hands of a silly, self-seeking entourage who encouraged him in his resistance to measures that had become inevitable, thus greatly embarrassing the position of the responsible Ministers of the Crown.

REPOSE.

After a Caricature by "H. B."

The Duke, as Premier, depicted as neglectful of and asleep over his work.

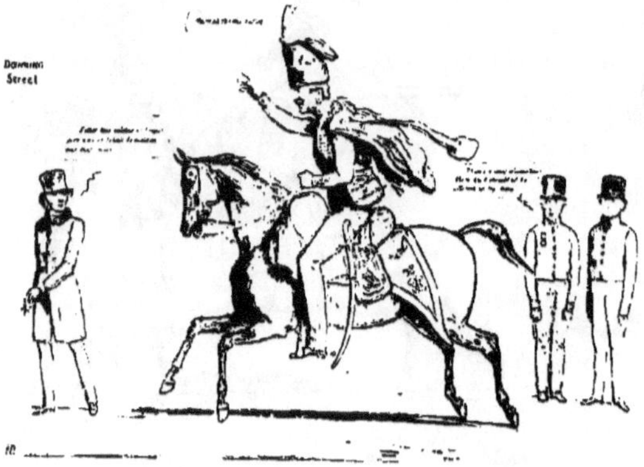

A DIS-ORDERLY.

After a Caricature by "H. B."

Sir Hussey Vivian, as Master General of the Ordnance, had dissented from the views of the Cabinet, of which he was *ex-officio* a member.

Many burning questions occupied the public mind and increased the difficulties of Government. The Duke and his colleagues, a good working team not easily got together, had to deal with the strained relations between Russia and Turkey, and the imminence of war; intrigues, vast and vexatious, were afoot in England to support Russia, and centring in a female Russian agent, the clever and attractive Madame de Lieven, who hated the Duke and got the ear of the King. Closely mixed up with this was the improper attitude taken by the King's brother, the Duke of Cumberland, who misused his power of access to the King and was intolerably meddlesome. These irresponsible agitators bent all their efforts to upset the Ministry, because it was patriotic in regard to foreign affairs, and they hoped much from any other Administration.

Then there was the question of the slave trade, the opposition to which had been accentuated by disturbances in Demerara, and the abolitionists were more than ever active in denouncing the traffic. The Government was willing to legislate, but its action was hampered by the attitude of France, which was not actually averse to the trade. French politics were an ever-present cause of trouble, and, as we shall see, George IV. would have shown his sympathy with the retrograde party, and seriously compromised the Duke's Government by paying a secret visit to Paris. The most pressing and disturbing question of all was the state of Ireland and the increasing clamour for the emancipation of the Roman Catholics. Some measure of relief was inevitable. The agitation and insecurity of the country was perhaps greater than at any period before or since. Daniel O'Connell had now been returned to Parliament, and the movement to secure the repeal of disabilities was organised on wide lines. Civil war was within measurable distance, but yet the King was inclined to concede nothing. Wellington wrote him, strongly urging that any Minister must see the paramount necessity for relief, and got at first a sullen permission to proceed with a Bill. But the King was not yet in earnest; he sought only to gain time, and at last, after a long and angry discussion, accepted the resignation of the Ministry sooner than yield.

THE COUNTESS OF MORNINGTON.

The Duke's mother, a woman of high intelligence [illegible] lived long enough to be proud [illegible] the son whom she [illegible]

The scene at Windsor was both pitiable and painful. Lord Ellenborough, who was present as Chancellor, has left a record. "The King," he writes in his diary, "talked for six hours. . . . . He was evidently insane. Had taken brandy and water before he joined us, and sent for some more, which he drank during the conference. . . . . He objected to every part of the Bill. Knighton (his medical adviser) said afterwards, "The King was in a deplorable state, and declared that he had not a friend in the world." At the end of the affair Lord Ellenborough writes: "It is impossible not to feel the most perfect contempt for the King's that. We should be justified in declaring we will have no farther intercourse with one who has not treated us like a gentleman."

The Duke was firm throughout, being satisfied that the measure must pass as proposed, believing, too, that the King must give way. The latter did in effect change his tone, but not until he found that it was impossible to form another Administration. The Duke of Cumberland, who had been mischievously active, and Lord Eldon, the King's secret adviser, were unable to get a Cabinet together, and on the very evening of the storm George IV. wrote to the Duke "my dear friend," and said he had decided to yield. The country must have a Government, and therefore he approved of the Duke proceeding as he wished. "God knows what it costs me to write these words," adds the wretched Sovereign in his abject despair.

Difficulties beset Wellington on every side. A whole crop of them grew up around the occupant of the Lord Lieutenancy. Lord Anglesea, who was then Viceroy, was favouring the Irish Catholics a little openly and prematurely. The King was greatly incensed with him, and pressed for his recall, but Wellington defended him, attributing his rash acts to an undue desire for popularity. The Duke felt bound, however, to take him to task, and some sharp letters passed. In one Lord Anglesea told Wellington that although he had marked his communication private, he (the Duke) had the power of making it public, and that he should assume the same right. This was

APSLEY HOUSE, PICCADILLY.

From a Modern Photograph.

[illegible] the end of the 18th century, and [illegible] The Duke bought it from his brother, [illegible] Wellesley, and made [illegible] changes in it [illegible]

more than the Duke would bear. "I feel that I could no longer correspond confidentially with Lord Anglesey, and that if this sort of relation was to continue he or I must go out." The Duke waited a month, feeling strongly the inconvenience of removing him, and hoping that time and reflection would have made him conscious of the unreasonableness of his conduct. But at last it was deemed impossible to leave him in Dublin, and the necessary recommendation was made to the King.

This is the same man who, as Lord Uxbridge, lost his leg by the Duke's side at Waterloo, a gallant comrade and old friend, although they fell out over political affairs. Wellington at this same period was involved in

A HINT TO DUELLISTS.
After a caricature by H. B.
The Duke of Wellington's duel with the Earl of Winchelsea was severely criticised. Some would have arraigned him for a gross breach of the law.

his only affair of honour—that with Lord Winchelsea, the last political duel fought in England. The great soldier had never been "out," as the phrase went, although he had been often enough under the enemy's fire. Yet he had ever been ready to give "satisfaction," as we know on the authority of Captain Gronow, who tells in his inimitable reminiscences how the great Field-Marshal was willing to "meet" a simple subaltern of the Guards who felt himself aggrieved by some supposed injury done him by the Duke. Now the Prime Minister, jealous of his own honour, called a political opponent to strict account for an unguarded expression, for which Lord Winchelsea would not apologise.

Lord Winchelsea gave dire offence by accusing the Duke in a public print of a secret understanding with the Catholics, and that in defending religion and morality he meant it as a blind to the Protestant and High Church party. This the Duke construed as imputing to him disgraceful and criminal motives, and in no measured terms, and sent a friend, Sir Henry (afterwards Lord) Hardinge, to Lord Winchelsea, but as the latter refused to withdraw the offensive expressions without further explanation from the Duke, there seemed no way out of it but a hostile meeting. The Duke declined to admit that because a gentleman happened to be a King's Minister, he need submit to be insulted by another, and declared that Lord

THE DUKE OF WELLINGTON.

Winchelsea was "alone responsible for the consequences." "I now call upon your Lord[illegible] W[illegible]ton "to give me that satisfaction for your conduct which a gentleman has a right to requir[illegible] [illegible] never refuses to give." From the earliest days to the last the Duke's highest [illegible] [illegible] gentleman, and he acted up to it consistently. The duel was fought in [illegible] [illegible] 182[illegible]. Lord Winchelsea would ma[illegible] no retractation, although strongly urged to do so by his own second, Lord Falmouth. But he wrote him that he did not mean to fire at the Duke, and after the first shot was ready to express his regret for what he had said. A third effort at arrangement was made upon the ground, but without result. When the opponents met and the signal was given, the Duke paused, seeing that Lord Winchelsea did not aim, but after a moment fired; then his antagonist raised his pistol above his head and fired deliberately into the air, and coming forward, immediately apologised, "in the most extensive, in every sense of the word," as his second afterwards said.

Sir Henry Hardinge now sharply lectured both for having so nearly jeopardised a valuable life, and after a few words the Duke touched the brim of his hat with two fingers in his well-known brief salute and said "Good morning, my Lord Winchelsea, good morning, my Lord Falmouth." Then he mounted his horse and rode away.

[illegible]

He was [illegible] [illegible] Wellington [illegible]

The Duke's attitude was much criticised at the time, and the well-known Jeremy Bentham, now advanced in years, addressed him a letter beginning, "ill-advised man," and [illegible] the confusion into which the whole fabric of Government would have been thrown if he had [illegible] [illegible] trial for murder come before the House of Lords instead of the Emancipation Bill. The [illegible] indispensable. He was living in an atmosphere of calumny, he declared, and to th[illegible] [illegible]. He

BARRACKS, DUBLIN.

Ireland, during the Viceroyalty of Lord Anglesea, was still so disturbed that a strong military force had to be maintained in the country. These are the Royal Barracks, which still form a prominent [illegible] in Dublin.

considered [illegible] duelling was as much a part of the Catholic question, and as necessary to carry it through, as any other step taken to attain the object in view. Whatever we may say of duelling in politics, there can be no doubt that it had the effect Wellington anticipated. "I am afraid that the event itself shocked many good men," wrote the Duke, "but I am certain that the public interests at the moment required that I should do what I did."

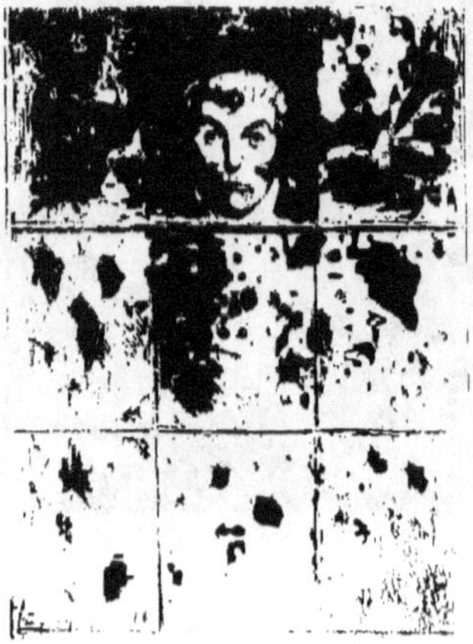

The Roman Catholic Relief Bill was duly passed, and by a large majority, but it was thought that the King would have refused his assent. He raged furiously and talked of preferring abdication; and had not the Duke insisted peremptorily, it might still have been delayed. The King's temper grew more and more trying after this, causing Wellington infinite vexation. They were widely at variance, the Sovereign and his subject, on matters of policy, patronage, and conduct. How heavy was the burthen laid upon Wellington may be gathered from one of his despatches of the period. "If I had known in January, 1828, one tithe of what I do now, and of what I discovered one month after I was in office, I should never have been the King's Minister, and so have avoided loads of misery. However, I trust God Almighty will soon determine that I have been sufficiently punished for my sins and will relieve me from the unlucky lot which has befallen me. I believe there never was a man who suffered so much for so little purpose."

The King was full of prejudices, of likes and dislikes, and under the influence of a lady whom he often pleased by perverting

STRATHFIELDSAYE, HANTS.

Wellington and Waterloo.

APSLEY HOUSE.
After an Engraving by Campion.
Shows the west angle of the house and the principal windows (first floor) of the banqueting-room and picture gallery.

justice or interfering with its procedure. He mitigated the death sentence in the case of an Irish gentleman who had committed forgery and perjury; he would not receive Denman, who had defended Queen Caroline, although in his official capacity, as representing the Recorder, he should have presented the "Report" of capital sentences, and the course of laws was impeded. He wished to have a baronetcy conferred upon his architect, although the man was under a cloud, and pressed it when the Duke demurred. He wrote to "his dear friend" insisting that the honour should be given, "not only as an act of justice to him, but to my own dignity. . . . For if those who have gone through the furnace for me and for my service are not protected, the favour of the Sovereign becomes worse than nugatory." But the King's favourite did not get the baronetcy.

The proposed visit of the King to Paris no doubt originated with the Duke of Cumberland, who hoped to curry favour with the reigning house in France. Although the revolution of 1830 was near at hand, the English Royalties could only see in thus siding with the Bourbons a way of damaging Wellington and his liberal views.

It would be tedious and out of place to follow out at any length the great Reform agitation, which all but landed England in revolution and was one of the most serious crises in our latter-day political history. It was the darkest period, too, in Wellington's whole life, when his conscientious but mistaken opposition to a necessary measure suddenly shipwrecked his popularity; when his great services were forgotten and the national hero became the finger-post of the national scorn. That immovable constancy which had gained him his military renown appeared now in an obstinate determination to resist reform. He could not [illegible] the least necessity for it; he at least was satisfied with Parliamentary representation as it [illegible] had been brought up to believe in [illegible] and rotten boroughs, and saw no [illegible] change. His [illegible] his unconcealed hatred [illegible] democracy [illegible] this, and he steadily [illegible] it

WALMER CASTLE.
After an Engraving by Campion.
The west front of the castle, with Deal in the background.

VISCOUNT CASTLEREAGH.

This great statesman and early friend of Welling[illegible] [illegible] 12th Au[illegible] 1822 that the time had come for increasing the electorate, for giving votes and members to the new centres of population still shut out from Parliament. He declined, being Premier at the time, to introduce any measure of reform in 1830 when it was demanded by Earl Grey, and declared that he should "always feel it his duty to resist such measures when proposed by others."

This peremptory defiance was fatal to his reputation. A wave of indignation swept through the country, fanned by the invective of stump orators and the diatribes of the Press. Other things helped to increase the storm. The creation of the new Metropolitan Police at that very juncture was denounced as an attempt on the Duke's part to ride roughshod over the liberties of the people. Again, when, in deference to dread rumours of outrage, the King's intention to make a royal procession to the City to open the new London Bridge was abandoned, the Duke was blamed fiercely. If the Sovereign was no longer safe in his streets it was because this martinet Minister had roused the worst passions of the people. The immediate result was disastrous. Panic prevailed in the city. The funds fell, trade stagnated, failures and bankruptcies followed. Abuse was poured out upon the undismayed but wrong-headed Duke, he was bitterly assailed in both Houses of Parliament; and seeing that his supporters dwindled away, and that public opinion was against him, he resolved to resign office, and did so in November, 1830.

"REFORM."

After a Caricature by "H. B."

Wellington and Peel discomfited at the base of the pillar surmounted by Earl Grey, to whom the country owed Parliamentary reform.

The new Ministry included Earl Grey and Lord John Russell, who in the spring of 1831 brought forward a scheme of reform so extensive, so revolutionary, that it was received by astonished enthusiasm on the one side, by indignation, almost terror, on the other. The struggle was fought out strenuously both in Parliament and beyond, not quite with judgment by the opposition headed by the Duke, with disgraceful excesses by the irritated people at large. Excited mobs collected in the streets to cheer or hoot public personages as they passed, according as they were friendly or hostile to the measure, and the more lawless in the crowd took to a larger exhibition of spite in smashing the windows of those obnoxious to them. Apsley House was marked down and attacked with great volleys of stones. This dastardly act was perpetrated at a moment of deep domestic affliction, when the Duke was sincerely and regretfully mourning the wife from whom he had been half estranged during life. The Duchess of Wellington actually lay dead in the house at the time of the outrage. It was after this that the Duke put up the

THE CHANCELLOR OF OXFORD AND HIS SUPPORTERS.

After a Caricature by "H. B."

The Duke heads the procession, and he is followed by his chief comrades in arms.

Wellington and Waterloo.

A GREAT DOCTOR OF CANNON LAW.

After a Caricature by "H. B."

The Duke in his robes as Chancellor of the University of Oxford.

iron shutters to which he would point sardonically, when in later years the fickle populace, having once more taken him into favour, would follow him with approving cheers.

A new Parliament was now summoned to deal with the Reform Bill, and the country sent an overwhelming majority to support it in the Commons. In the Lords the attitude of defiance was unchanged, and after a magnificent exhibition of eloquence on both sides, the Bill was finally rejected amidst a storm of indignation. The whole kingdom was convulsed; the entire nation lapsed into anarchy. There were riots in Bristol and Nottingham, in Edinburgh and Glasgow, with scenes of the grossest violence. The noble Lords who had voted against the Bill were hunted through the streets; before the new iron shutters could be closed, the windows of Apsley House were again wrecked; the hatred of the Duke of Wellington was so intense that he went in danger of his life. A plan was laid to intercept the Duke on his journey to Walmer, and although the gallant old soldier carried arms and resolved to fight as he was always ready to fight, his safety was really assured by a party of chivalrous gentlemen who met his carriage and escorted it within the gates of his castle.

But it was the voice of the nation that was speaking, even with this illegitimate and indefensible language, although the Duke of Wellington would not consent to listen to it. Parliament reassembled, but he would not yield an inch. He still honestly believed that the Reform Bill, if passed, would destroy the constitution of the country. He had no doubt a good backing in the learned profession, the universities, among leading merchants, clergy, and landed proprietors, and it was long before he admitted that any Parliamentary reform must be conceded. When this was forced upon his mind he bent every energy to make the change as little subversive and gradual as possible, by modifying the provisions of the Bill. The Government resented this, and claiming to pass it unmutilated, called upon the King to create Peers to give them a majority in the House of Lords. Another anxious period followed, during which the Duke tried in vain to form an Administration and was more than ever unpopular. His life was constantly threatened; he was actually mobbed in the City on Tower Hill, and only escaped by his own fearlessness

UNIVERSITY DISCIPLINE.

After a Caricature by "H. B."

The Duke, as Chancellor, is seen drilling the heads of colleges in their duties.

A CABINET COUNCIL.
After a Caricature by "H. B."
The Duke, in the absence of Sir Robert Peel abroad, takes upon himself the whole duty of Government, and fills all the great offices himself.

and with the active assistance of two bystanders, one of whom was afterwards Lord St. Leonards. At last the opposition so far gave way that the dissidents withdrew in a body from the House of Lords and abstained from voting. They would do no violence to their consciences, but yet saw that further resistance would ruin their order by swamping the body of the Peers. Then the Reform Bill became law, and the Duke lived to see that he had been wrong and its promoters right.

Within a year or two the public mind regained its balance, and the great soldier was gradually reinstated in popular esteem. The old cry was soon revived as the Duke passed, "There he goes, God bless him." People saluted him again respectfully. "I am getting up in the market," he would say with seeming contempt, but yet touched by the plain proof of his revival of popularity. Within a couple of years he was again at the head of affairs, only temporarily, it is true, but under circumstances that were highly complimentary. A change in parties led to the necessity for a new Ministry, and the Duke was summoned by the King. He refused to form a Cabinet himself, and recommended Sir Robert Peel, who was unfortunately at a distance, in Rome. Whereupon the Duke took upon himself the entire business of Government until Peel could return, and held in his own person, for the first and so far the last time in history, all the great offices of State. He was First Lord of the Treasury, Home Secretary, Foreign and Colonial Secretary, and Secretary at War. He was thus for nearly a month sole Minister and almost absolute dictator in England. Perhaps no greater tribute could be paid to his unimpeachable honesty and trustworthiness as the servant of the Sovereign and the people.

HER MAJESTY QUEEN VICTORIA.
After a Contemporary Sketch, [illegible]
Military costume worn by the Queen at her first review.

Yet another great honour was in store for him. The University of Oxford, contrary to all precedent, offered him the post of Chancellor, preferring a strong, sensible head who could do battle for its interests to any distinguished scholar. The Duke's installation at Oxford was one of his greatest triumphs. His reception was a scene of the wildest enthusiasm; the undergraduates cheered him to the echo and with a boisterous enthusiasm that made a great impression on the Duke. "Let

QUEEN VICTORIA.

Her Majesty [illegible]

Wellington and Waterloo.

ON A WRONG SCENT.
After a Caricature by H B.

OPPOSITION 'BUSES.
After a Caricature by H B.
J— Bull is being "touted for" by the Duke of Wellington.

those boys loose in the state in which I saw them," he said afterwards, "and give them a political object to carry, and they would revolutionise any nation under the sun."

Now soon the Duke came under the rule of our present Most Gracious Sovereign, to whom he ever rendered the most loyal and devoted allegiance, which was heartily repaid so long as he lived. The young Queen gave him her fullest confidence, and treated him with the warmest respect. He was on the best terms with her responsible advisers, but still spoke out his mind. He entered too, in fact, upon the last phase of his political and public life, that of general arbitrator and adviser, one altogether superior to party, who was ready to support every measure that he thought deserved it, and this independently of the side from which it came. He had more than ever at heart, strengthened and emphasised, the honour of the Crown and the welfare of the country. This end he strove constantly to secure by his counsels and his criticism.

WATERLOO CHAMBER.

From a Modern Photograph

The great dining-hall in which the Waterloo banquet was given yearly by the Duke of Wellington. It is also the principal picture gallery in Apsley House.

CHAPTER XII.

Closing days of Wellington's life. His widespread popularity. Latest public services. General adviser to Crown and Government. His attitude towards the Corn Laws. Last services as a soldier. Ready to take the field in India. His letter on the defenceless state of the country. His fine preparations to meet the Chartists. Last hours and peaceful death. His character and distinctive personal traits. "Duty" the mainspring of his conduct. His true kindliness and charitableness. Simplicity of his daily life.

WELLINGTON now entered the last phase of his great and useful career, secure in the gratitude and goodwill of all classes of his countrymen. Except for the one disgraceful episode when his transcendent services were forgotten in a fierce outburst of popular disfavour, he was ever appreciated as he deserved, and never more than in the closing days of his life. He was the centre of interest at every public celebration. When, as Lord High Constable of England, he carried the Sword of State at the Coronation, the veteran warrior shared the honours of the occasion with the girl Queen. When, a few months before his death, he walked arm-in-arm with his old comrade and former political antagonist, Lord Anglesea, at the opening of the Great Exhibition of 1851, he was vociferously cheered. The man who had spent his manhood in fighting his country's battles now gave his willing sanction to what was vainly deemed the dawning of an epoch of perpetual peace among men. Whenever the Duke went abroad in these latter days, he was attended by an admiring crowd. A little knot of spectators watched him leave Apsley House for the Horse Guards, and were again in waiting as he crossed from Whitehall to the House of Lords; others were there to see him home. Country cousins, Colonial visitors, the rising generation, all collected to get one glimpse of the grand old soldier; and there are some of us left who remember, as a hallowed tradition, the slight, straight figure, the strongly-marked profile, and the two fingers raised in courteous recognition of the universal greetings.

APSLEY HOUSE, HYDE PARK CORNER.

From a Modern Photograph.

Named after Lord Chancellor Apsley, and built at the end of the 18th century. The Duke bought it in 1820, and spent £130,000 in improvements.

BOEHM'S EQUESTRIAN STATUE.

From a Modern Photograph.

The Duke i[illegible] charger he rode at Waterloo.

His public life was by no means ended after the Queen's accession, although he was raised above the strife of parties, and filled a position unique in our political history. He was actively engaged on neither side, but spoke out clearly and independently, according to his own judgment, on measures proposed. Disputes and differences were constantly referred to him, and his decision was generally respected as that of one absolutely disinterested, the faithful servant of his Queen and country, who had no thought but to staunchly support the one and wisely befriend the other. We have seen how, in the crisis after Lord Melbourne's death, he stepped in alone to fill the gap until Sir Robert Peel's return to England. Again, on the question of the Corn Laws, when Sir Robert Peel announced that he could not carry on the business of the country unless they were repealed, and became an avowed Free Trader, the Duke wisely cast in his lot with him. Wellington might have successfully resisted the Bill, for, although it had passed the House of Commons, he had commanding influence at this time in the House of Lords. But the Duke had not forgotten the Reform agitation, and was nowise prepared to again oppose the sovereign will of the people. He gave his support to Peel, therefore, and Protection was doomed.

A last political service rendered by the Duke was on the resignation of Lord John Russell in 1851. The Queen sent for

SIR ROBERT PEEL.

After a Portrait by Sir Thomas Lawrence

The great statesman was at this time Home Secretary and in the very prime of life.

Lord Stanley, who was unable, however, to form an Administration, and there seemed no remedy but to dissolve Parliament. The Queen was loth to commit the country to a general election on the very eve of the Great Exhibition, and the Duke's advice was sought. He gave it with characteristic force and brevity. The Sovereign should lay her commands upon Lord John Russell and his colleagues to retain office until a more convenient season, and the result was an armed truce between parties, the weakest still holding the reins of Government until the Exhibition was over.

Wellington's military services were not yet ended. In 1842, on the resignation of his old friend and comrade, Lord Hill, he resumed his place as Commander-in-Chief of the Army, and held it till his death ten years later. It has been often stated, in the Duke's disparagement, that he did little for the Service or for his brethren-in-arms, that he suffered the Army to be reduced nearly to extinction, and that there was no strong bond of sympathy between him and his old officers. We now understand that he kept the Army in the background [illegible] ly means of [illegible] and Manchester economists, who would [illegible] have done, [illegible] weaken it. It was [illegible] the [illegible] necessitated its [illegible] escape

THE DUKE'S BEDROOM AT APSLEY HOUSE.
After a Contemporary Drawing.
This represents the interior as in the Duke's lifetime. The room is on the ground floor.

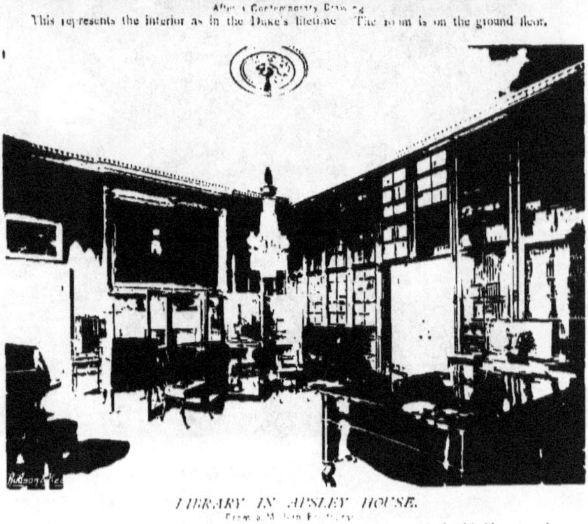

LIBRARY IN APSLEY HOUSE.
From a [illegible]
The Duke's [illegible] communicated with this library, where he worked with his secretaries.

LADY JULIA PEEL.

THE HALL, APSLEY HOUSE.

From a [illegible]

The busts on each side of the door are of the Duke himself and the Marquis of Wellesley.

THE MUSEUM, APSLEY HOUSE.

From a [illegible] Photograph.

[illegible] cases are preserved the [illegible] decorations, and insignia conferred on Wellington.

observation, and if the result was that troops were never assembled for manœuvres in large bodies, so that all ranks missed necessary training, the blame does not quite rest with the Duke. As for his neglect of the men who had helped him to win his victories, his refusal to issue a Peninsula medal, his coldness towards his former supporters—these are all charges that rest on some foundation, but have never been positively made out. The Duke was on the surface a cold, hard, undemonstrative man, little inclined to show enthusiasm, imbued with so strong a sense of duty, that the strictest performance of it called, as he thought, for no especial reward. He was not himself greedy for honours and distinctions, although they were never more freely lavished on anyone, and he could not understand why others craved for them.

That he did not associate more freely with military men, and had few close intimate friends among them, is to be explained, if not justified, by the fact that he belonged by birth and predilection to another set—to the aristocratic caste, not then represented largely in the Army. He began as a sprig of nobility, he ended as one of the heads of the order, and throughout his favourites and companions were the "curled darlings" of Society. This was very apparent in his campaigning days, when he surrounded

himself with two distinct classes of staff officers. There were the men who did his work, and the men with whom, so to speak, he played. The first were stern soldiers, who had given good earnest of military efficiency; the latter were princes and lordlings, whom Wellington called by their Christian names and gossiped with about home. Gallant gentlemen all of them, brave as lions and unsparing of effort, but chosen as members of the personal staff for the reason above given.

Wellington to the last was like an old war-horse, ever eager to re-enter the fray. It was in his seventy-eighth year that he seriously proposed to take the field in India when Sir Charles Napier at first declined to accept the command in supersession of Lord Gough. The Duke was as usual consulted by the Government, and asked to submit three names from which a choice might be made. He gave as the first name that of Sir Charles Napier, as the second the same name, and again as the third. He had no doubt whatever as to the narrow limits of selection, for when Sir Charles hesitated, as has been said, the Duke declared with characteristic directness, "Very well! If he won't go, I must." There is no reason to suppose that he would not have carried out his intentions, still less that he would have failed. Not long afterwards the veteran Austrian, Marshal Radetzky, won the battle of Novara, in his eightieth year. The fact is worth recalling in these days, when the worship of mere youthfulness is carried to an absurd extreme, and great age is counted an absolute disqualification for command.

No. 1 (of shield).—The taking of Seringapatam and battles in India.

No. 2.—Wellington's landing in Portugal and the battle of Vimiera.

The Duke's ardent patriotism was evoked about this time by the occurrence of one of those threats of invasion that periodically disturb the public mind. The vapourings of the Prince de Joinville, who had demonstrated the ease with which a French descent might be made, brought out his celebrated letter to Sir John Burgoyne on the defenceless state of the country. Alarm was general, but no sufficient steps were taken to build fortifications, which even now, fifty years later, are not completed. The Duke, it may be added, held strong views as to the necessity of Naval stations and harbours of refuge, and it was on his initiative that those of Holyhead and Portland were undertaken. The harbour now in process of construction at Dover was also recommended by the Duke, and, in his capacity of Warden of the Cinque Ports, he gave close attention to all that concerned the southern coast of Kent.

His consummate skill in handling troops was once more and finally called into play when the Chartist agitation threatened London with riot and bloodshed. At this moment revolutions were rife all over the Continent, and the English Government [illegible] vely alarmed. But it was resolved to meet force with force, and that London should be fully garrisoned [illegible]. The Duke of Wellington was consulted and put in chief command, although the Government, nervous and fussy, was disposed to interfere. His arrangements were comprehensive and masterly.

No. 3. The assault and capture of Ciudad Rodrigo and Badajos.

No. 4. The battles of Vittoria and in the Pyrenees.

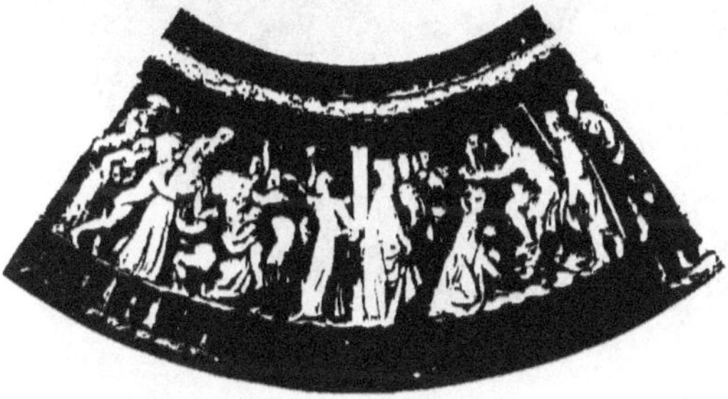

No. 5. Wellington's triumphant reception after the peace.

Various portions of the great gold shield presented to the Duke after Waterloo by the City and Corporation of London.

From [illegible]

Carefully avoiding the irritation that must follow any public display of soldiers in the streets, he kept them out of sight, within enclosures and buildings, such as the palaces, banks, and Millbank Prison. Not a single point was left unguarded, and the whole plan was so contrived that masses could appear in a moment wherever most required. As is well known, there was happily no collision, and the Chartists were dispersed by a handful of police.

The Duke's end was peaceful; his mind was clear, his faculties unimpaired to the last. He had suffered from a slight cold, but did not keep his room. On the morning of the 14th September, 1852, he was called as usual soon after 6 a.m. He answered, but woke with difficulty and did not rise. An hour or two later his breathing became heavy, medical advice was summoned, but life was failing fast. The Duke lingered till after noon, then passed quietly away. The news of his death was received far and wide with profound sorrow. All classes in this and many neighbouring countries paid a tribute of sad respect to the man who had played so great a part in the world's history. His funeral was a great public pageant, and the departed soldier was laid with all honourable pomp in St. Paul's side by side with our great Naval hero, Nelson.

It remains only to take a general survey of Wellington's character, based upon his performances and his personal traits. The first have been described in the preceding pages, but not the qualities that made them uniformly successful. We have seen him winning victory after victory without realising, perhaps, why he must take such high rank among the masters of the art of war. Wellington was a great soldier, because he made circumstance subserve his purpose; he could be bold or cautious, firm or yielding,

CENTRE OF THE GREAT SHIELD.

From a Modern Photograph.

The Duke being crowned with a laurel wreath as he rides down his fallen foes.

according to the end he had in view. He dared all in his assaults on Ciudad Rodrigo and Badajos because all depended on their capture. He cowered behind the lines of Torres Vedras, despite calumny and derision, till the time was ripe to expel Massena from Portugal. He triumphed over lukewarm supporters at home, faithless allies, and an often incompetent staff by a mixture of concession and strength. His operations in the field were planned astutely, and executed with vigour and decision. He was a strategist of the highest order, and, as a tactician controlling the events of the battle-field, he was unrivalled by any of his contemporaries. Even more marked than his power to strike was his patience to prepare. The foresight, fertility of resource, the unwearied industry with which he met shortcomings and overcame transcendent difficulties, scarcity of means, supineness of agents, physical obstacles, are beyond all praise. If we add to these marked characteristics an unvarying steadfastness of aim, extraordinary breadth of view, and a quick unerring grasp of men and things, we see combined in him the chief qualifications of success. His reputation is now firmly fixed on an enduring basis. The story goes that someone, once addressing Lord Palmerston, began, "The great Duke of Wellington——" "Ah! but was he a great man?" interrupted Lord Palmerston. If the great statesman thus hazarded an ungenerous doubt, history has decided in favour of the great soldier.

THE COUNTESS OF JERSEY.
After a Portrait by C[illegible]on.
A well-known leader of Society, wife of the 5th Earl of Jersey, and an intimate friend of the Duke's.

The mainspring of Wellington's conduct through life was his stern sense of duty. The point cannot be too strongly emphasised, nor his example too often held up for imitation. Nothing was too small, nothing too tedious for his attention, nothing too great or too arduous to face where duty called. No man worked harder than Wellington, however he might be placed, whatever might be expected of him. His despatches, that extraordinary monument to his knowledge, his industry, his intellectual powers, show the infinite pains he brought to bear on every subject, every branch of business. He exacted the same

THE DUKE OF WELLINGTON.

STRATHFIELDSAYE.

[illegible]

A full view of the house which was [illegible] of the nation to Wellington after Waterloo.

WALMER CASTLE.

From a Modern Photograph.

The Duke's residence as Warden of the Cinque Ports.

unflagging energy from all his subordinates. When clerks in the Treasury protested against the labour involved in carrying out some of his views, he quietly told them he would call in half-a-dozen pay-sergeants to do what he wanted. We owe to the Duke the famous apothegm that to get a thing well done you must do it yourself. He devoted the same punctilious care to all his private affairs. He audited his own house accounts, supervised his estate of Strathfieldsaye, and chose and controlled his own servants. He conducted much of his correspondence with his own hand, and his laconic replies to fussy critics of his policy, to bores seeking autographs, and to the thousands of applicants for charity are still remembered as models of their sort.

WELLINGTON'S DEATH CHAMBER.

After a Contemporary Print

The room in Walmer Castle in which the Duke died. The simple furniture and small bed were what he always preferred.

Wellington had really a kindly heart under a cold exterior. He was warmly attached to his personal friends. When any member of his staff was taken off suddenly, he mourned his loss sincerely. Authentic stories are told of his bitter grief at the loss of Sir Alexander Gordon, long one of his devoted supporters. He showed infinite tact when Lord Fitzroy lost his arm at Waterloo, and gave the acting appointment to Colonel Felton Harvey, who was maimed in the same way. The Duke was singularly fond of children. He was a noted admirer of the *beau sexe*. He loved a joke, and would laugh loud and long at the dinner-table. His language, as seen in his despatches, took often a quaint turn that showed anything but a gloomy spirit. "If I had done half what had been expected of me, I should have been long before this in the moon." "God help me if I fail, for no one else will."

The Duke aspired first and before all to be deemed an English gentleman, and was ever ready, according to the code of the day, to defend his honour at the risk of his life. He fought only one duel, that with Lord Winchelsea, but he offered to "go

THE DEAD FIELD-MARSHAL'S HORSE.

After a Sketch by Herring

The empty boots reversed are a special feature at a military funeral.

THE DUKE'S FUNERAL.

After a Drawing by Louis Haghe.

The interior of St. Paul's during the funeral service.

out" with Captain Gronow in Paris in 1815, when that young officer felt aggrieved at some fancied injustice from the Duke. Although given to abrupt speech at times, the result of years of commanding authority, he was scrupulously polite to all comers, and would talk freely with all classes. He was easy of access, but had an inconvenient habit of appointing early hours for interviews, and would be at home to visitors at 8 and even 7 a.m. There was nothing sordid or mean about his character; he cared little for money, and was very generous and free-handed. His purse was open to his friends; he offered to lend money to Lord Hill when in trouble; he welcomed Alava, his Spanish attaché, when in exile, and gave him *carte blanche* at the bankers. His charities were unostentatious but unceasing. He was generally his own almoner, and kept a quantity of notes and cash upon his desk ready to meet the numerous appeals that reached him, and which he always answered himself. Designing people constantly preyed upon him; he could never resist a tale of distress. "What could I do?" he would ask when tackled; "I thought the fellow might starve."

His habits and ways of life were singularly simple and unpretentious. From first to last he disdained the services of a valet; he slept for choice on a narrow camp bed, and was so little of a sluggard that he invented another famous phrase, "When it is time to turn over it is time to turn out of bed." He was temperate and abstemious to a high degree, and this in an age when drunkenness was no more than a gentlemanly failing, and, till his strength began to fail, he found his reward in unvarying good health. Only latterly he carried his asceticism too far, and nearly lost his life by refusing all sustenance and stimulant and treating himself with frequent cold baths. He had no extravagant tastes, if we except an amiable liking for collecting watches and clocks; for all his life he was a rigid observer of punctuality, and could never tolerate a bad time-keeper. He dearly loved a good horse too, and, although never a fine rider, was an ardent sportsman who kept his own pack of hounds in the Peninsula, "The Peer's," as it was known in the Army, and who, till quite late in life, hunted regularly with the hounds in his neighbourhood, and rode very straight.

He was seen at his best in English country life at Strathfieldsaye, at Walmer, or the houses of his friends. He was much given to hospitality of a quiet kind. Except when he assembled all survivors at the annual Waterloo banquet in the great gallery of Apsley House, his circle was small, made up of intimates with whom he could talk unreservedly on current topics, and more rarely on the scenes and people of the great past, discussing then the comparative merits of the men opposed to him, the narrowness of some of his victories, the qualities of his own and his enemies' troops. As to Waterloo he long showed great reticence, and it was not till thirty years or more after the event that he spoke at all freely of his intentions and movements at the battle. By that time memory was failing, and it is to be feared that he did not dispose entirely of the many problems and conjectures that were and still are, some of them, afloat as to that "battle of giants."

www.ingramcontent.com/pod-product-compliance
Lightning Source LLC
Chambersburg PA
CBHW032102220426
43664CB00008B/1098
* 9 7 8 3 3 3 7 1 4 4 3 5 7 *